RICS
Research

The Royal Institution of Chartered Surveyors is the mark of property professionalism worldwide, promoting best practice, regulation and consumer protection for business and the community. It is the home of property related knowledge and is an impartial advisor to governments and global organisations. It is committed to the promotion of research in support of the efficient and effective operation of land and property markets worldwide.

Real Estate Issues

Series Managing Editors

Stephen Brown Head of Research, Royal Institution of Chartered Surveyors

John Henneberry Department of Town & Regional Planning, University of Sheffield

David Ho School of Design & Environment, National University of Singapore

Elaine Worzala Professor, Director of the Accelerated MSRE, Edward St. John Department of Real Estate, Johns Hopkins University

Real Estate Issues is an international book series presenting the latest thinking into how real estate markets operate. The books have a strong theoretical basis – providing the underpinning for the development of new ideas.

The books are inclusive in nature, drawing both upon established techniques for real estate market analysis and on those from other academic disciplines as appropriate. The series embraces a comparative approach, allowing theory and practice to be put forward and tested for their applicability and relevance to the understanding of new situations. It does not seek to impose solutions, but rather provides a more effective means by which solutions can be found. It will not make any presumptions as to the importance of real estate markets but will uncover and present, through the clarity of the thinking, the real significance of the operation of real estate markets.

Books in the series

Greenfields, Brownfields &
Housing Development
Adams & Watkins
9780632063871

Planning, Public Policy &
Property Markets
Edited by Adams
Watkins & White
9781405124300

Housing & Welfare in
Southern Europe
Allen, Barlow, Léal
Maloutas & Padovani
9781405103077

Markets and Institutions in
Real Estate & Construction
Ball
9781405110990

Housing, Neighbourhood Renewal
& Community Engagement
Edited by Beider
9781405134101

The Cost of Land Use Decisions
Buitelaar
9781405151238

Urban Regeneration in Europe
Couch
Fraser & Percy
9780632058412

Urban Sprawl
Couch, Leontidou & Petschel-Held
9781405151238

Economics & Land Use Planning
Evans
9781405118613

Economics, Real Estate &
the Supply of Land
Evans
9781405118620

Development & Developers
Guy & Henneberry
9780632058426

The Right to Buy
Jones & Murie
9781405131971

Economics of the Mortgage Market
Leece
9781405114615

Housing Economics & Public Policy
O'Sullivan & Gibb
9780632064618

International Real Estate
Seabrooke, Kent & How
9781405103084

British Housebuilders
Wellings
9781405149181

Urban Sprawl in Europe

Landscapes, Land-Use Change & Policy

Edited by

Chris Couch, Lila Leontidou and Gerhard Petschel-Held

Blackwell
Publishing

© 2007 Chris Couch, Lila Leontidou, Estate of Gerhard Petschel-Held

Editorial offices:
Blackwell Publishing Ltd, 9600 Garsington Road, Oxford OX4 2DQ, UK
    Tel: +44 (0)1865 776868
Blackwell Publishing Inc., 350 Main Street, Malden, MA 02148-5020, USA
    Tel: +1 781 388 8250
Blackwell Publishing Asia Pty Ltd, 550 Swanston Street, Carlton, Victoria 3053, Australia
    Tel: +61 (0)3 8359 1011

First published 2007 by Blackwell Publishing Ltd

ISBN: 978-1-4051-3917-5

Library of Congress Cataloging-in-Publication Data
Urban sprawl in Europe: landscapes, land-use change & policy / edited by Chris Couch, Lila Leontidou, and Gerhard Petschel-Held.
    p. cm. – (Real estate issues)
  Includes bibliographical references and index.
  ISBN-13: 978-1-4051-3917-5 (pbk. : alk. paper)
  ISBN-10: 1-4051-3917-X (pbk. : alk. paper)
    1. Cities and towns–Europe–Growth. 2. Urbanization–Europe. 3. City planning–Europe.
4. Urban policy–Europe. I. Couch, Chris. II. Leontidou, Lila. III. Petschel-Held, Gerhard.
HT384.E85U94 2007
307.76094–dc22

A catalogue record for this title is available from the British Library

Set in 10/13 pt Trump Mediaeval
by Newgen Imaging Systems (P) Ltd, Chennai, India
Printed and bound in Malaysia
by KHL Printing Co Sdn Bhd

The publisher's policy is to use permanent paper from mills that operate a sustainable forestry policy, and which has been manufactured from pulp processed using acid-free and elementary chlorine-free practices. Furthermore, the publisher ensures that the text paper and cover board used have met acceptable environmental accreditation standards.

For further information on Blackwell Publishing, visit our website:
www.blackwellpublishing.com

Forthcoming

Building Cycles & Urban Development
Barras
9781405130011

Mortgage Markets Worldwide
Ben-Shahar, Leung & Ong
9781405132107

Real Estate & the New Economy
Dixon, McAllister
Marston & Snow
9781405117784

Towers of Captial
Lizieri
9781405156721

The Cost of Land Use Decisions
Buitelaar
9781405151238

Affordable Housing & the Property Market
Monk & Whitehead
9781405147149

Property Investment & Finance
Newell & Sieracki
9781405151283

Housing Stock Transfer
Taylor
9781405170321

Real Estate Finance in the New Economic World
Tiwari & White
9781405158718

Housing Markets & Planning Policy
Jones & Watkins
9781405175203

This book is dedicated to the memory of

Gerhard Petschel-Held

GERHARD PETSCHEL-HELD (1964–2005)

The work presented here was developed within the EU Framework V project URBS PANDENS, a research project of nine European partners investigating seven European cities with respect to city development and urban sprawl. URBS PANDENS was led by an excellent scientist, Dr. Gerhard Petschel-Held from the Potsdam Institute for Climate Impact Research. Gerhard Petschel-Held passed away in 9 September 2005. This book is a small tribute to his life and work as it disseminates the scientific achievements made within the project.

Gerhard Petschel-Held was a person full of character and a very passionate scientist. He led the project with great enthusiasm, patience and force. A project about urban sprawl and city development calls for a strong interdisciplinary focus which he was able to perfectly and sensitively coordinate.

He was born in Nuremberg and trained as a physicist. He studied in Würzburg and Albany (New York) and obtained his doctorate in 1992 in Frankfurt/Main, with a thesis about the borders between classical chaos and quantum mechanics. In 1993 he joined the Potsdam Institute for Climate Impact Research (PIK). Soon after his arrival at PIK, he was appointed as deputy head and some years later as acting head of the department of Integrated Systems Analysis. Despite his young age, his intelligence, his empathy, his creativity and not least his humour, resulted in Gerhard Petschel-Held being the leader of a group of scientists with widely differing backgrounds, who became a productive and highly innovative team with a shared vision. He led projects which approached an interdisciplinary understanding of the Earth system in the light of critical changes in the relationship between human societies and environment.

These ambitions and experiences made it possible for him to suggest, implement and lead a unique project like URBS PANDENS. It is characterised by a broad range of disciplinary orientations of the participating scientists from physics and hydrology to geography and planning, and a broad range of scientific schools from generalising, quantitative modelling to qualitative restructuring and cultural approaches. Reflecting the great chances for innovation inherent to this large variety, the project started in a scientifically very open way and was thereby confronted with the tremendous heterogeneity in describing and understanding urban sprawl. There are not many coordinating scientists that are on the one hand open to all of these disciplinary orientations – which to some degree conflict with one another – and who are also able to keep the collective scientific process in a direction that allows for mutual understanding and progress towards the project's objectives. Interest and commitment were coupled with an ability for complex thinking, never losing sight of what was most important. Gerhard Petschel-Held was a good listener and was therefore asked for advice and feedback by all the project scholars. Besides this being very advantageous for the project's cohesion, it was also a reason for his successful contribution to broader international activities. In parallel with scientific projects, he contributed in the Millennium Ecosystem Assessment, the UNEP-Global Environmental Outlook and the Intergovernmental Panel on Climate Change. In his personal style of approaching everyone with appreciation, he demonstrated integrity and humanity which was met with respect and deep trust by his colleagues and project partners. He nevertheless did not hold back with criticism or his independent views, but he was never condescending, as he sought out – without compromise – his own quest for scientific quality. Losing him at such a young age left an immense gap among us and several unfinished innovative projects.

Matthias Lüdeke
Diana Reckien

Contents

Contributors

Alex Afouxenidis
Alex Afouxenidis is a sociologist (PhD, Durham University) who teaches in the Program of European Culture at the Hellenic Open University. Previously he taught European spatial change, Social Geography and Method in Social Science at the Department of Geography of the University of the Aegean; and Sociology and European Social and Economic History at the Hellenic-British Educational Association in Athens, and worked in London. His main scholarly and research interests lie in political sociology and theory with particular reference to exclusion, shifting borders and the third sector.

Karl-Olov Arnstberg
Karl-Olov Arnstberg is an ethnologist and formerly professor at Stockholm University. He is also the former head of the Institute for urban studies at Stockholm University. He is the author of many books including *Eight Postulates on Planning* (Formas, 2003) [with Bergstrom], and *Sprawl* (Symposion, 2005) [in Swedish].

Inger Bergstrom
Inger Bergstrom is an architect, practicing planner and docent (associate professor) at Chalmers University in Gothenburg. Among other books, she has together with Karl-Olov Arnstberg written *Eight Postulates on Planning* (Formas, 2003).

Chris Couch
Chris Couch is Professor of Urban Planning at Liverpool John Moores University and formerly Head of Planning and Housing Studies. He also teaches at Liverpool University. His main research interests lie in the application of socio-economic and planning theory to aspects of urban planning and regeneration, particularly in a European comparative context; also the study of urban change and policy in the Liverpool area. He is author of a number of books on planning including *City of Change and Challenge: Urban Planning*

and Regeneration in Liverpool (Ashgate, 2003) and co-editor (with Charles Fraser and Susan Percy) of *Urban Regeneration in Europe* (Blackwell, 2003).

Małgorzata Gutry-Korycka

Małgorzata Gutry-Korycka is Professor and Head of the Department of Hydrology, Faculty of Geography and Regional Studies, University of Warsaw. Her research interests are focused on hydrology science and water management, particularly investigations connected to urbanisation and global change processes with hydrological and sustainable development dimensions. She also has expertise in mathematical modelling for the long-term prediction of hydrological responses to global change in catchments, and the mathematical modelling of urban impacts on hydrological processes (both issues of water quality and quantity). She has recently co-authored and edited *Urban Sprawl: Warsaw agglomeration* (Warsaw University Press, 2005).

Jay Karecha

Jay Karecha is a Researcher in the European Institute for Urban Affairs at Liverpool John Moores University. He has a number of years of experience in examining UK cities in a European context. His research interests focus on the measurement of change in cities, quantitative data collection and analysis, economic and social trends, and urban sprawl. He has co-authored a number of publications. His recent work includes a quantitative study into the economic and social performance of Cardiff and an analysis of area change in New East Manchester for the New East Manchester Urban Regeneration Company.

Elias Kourliouros

Elias Kourliouros is Professor of Economic Geography & Spatial Planning and Dean of the School of Social Sciences at the University of the Aegean. He studied Architecture at the National Technical University of Athens and Geography at the London School of Economics, where he was awarded his second Ph.D. He is author of several articles and books, including *Itineraries to the Theories of Space* (in Greek, Hellenica Grammata, 2001). His main research interests are in critical economic geography, regional development and planning, urban restructuring, urban sprawl and sustainable development.

Lila Leontidou

Lila Leontidou is Professor of Geography & European Culture and Dean of the School of Humanities, Hellenic Open University, Greece. She studied Architecture at the National Technical University of Athens and was awarded her MSc in Geography and her PhD at the London School of Economics. She was previously a Professor at the University of the Aegean, a Senior Lecturer at Kings College, University of London, and an Associate Professor at the National Technical University, Athens. She is author of over 100 articles and books, including *Cities of Silence* (in Greek, ETVA & Themelio 1989/2001), *The Mediterranean City in Transition* (Cambridge, 1990/2006), *Geographically Illiterate Land* (in Greek, Hellenica Grammata, 2005). She has also co-authored several books and co-edited *Mediterranean Tourism: Facets of Socioeconomic Development and Cultural Change* (Routledge, 2001). She is on the editorial advisory board of a number of journals including *City, Geografiska Annaler, Urban Studies* and *Urban History*.

Matthias Lüdeke

Matthias Lüdeke studied theoretical physics and sociology at the Johann Wolfgang Goethe-University in Frankfurt am Main and received his PhD in natural sciences at the same university in 1992. Since 1995, he has worked as a scientist at the Potsdam Institute for Climate Impact Research PIK, Department for Integrated Systems Analysis, focusing on interdisciplinary modelling of coupled man-environment systems in relation to global change. He contributed to the formalisation and further development of the Syndrome Concept. He is leader of the Group for Integration and Place-based Approaches and coordinates the Triple-Q project on methods of qualitative modelling.

Emmanuel Marmaras

Emmanuel Marmaras is Professor of Urban Development & Town Planning at the Technical University of Crete. He studied Architecture at the National Technical University of Athens and was awarded his MA at the University of Sheffield and his second PhD in Urban History at the University of Leicester. He is author of several articles and books, including *The Urban Apartment Building of Interwar Athens* (in Greek, ETVA & Themelio 1991), *Planning and Urban Space* (in Greek, Hellenica Grammata 2002). His areas of interest include Urban Geography, Urban Development and Planning, Renewal in the Historical Urban Cores, Urban and Planning History, and travel writing.

Nataša Pichler-Milanovič

Nataša Pichler-Milanovič is a senior researcher at the Department of Geography, Faculty of Arts, University of Ljubljana. She was trained as a geographer and spatial planner at the University of Belgrade (Yugoslavia) and the London School of Economics and Political Science (UK). Since 1990 she has been involved in many comparative EU-funded projects on urban and regional development in Europe. Her fields of expertise are in studies of urbanisation, housing and planning policy and practice published in Urban Studies, European Journal of Housing Policy and several books. She has recently co-authored and edited a book on urban transformation in Central and Eastern Europe, published by the United Nations University Press.

Henning Nuissl
Henning Nuissl is a sociologist and planner who studied at the Universities in Heidelberg, Hamburg and Hamburg-Harburg. He obtained his doctorate from the Brandenburg Technical University Cottbus. He is a senior researcher at the Helmholtz Centre for Environmental Research - UFZ, Department of Urban and Environmental Sociology; and a lecturer at Technical University Berlin. His fields of expertise are in land use policy and urban sprawl; milieu, social capital and trust; urban governance and planning theory. He has recently published articles on these subjects in *Landscape and Urban Planning; Cities; European Planning Studies and European Urban and Regional Studies.*

Diana Reckien
Diana Reckien works at the Potsdam Institute for Climate Impact Research, the co-ordinating institute for the URBS PANDENS research project. She studied human geography at the Technical University of Dresden/Germany, geography, ecology and economics at the University of Greifswald/Germany, and Geographical Information Systems at the Rijks-Universiteit at Utrecht/Netherlands. One of her main scientific interests is urban processes in both the physical and anthropogenic sphere. She has contributed to projects that investigated the transport energy consumption of people in urban areas, e.g. to discuss possible carbon dioxide reduction measures and their implementation. Currently, she is finishing her PhD in Geography at the University of Marburg/Germany with a work about urban sprawl in old industrial areas.

Dieter Rink
Dieter Rink studied Cultural Science and Humanities at the University of Leipzig from 1981–1986 and worked after his studies at the Philosophical Institute of the University of Leipzig, where he completed his PhD in philosophy. From 1991–1994 he researched social movements at the Science Centre Berlin. Since 1994 he has been a member of the staff at the Environmental Science Centre Leipzig-Halle, and since 2000, an honorary professor at the University of Applied Sciences, Mittweida. His main research interests are in urban development, sustainability and social movements.

Preface

Writing in 1933 Sir Patrick Abercrombie commented that:

> 'the biggest challenge will be to withstand the pressure throughout the
> world to suburbanize the country as well as the towns…with modern sys-
> tems of mass production and distribution it is all too easy to proliferate
> man's modern technical products; but, if the countryside is not to be over-
> run, the need to maintain nature reserves of wilderness and plain, coastal
> belt and sea, is all-important … it is essential to create both urban and
> rural aesthetic standards to avoid the universal spread of subtopia'.
>
> (Abercrombie, 1933, p. 275)

Whatever the changing terminology, urban sprawl has been a matter of
concern to planners for many years. Abercrombie and his generation were
particularly exercised by the aesthetics of urban development and, it should
be said, the efficiency of different forms of urbanisation in providing for the
needs of the population. This alone provides reason enough to study urban
sprawl in the new millennium. But times have changed and new agendas
have appeared. Traffic congestion and the knowledge that traffic growth is
related to land use, demands planning strategies that minimise the need
for travel. The crisis of de-industrialisation and dis-investment that rav-
aged so many older urban areas in the last quarter of the twentieth century
(especially in Northern Europe) demands planning decisions that encourage re-urbanisation and re-investment in existing urban areas. Throughout
the developed world urban populations are becoming increasingly spatially
segregated by social characteristics: wealth, age, ethnicity, life style; and the
larger the area of the city, the greater these spatial divisions become. Climate
change and the loss of non-renewable natural resources and the knowledge
that urban form has a role to play also demands action by planners. Each of
these problems have one thing in common, they are all exacerbated by urban
sprawl.

It was the last of these problems, climate change, which provided the initial driving force behind the process that has culminated in the writing of this book. Colleagues at the Potsdam Institute for Climate Impact Research (PIK) undertake a number of streams of research related to global climate change. Whilst much of the work of the Institute is defined by the natural sciences and is concerned with understanding and modelling the dynamics of climate change, one stream of work, which has been of growing importance, is that of understanding the 'socio-economic causes of global climate change'. Amongst their concerns are the production and use of energy; urban form and dynamics; the nature and location of economic development. It was evident to PIK that urban sprawl is an important cause of inefficiency in energy use (particularly through the transport system) and in the consumption of land and consequent damage to ecosystems. Amongst the principal methodologies used by PIK is modelling and it was felt that a novel form of model, known as Qualitative Dynamic Modelling, developed by Gerhard Petschel-Held and his scientific team, might prove a useful tool, both in understanding the dynamics of urban sprawl and in policy formulation.

It can be argued that there is already a body of literature on urban sprawl and that further research and an additional book are unnecessary. However, a cursory look at the literature reveals that much of it is from and about North America and particularly the United States. It was our feeling, and we argue this in the book, that Europe is sufficiently different, with a greater diversity of urban contexts, to justify its own research and body of literature.

Thus in 2002, with the initiative and under the project leadership of Gerhard Petschel-Held, PIK led an international consortium of universities and research institutes that secured funding from the European Commission under its Framework V research programme on *City of the Future*, for a project entitled *'Urban Sprawl: European Patterns, Environmental Degradation and Sustainability'*, with the acronym URBS PANDENS. The other establishments involved were: University of the Aegean and Hellenic, O.U.; UFZ Centre for Environmental Research Leipzig-Halle; Liverpool John Moores University; Urban Planning Institute of the Republic of Slovenia and the University of Ljubljana; Stockholm University; Vienna University of Technology; and Warsaw University. Additionally the International Council for Local Environmental Initiatives (ICLEI) provided support in organising workshops with planning practitioners and in the dissemination of findings.

Colleagues from each of these establishments worked as a loose team for a period of three years, coming together every six months or so for coordination meetings and workshops. These colleagues, many of whom are contributing authors to this book, each had their own disciplinary backgrounds and own particular interests in urban sprawl. These backgrounds included: sociology; ethnology; economics; town planning; architecture; geography; and natural sciences. Also, being drawn from different parts of Europe with different urban experiences, colleagues had very different perspectives on what urban sprawl meant for them and their home cities.

This broad spectrum of backgrounds, knowledge and skills proved to be an immense strength of the project but quickly led to the realisation that reductionism, generalisation, and simple theory formulation would not be characteristics of our work. It soon became evident that diversity would be the key to understanding the nature of urban sprawl, its causes and consequences, and the policies to reduce or ameliorate sprawl. Thus our approach is primarily qualitative. Whilst we did undertake various surveys and data gathering exercises and we did use a lot of secondary data, our aim was always to understand and explain the nature and dynamics of urban sprawl, to accept diversity and appreciate the differences in causes and consequences in different places and at different times.

This book does not directly report the project. That was done in a document prepared for the European Commission in 2005. Gerhard Petschel-Held, who was the inspiration behind the original proposal and leader of the project, sadly died in 9 September 2005 shortly after completing that report.

This book does draw very substantially upon the work that he led and the process of writing has been informed by the formal research undertaken during the project, the meetings, workshops with practitioners, study visits and many informal discussions and conversations over a coffee or a beer in the case study cities around Europe. Whilst this is an edited book, all the authors worked closely together, with each contributing to and commenting on the work of others. Thus we have tried to produce a text that tells one story, with different authors taking up the tale where their knowledge is greatest. As editors we are indebted to all the individual authors for their expertise and their endeavour. The book is theirs and could not have been completed without them. Nevertheless, as editors we must take responsibility for the final text and for any errors that remain.

Chris Couch, Lila Leontidou

References

Abercrombie, P. (1933) *Town and Country Planning*. Oxford University Press, Oxford.

European Commission (2005) *Urbs Pandens Final Report*. CEC, Brussels.

Acknowledgements

The authors are grateful to all those who took part in the URBS PANDENS project for their contribution to the research which forms the foundation for much of this book. In addition to the current authors these include Mirosława Czerny, Jens Dangschat, Mirosław Grochowski, Alexander Hamedinger, Holger Robrecht, Susanne Kratochwil, Marko Krevs, Barbara Lampič, Andrzej Lisowski, Andrea Mann, Kostas Rondos, Ulrike Schwantner, and Kyriakos Tourkomenis.

The maps in Chapters 2 and 8 were drawn by Paul Hodgkinson and those in Chapter 3 by Thomas Hadzichristos, Lila Leontidou, and Dora Manta. The cover photograph was taken by Henning Nuissl. Other photographs were taken as follows: photographs in Chapter 3 by Lila Leontidou; in Chapter 4 by Jaroslaw Suchozebrski, Biba Tominc and Matej Nikðiè; in Chapter 5 Chris Couch; and in Chapter 6 Karl-Olov Arnstberg.

Chapter 5 is substantially drawn from an earlier article by the same authors published in *European Planning Studies* **13**(1) (2005) [http://www. tandf.co.uk/journals]. The authors are grateful to the publishers, Taylor & Francis, for kind permission to reproduce that material here.

Part I

Theory and Method

1

Introduction: Definitions, Theories and Methods of Comparative Analysis

Chris Couch, Lila Leontidou and
Karl-Olov Arnstberg

Background

This book has its origins in a pan-European research project examining aspects of 'Urban Sprawl in Europe' undertaken for the European Commission under its Framework V research programme. That project went under the acronym of 'URBS PANDENS' and sought to understand recent trends in urban sprawl in a number of case study regions and to advise the Commission on policy development with regard to the control, management and amelioration of the effects of urban sprawl. That work was completed and reported in 2005 (European Commission, 2005).

Themes that emerged from that work are developed in this book. Our aim is to provide a more general discussion of the nature of urban sprawl and to consider:

- the extent to which common European patterns and processes of sprawl can be found, distinct from those previously identified in the USA;
- whether new theories can be formulated to explain urban sprawl, particularly in terms of formal qualitative modelling; and
- what innovations might be suggested regarding the management of urban sprawl.

The term 'urban sprawl' is often used today rather negatively, typically to describe low density, inefficient, suburban development around the periphery of cities. Many of the definitions found in the literature tend to emphasise the idea of urban sprawl being a type of urban form or a pattern of urbanisation, rather than a process of urban change. However, in our view the latter may be a more useful perspective, since it is the process of sprawling that leads to undesirable side effects and it is in the process of sprawling that policy must intervene. A feature of our discussion is therefore that it concentrates on urban sprawl, not as a *pattern of urbanisation*, as is more usual in the literature, but rather as a *process of urban change*. This book therefore takes its own particular approach to the definition and measurement of urban sprawl. The analogy of a sandcastle may be used: imagine building a conical sandcastle with firm wet sand – it has a certain height, the sides slope at a certain angle and it has a certain circumference. Now imagine pouring on more water. The structure becomes waterlogged and the sand does not bind together so well and slips downwards and outwards. The height of the peak at the centre of the cone is less, the angle of slope is reduced and the circumference is enlarged. The volume of sand in the castle remains unchanged but it has spread over a larger area: it has sprawled. Similarly with the city: social, economic and environmental pressures may cause a relative fall in demand for land and development in the central city whilst they may cause a rise in demand at the periphery. Thus, urban sprawl may be considered as the *process* by which this spreading occurs.

Much of the discussion on suburbia, in terms of urban sprawl, is American. Among the many reviewers of the literature on urban sprawl, Chin (2002) has identified four types of definitions based upon urban form; land use; impacts and density. In terms of urban form, urban sprawl is generally measured against an ideal type of 'compact city'. Thus any deviation from this compact city in the form of suburban growth, ribbon development, leapfrogging and scattered development may all be regarded as urban sprawl. Definitions based on land use tend to associate sprawl with the spatial segregation of land uses, and with the extensive mono-functional use of land for single-family residential development, freestanding shopping malls and industrial or office parks. Ewing and others have devised alternative methods of defining urban sprawl based upon its impacts. Under this approach 'poor accessibility among related land uses' or 'a lack of functional open space' would be examples of the defining characteristics of urban sprawl (Ewing, 1994). Chin argues that this approach creates a temptation to label any development with negative impacts as sprawl, thus creating a tautology that is unhelpful. Many definitions use the notion of low density to identify urban sprawl, however, according to Chin, this is frequently neither quantified, nor explained, adequately (Chin, 2002, p. 5). In addition, there are definitions based upon example, in which 'Los Angeles is often given a place of honour,' and aesthetics, in which sprawl is ugly development (Galster *et al.*, 2001, p. 683).

Amongst the most recent definitions, Peiser (2001) proposes that:

> 'the term is used variously to mean the gluttonous use of land, unin-
> terrupted monotonous development, leapfrog discontinuous development
> and inefficient use of land'.   (Peiser, 2001, p. 278)

In a similar vein, Squires defines sprawl as:

> 'a pattern of urban and metropolitan growth that reflects low-density,
> automobile-dependent, exclusionary new development on the fringe of
> settled areas often surrounding a deteriorating city'.   (Squires, 2002, p. 2)

Galster *et al.* (2001), suggest that the term has variously been used to refer to:
patterns of urban development; *processes* of extending the reach of urbanised
areas; *causes* of particular practices of land use; and to the *consequences* of
those practices (Galster *et al.*, 2001, p. 681). In place of this confusion they
suggest that sprawl is:

> 'a pattern of land use in an urbanised area that exhibits low levels of some
> combination of eight distinct dimensions: density, continuity, concentra-
> tion, clustering, centrality, nuclearity, mixed uses and proximity'.
>   (Galster *et al.*, 2001, p. 685)

One of the advantages claimed for this definition is that it suggests and
can accommodate different types of sprawl. Furthermore, it permits sprawl
to be considered as a *process* and not merely a *pattern* of urbanisation.
Galster *et al.* (2001), develop conceptual and operational definitions of each
of these eight dimensions of sprawl. These operational definitions, which
only measure patterns of sprawl, were tested through their application in
13 large urbanised areas in the USA. Although the study did not attempt
to develop measures of sprawl as a process, the authors argue that the measurement of patterns of sprawl at different points in time would reveal the
processes at work (Galster *et al.*, 2001, p. 687). This approach is conceptu-
ally interesting and does attempt to bring some quantitative rigour to the
measurement of patterns of urban sprawl. However, it is very demanding
on data, which makes its widespread application difficult, as the definitions
of urbanised areas and the nature and availability of data vary so widely
between individual cities, regions and countries: a particular problem when
looking comparatively across the European continent.

Traditional urban models usually show the intensity of urban activity to be
greatest in the city centre and gradually declining towards the edge of the
urban area. In other words, there is a density gradient that tends to slope

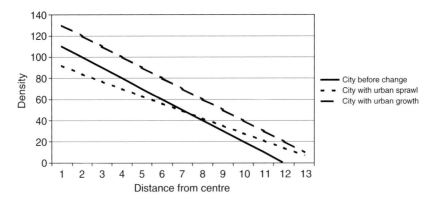

Figure 1.1   Distinguishing urban sprawl and urban growth.

downwards away from the city centre. The slope and precise shape of this line will vary with the nature of the activity being measured. Thus, the gradient for employment density will differ somewhat from that for population, housing or floorspace. In reality, a whole range of factors including local topography, transport routes, suburban centres, and so forth will distort density gradients. Furthermore, post-modern urban analysis recognises a whole host of additional influences on urban change and urban form (see, e.g. Harvey, 1989). Leontidou (1993), in particular, has pointed out the structural differences between the Mediterranean city and the northern European or Anglo-American city.

Nevertheless, if this initial idea of a downward sloping density curve can be accepted for a moment, then, as shown in Figure 1, urban sprawl will always result in the density gradient becoming less steep. It is this change in the gradient of the density line that is for us a key defining feature of urban sprawl. This also enables us to distinguish urban sprawl from urban growth. Urban growth can be defined in terms of either an expansion of population, or economic activity within an urban area. All other things being equal, urban growth will cause the density gradient line to shift to the right, whilst retaining the same gradient, whereas urban sprawl will cause it to become less steep (Couch *et al.*, 2005). This analysis leads to an important indicator of urban sprawl that can be tested empirically: changes in urban density at different distances from the city centre.

The origins of suburbia and urban sprawl in Europe and the USA

At the end of the eighteenth century, London had long since succeeded Paris as Europe's largest and most powerful city; in the year 1800 its metropolitan area already had a population of 1.1 million inhabitants (Fishman, 1987, p. 18). London became not only a very big, but also a very dense city. Home and work were inseparable and there were few neighbourhoods exclusively given over to commercial office, or residential functions. Production took place in the small shops of artisans; public buildings, hotels, churches, warehouses, shops and homes were interspersed, often located in the same structure (Jackson, 1985, p. 15). The density was so high that it took only a couple of hours to walk from the very edges of the city to the centre.

Amongst the industrialising nations of Europe, especially in Britain, the first half of the nineteenth century saw the emergence of a substantial middle class, based upon the rapid expansion of professional and managerial work. 'This "new" class was the most family-conscious and home-centred generation to have emerged in English history' (Burnett, 1986, p. 98). But, initially, this growing middle class had to live in the extremely congested urban core. Even for the wealthy urban elite everyday life was, in some ways, pretty much the same as for the urban poor: crowded, dirty, noisy and unhealthy. The city became economically more and more important, but at the same time more and more difficult to inhabit. The bourgeoisie both hated and feared city life. No wonder they developed two strong withdrawals, both also highly relevant today: one was *domesticity*, the other was the *suburb*.

In 1864, the British art historian and author, John Ruskin, delivered a series of lectures in Manchester. They concerned domesticity and for him the ideal Victorian suburban wife was a kind of home manager. The Evangelical church also gave women the role of guardians of the Christian home. In their opinion, a decent woman's only task outside the home was charity work among the local poor. Her responsibilities at home could be specified, just as the male responsibilities in the outer world. It was her duty to supervise the servants, educate her children and master the household accounts. She had important *work* to do in order to secure the home's tidiness, comfort and loveliness.

'This is the true nature of home – it is the abode of peace; the protection not only against damage but also against terror, doubt and division. If it does not work that way it is not a home. When the anxiety of the outer world penetrates into it, when an incoherent, uncharitable and hostile world is allowed to cross the threshold by a husband or a wife, it ceases to be a home. It becomes just a part of the outer world, with a roof over it and a fireplace. But as long as it is a sacred place, an exalted temple, a temple of the heart ... it is a home'.   (Ruskin, 1905, p. 73)

This new and emotional type of family motivated the middle class to create the suburban life style. The aim, as Ruskin pointed out, was to protect the individual against external threats, against what was 'out there' in a world inhabited by strangers. One may talk about a division between the three historic functions of a home: to work in, to live in, and to sell or exchange the fruits of one's production from. In the nineteenth-century middle-class English suburb, only the function of living remained within the home. A characteristic of this style of living was its privacy, which meant that it became exceptionally difficult to build an organic and well-functioning society around it. The home turned into a symbol for the family in general, and for the nuclear family in particular.

The nuclear family is a nineteenth-century invention. In his famous book *The Family, Sex and Marriage in England, 1500–1800*, Lawrence Stone describes the domesticated nuclear family as a handful of individuals bonded to each other by warm affective ties. The older nuclear family was open, in the sense that influences from neighbours and kin usually were more important than the ties between father, mother and children. It was also fragile and often very short lived and Stone writes that it was neither very durable, nor emotionally or sexually very demanding (Stone, 1977, p. 7).

Richard Sennett claims that what happened was that a wall was built between our subjective experiences – those we have in our consciousness – and our outer, physical environment. Our cities look the way they do because we are afraid to reveal our inner thoughts. The reason behind this is that city-dwellers are forced to share their everyday existence with others who are and remain strangers, and strangers cannot be expected to be benevolent. If outer life were just a simple reflection of inner life we would all be exposed to each other. Therefore, we have to create a contrast between an inner life, which does not correspond to the outer life, to the extent that this is in our powers. And vice versa, an outward existence, which does not relate to what is going on inside us. The city is on the outside, home on the inside. The family is its own kingdom and, until liberated by the gender equality and new working patterns of the late twentieth century, it bound women in, what Sennett calls, both a secular *purdah* and an *émigration intérieure*. He writes: 'stated baldly, "home" became the secular version of spiritual refuge; the geography of safety shifted from a sanctuary in an urban centre to the domestic interior' (Sennett, 1990, p. 21).

This was the situation when the wealthy merchant elite of London, in the eighteenth century, started to acquire weekend villas, where they went by private carriage each Saturday afternoon and returned to the city Monday morning. One could say that the suburban life started by the wife and children remaining in the weekend house, while the male breadwinner commuted. Robert Fishman writes that the weekend houses were the ready-made materials from which the bourgeoisie created suburbia (Fishman, 1987, p. 40)[1]. To give just one example, Clapham was one of the favourite sites for wealthy Londoners in the eighteenth century. There they raised the new domestic suburban architecture, with detached country houses, and could escape from the urban poor and messiness of the city. They created a new kind of community for likeminded evangelical people, worshipping family life and having direct contact with nature. The functions of the home gradually became differentiated. The children got their own room, the parents got one room to receive guests and represent the family in, another to sleep and make love in (quietly so the children could not hear). A separate eating room was also required, in which a specific behaviour ('table manners') evolved. The social graces were directed inward, toward the mutual education and moral betterment of the nuclear family itself. With this kind of ideal home, they unintentionally shaped a new urban quality, the urban landscape, with houses in private gardens: the first version of suburban sprawl.

Before this middle class exodus from towns like London and Manchester, the suburbs were just the urban outskirts: the latest developments of housing on the next available parcels of land. With the sharp rise in urban populations in the late eighteenth century this expansion gathered pace. But:

> 'These were not places of escape for the middle class but housing for the masses: designed to be overcrowded, planned not only to save expenditure on land by covering sites as closely as possible, but also to avoid the expense of road building as far as possible'. (Gauldie, 1974, p. 84)

And the French historian Fernand Braudel writes in *The Structures of Everyday Life*:

> 'Every town in the world, beginning with the West, has its suburbs. Just as a strong tree is never without shoots at its foot, so towns are never without suburbs. They are the manifestations of its strength, even if they are wretched fringes. Shoddy suburbs are better than none at all. Suburbs housed the poor, artisans, watermen, noisy malodorous trades, cheap inns, posting-houses, stables for post horses, porters' lodgings. Bremen had a face-lift in the seventeenth century; its houses were constructed in brick, roofed with tiles, its streets paved, a few wide avenues built. But in the suburbs around it the houses still had straw roofs. To reach the suburbs was always to take a step downwards, in Bremen, London and elsewhere'. (Braudel, 1979, p. 503)

In the fourteenth century, and thence for more than 300 years, the suburb was an inferior place. In Chaucer's *Canterbury Tales* the suburbs are described as 'corners and blind alleys where robbers and thieves instinctively huddle secretly and fearfully together'. In Shakespeare's London, a whore could be called 'a suburb sinner', because of the many brothels on the urban fringe, and to call a man a 'suburbanite' was a serious insult (Fishman, 1987, p. 6). Early seventeenth-century Southwark, home to Shakespeare's Globe theatre on the outskirts of London 'was the principal nest of crime in the capital, it was filthy, crowded and dangerous' (Bragg, 2003, p. 139).

These negative connotations had to change when wealthy Londoners started to move out to their weekend houses. The emergence of *suburbia* needed a complete transformation of urban values, since the modern suburb had no precedents in the pre-industrial city. Suburbia was a contradiction of the older principle that said that the central city was the only proper place for the elite to live in. It also contradicted the nobility's definition of land as *productive*: in the emerging suburbia, land was organised for *consumption*. Nevertheless, this new and exemplary version of suburbia was the result of improvisation, not a designed idea such as, for example, Ebenezer Howard's *Garden City*. Maybe Lewis Mumford gave the best explanation of the change, when he wrote that suburbia is 'a collective effort to live a private life' (Mumford, 1938). With the suburban detached house situated in a wholly residential area, the bourgeois family could escape both from the industrial estates, and the working poor with their horrible dwellings. It really was a flight from the industrial world they themselves were creating. But, more than that, suburbia could well be seen as the birth of the spatially class-segregated society, the end of the mixed society that planners of today often romanticise.

Friedrich Engels' description, from 1844, of what happened to Manchester, is famous. The town had an elegant business district with principal buildings in Gothic and Venetian styles; warehouses, banks, counting-rooms, offices, commission houses and agencies. Visitors met for the first time ever in an urban core that was quiet and empty after business hours, since nobody lived there. A factory zone, densely packed with workmen's dwellings, chimneys and the factory buildings with their steam driven machines, surrounded this business district. Beyond the region of smoke, in the suburbs, the bourgeoisie had their villas. An observer, Thomas Parkinson, believed that there was no town in the world where the distance between the rich and the poor was greater. There was said to be far less personal communication between the master cotton-spinner and his workmen than between the Duke of Wellington and the humblest labourer on his estate (Parkinson, 1841).

The Americans were not far behind. Frederick Law Olmsted, the famous landscape architect and planner who had his greatest success with Central Park in New York, together with his partner, Calvert Vaux, laid out sixteen suburbs. He was convinced that no great city could any longer exist without great suburbs (Jackson, 1985, p. 79). To summarise, there is strong evidence that the notion of *suburbia* is substantially Anglo-American in origin. European cities would experience the development later, in a very different way.

But the growth of the suburbs could not occur without improvements in urban transport systems. It was all very well for those who could afford a horse and carriage to move out to new suburban villas where the air was cleaner and the neighbours more polite (Burnett, 1986, p. 13), but it was not until the emergence of suburban railway systems, in the latter half of the nineteenth century, that the great age of suburbanisation could begin. Again, amongst the great cities of Europe it was London that took the lead. The building of the London underground and suburban railway systems extended deep into the surrounding countryside, bringing many new areas within daily commuting distance of the capital and creating a multitude of opportunities for speculative suburban housebuilding.

'Underground (railway) extensions such as that from Golders Green to Edgware in 1924 had quite consciously opened up a whole sector of the urban fringe for development, which in turn generated more passengers'.
(Ward, 1994, p. 44)

In contrast the Paris 'metropolitan' railway did not extend beyond the city's tightly drawn boundary, whilst in Berlin the development of the underground railway was held up by legal wrangles (Hall, 1988, p. 33). But the continental European experience was different in other ways too.

When Olmsted believed that no great city could exist without suburbs for the affluent citizens, he was wrong. Not completely of course, in the same way as a minority of wealthy Englishmen insisted on staying in the city core, there where some new suburban villas in France, but they were indeed considered quite eccentric. The French bourgeoisie favoured the city core that the English saw as more or less unliveable in and rejected. French cities belong to a more Mediterranean tradition of urban form – almost the reverse of the Burgess model (see Leontidou, 1990; 2001; and Chapter 3 below).

The French ideal was an apartment in a large building located on a busy boulevard near the centre of the city: how come? Robert Fishman tells the story. During the 1840s, successful Parisian merchants created a new urban district, *Chaussée d'Antin*, where they could practice the same principles as the English did in the suburb: domesticity, privacy and class segregation. In contrast to the house plans in London, in these elegant French houses workspace and family space were kept apart. The apartments often occupied a whole floor with elegant suites of rooms. The shops with their large windows did not have any connection with the residences. Servants and tradesmen had to use back doors and back stairs: only the residents and their guests used the main stairways. To make differences between the servant's and the family's space was important. The latter was decorated with parquet floors, elaborate plastering, marble fireplaces and gold-framed mirrors. The servant's space consisted of the kitchen and the rooms facing the courtyard. Thus, the French elite acquired the domestic isolation that the English had achieved by fleeing to suburbia. Emile Zola (1999) captured the atmosphere exactly in his cutting satire of bourgeois life in 1860s Paris: *Pot-Bouille*. These apartment houses of *Chaussée d'Antin* served as models for future middle class housing in the same way as the suburban villas did in London and Manchester. Instead of combining domestic values with a countryside lifestyle, the French elite preferred to combine privacy with urban pleasures such as theatres, balls, cafés and restaurants (Fishman, 1987).

When the English suburb developed, really no great concentration of capital was needed. But for Paris the situation was different. Napoleon III wished to transform the chaotic and still medieval Paris with its winding and narrow streets into a grand imperial capital and, in his view, a large city could not be modernised piecemeal. In order to accomplish his vision, he gave almost dictatorial powers to the prefect of Paris, Baron Georges-Eugène Haussmann. To summarise a complex and dramatic change in a few words, Haussmann transformed Paris into an elegant modern city – where it was easy to control the revolutionary crowds – with boulevards and prestigious apartment houses, symbolising the adherence to the Napoleonic regime (Harvey, 2003). The poor, who received none of the largesse that Haussmann bestowed on the favoured bourgeoisie, found their neighbourhoods demolished, and were forced by government policy to move to the outskirts of the city. Industry too was forced to the periphery, and a working-class industrial belt was formed in precisely those picturesque areas that might have attracted middle-class villas (Fishman, 1987, p. 115). Urban planning here achieved what in other cities, especially those of Southern Europe, happened spontaneously: the exclusion of the poor to the periphery of the city (Leontidou, 1990; 2006).

In a period of two decades, Paris achieved its classic form and inspired many other European cities, from Lyon and Marseilles to Berlin and Stockholm. Vienna and Prague, especially, used Paris as a model and developed urban cores with monumental apartment houses. This style of urban design soon spread through central and eastern Europe. No wonder Paris is seen as the cultural capital of the nineteenth century and as the capital of modernity (Harvey, 2003). However, it should also be said that the Parisian model was more authoritarian by far than the Anglo-American. The great Parisian boulevard was possible to accomplish in the nineteenth century – and so was the Viennese Ringstrasse (Schorske, 1981) – but could hardly be repeated in the Western world today.

In the late 1800s, with the industrial revolution, many Americans moved from rural areas into towns and cities. Immigrants also usually started their new lives there, and they fuelled urban growth even more than in-state people relocating to cities. The reason was the same as today: the poor make cities around the world grow very fast through necessity, as it was in cities and urban areas they could hope to find a job. This process accelerated in the early 1900s and by the early 1930s only 30% of the population of the USA lived in rural areas. North America's future was urban. But it was also suburban: like a tide turning, people started to move outwards again, to the suburbs.

The process of urban sprawl in the USA appears to have its origins in the early years of the twentieth century with the expansion of bus services, the electric streetcar and metropolitan railway systems, making possible daily commuting into the central city and back to the suburbs. Later, rapidly rising automobile ownership opened up for development areas that had not been well served by public transport. Responding to the emerging growth in traffic, public agencies built new highways that reduced travel times and costs still further and made suburban development yet more attractive. There were other factors too. By the 1950s, a combination of rapid population growth, migration from rural to urban areas, rising household incomes and the availability of low-cost long-term mortgage finance all fuelled an increased demand for new suburban housing. Local governments also encouraged sprawl through zoning and sub-division regulations (GAO, 1999, pp. 6–7). In contrast, over the same period, most European countries saw a slower acquisition of automobiles, slower growth in household incomes, less investment in highway construction, a stronger commitment to planned higher-density development – including public housing, and in some countries, huge redevelopment costs following the World Wars.

According to Squires, between 1950 and 1990 metropolitan areas in the USA expanded by 181% – from 208 000 square miles to 585 000 square miles – whilst the metropolitan population increased by only 128% – from 84 million to 193 million people. This represents a fall in density from 407 to 330 persons per square mile. Within this expansion, many cities saw a major shift in households, especially those of the more affluent, from the central cities to the suburbs (Squires, 2002, pp. 5–6). Furthermore, the percentage of people living outside the central city in the 10 largest U.S. metropolitan areas increased from about 40% in 1950 to about 60% in 1990 (GAO, 1999, p. 4). There are urban areas that both decline and sprawl: between 1970 and 1990, the population of Detroit in Michigan declined by 8% while its land area increased by 28%. Economic activity, especially commerce and retailing, has followed this trend towards the suburbs, and many of those formerly rural counties on the edge of metropolitan areas have become some of the fastest growing locations in the country (Isserman, 2001).

There has also been a racial dimension to sprawl, as middle-class white Americans detached themselves from the black and multiethnic inner-city areas. Today, the 'white flight' continues, and often people move to quite distant suburbs and communities – sometimes even gated (Blakely & Snyder, 1999). No wonder there is an expanding discussion on *demographic balkanisation*, a term that refers to the separation by race, ethnicity, class and age across urban regions. Data from the 2000 Census shows that, between 1970 and 1990, the inner-city population in the US was reduced by 23% in favour of the suburbs (Simmons & Lang, 2001). Here one should also remember that America is growing faster than Europe. According to the Population Reference Bureau, the USA has a 1% annual increase in population – 30% comes from migration and 70% from the excess of birth over deaths. During the present century, the population of the USA will probably more than double (Riche, 2000).

For individual residents, the problem of sprawl is not always easy to see, with many people being quite obviously happy living in sprawled urban areas. However, from an ecological perspective, sprawl is harder to accept. No one could deny that sprawl increases the energy intensity of modern lifestyles. The USA has no more than 5% of the world's population, but consumes one-quarter of the world's oil. More than 60% of this is for transport. In 'Realty Times', the leading Real Estate News Site on the internet, the columnist Lesley Hensell, in April 2001, wrote that sprawl was so serious a problem it threatened the American way of life, including those 'values' of motherhood and apple pie. Maybe one could say that suburbia has succeeded too well. In extreme cases it has become an *edge city*:

> 'Our new city centers are tied together not by locomotives and subways, but by jetways, freeways, and rooftop satellite dishes, thirty feet across. Their characteristic monument is not a horsemounted hero, but the atria reaching for the sun and shielding trees perpetually in leaf at the cores of corporate headquarters, fitness centers, and shopping plazas. These new

urban areas are marked not by the penthouses of the old urban rich or the tenements of the old urban poor. Instead, their landmark structure is the celebrated single-family detached dwelling, the suburban home with grass all around that made America the best-housed civilization the world has ever known'.   (Garreau, 1991, p. 4)

Even the most ardent advocates of suburban growth never desired this – a new form of city, neither the Dickens-styled nineteenth-century city nor the middle class suburb. It is a decentralised and fragmented hybrid landscape, without either the traditional urban concentration or the segregated suburb. These new developments, such as that centred on Boston's intersection of Route 128 and the Massachusetts Turnpike, are neither married to the city nor to the country. They exist in their own right, privatising the domains in which large numbers of strangers come together. According to the Sierra Club, Americas oldest, largest and most influential grassroots environmental organisation, sprawl is irresponsible and poorly planned development that destroys green space, increases traffic and air pollution, crowds schools and even drives up taxes. 'Good' cities solve this by having people stacked in apartment houses, while 'bad' cities continue to favour single-family houses on green lots.

In summary, it could be said that modern urban sprawl in the USA has five quite homogenous components:

- Housing subdivisions, sometimes misleadingly called villages, towns and neighbourhoods. They consist of residences only.
- Shopping centres, from small to big. What they have in common is that consumers cannot make use of them without a car.
- Office and business parks, often with dispersed towers and large parking lots.
- Civic institutions such as churches, schools and places where people go for municipal services and cultural events, are spread out and located nowhere in particular.
- Roadways, miles of sealed surface, necessary to the functioning of urban sprawl (after Duany *et al.*, 2000, p. 5).

Some differences between Europe and the USA

The literature and theory on urban sprawl is substantial and already provides a good explanation of its nature, causes and consequences. The question then is whether there is any need to write another book on sprawl. A closer examination of that literature reveals, however, that most of it has been written by North American scholars, particularly about the cities of the USA, while few and only very recent books concern Europe (Hoggart, 2005; Phelps *et al.*, 2006), or the Third World (McGregor *et al.*, 2006). Also, the scientific discussion on how to develop policies to control sprawl is still at an early stage; although some individual cities and governments appear to be having some notable successes, many others are not.

In our project we have used the North American findings combined with our own material to develop a different approach adapted to the European situation. It is true that sprawl in Europe sometimes has much in common with sprawl in North America, but it is also true that European sprawl has its own different characteristics, especially in South and East Europe. It may be that the European situation is more complex. Many European cities have large inner districts with poor housing conditions and socially excluded residents, but rarely on the scale of some US cities. European cities are frequently surrounded by sprawling suburbs but, again, with a different social class basis than US suburbs and rarely on the scale, or at the low density, or with the car-dependency found in many US cities. Furthermore, many European cities are seeing a return of population and rapid gentrification of the central city and regenerated areas such as former docklands. For these reasons, urban sprawl in Europe requires a different definition and different theoretical explanations of causes and consequences from those developed to explain urban sprawl in North America.

The topic of urban sprawl appears to be of much greater concern to policy makers in North America than in Europe. For example, a quick look at the search engine 'Google Scholar' in January 2006 revealed that, of the first 50 publications cited under the term 'urban sprawl', 45 were written in or about North America, 4 were written about Europe and 1 about Asia. In part this may simply be a consequence of terminology. Much of the equivalent debate in Europe is shaped around such concepts as 'sustainable urban development', 'suburbanisation' or 'urban regeneration'. Also the theories are different. Peter Hall makes a clear distinction between the Anglo-American and the European tradition in urban planning (Hall, 1975). Since at least the writings of Ebenezer Howard there has been a strong attachment to suburban development and the linking of town and country in Anglo-American urban theory. As a reaction against the hard and unhealthy urbanity of the nineteenth-century city, Howard (1902) conceptualised the idea of the 'Garden City', which would bring together the virtues of the town (jobs, culture, opportunities), with the virtues of the countryside (greenery, fresh air, quietude). Both in Britain (his home) and in the USA this ideal struck a chord with professionals and public alike, and was taken up as a powerful normative theory of planning. It has played a key role in shaping the form of urban growth through the twentieth century. In Britain, his ideas led to the development of two garden cities, many so-called 'garden suburbs' and eventually to the 'New Towns' programme of planned overspill.

In the USA, Clarence Perry developed the concept of the suburban 'neighbourhood' as a means of bringing order to the fast growing suburbs of the New York region. In the 1930s, Clarence Stein went further by separating vehicular traffic from pedestrians in what later became known 'Radburn' housing layouts, after the town of Radburn, New Jersey where his ideas had first been put into practice. Around the same time, Frank Lloyd Wright developed his vision for *Broadacre City*, consisting of single-family homes, each surrounded by a large plot of land on which each household could grow their own food. Back in Britain, in his Greater London Plan (1944), Patrick Abercrombie advocated a concentric ring approach to the planning of London. Densities would be reduced in the innermost ring through slum clearance; there would be no action in the second, suburban ring, but its outward growth would be restricted by a 'green belt' (the third ring); and in the final, outermost ring a series of planned satellite towns would absorb overspill and sprawl. Thus, both Britain and the USA had strong advocates who legitimised the low-density residential neighbourhood as a desirable urban form. In Britain, perhaps rather more than in the USA, there was an attempt to bring some coherence to urban growth by grouping these neighbourhoods into planned overspill developments and new towns.

Although the garden city has its examples in continental Europe, for example in some German mining settlements, the idea never obtained the dominance it had in Britain and the USA. More influential were the ideas of Le Corbusier who, although addressing the same problems of urban failure as Howard, came to radically different conclusions. For Le Corbusier, it was the inner city that required remodelling besides the suburbs, and his solution was to use modern technology to increase urban densities by building a high-rise city that freed the ground for landscape and public use. Furthermore, he argued for equally high densities across the city – even in central Paris, along the banks of the Seine – to reduce the pressure on the central business district. The result was *La Ville Radieuse* (The Radiant City), published in 1933. In continental Europe, much more so that in Britain or the USA, these ideas had an effect on urban form throughout subsequent decades, although the Radiant City itself was never implemented.

Beyond urban theory and planning ideals, there are other contextual differences that differentiate urban sprawl and its control between USA and Europe. The most important of these are briefly discussed below.

Policy and governance

- Urban and environmental policy in the USA appears, from a European perspective, to be embedded within a fundamental orientation of all tiers of government towards a belief in the primacy and supremacy of the market and market-led solutions. In most European countries, there is a more ambivalent and complex relationship with the market. European politics and society generally accept and encourage more market intervention and market replacement than often appears to be the case in the USA.
- There appears to be a fundamental orientation in US politics towards 'small' government and significantly lower levels of taxation and public spending to those typically found in Europe. Even where, in the 1990s, European countries elected 'right-wing' parties to government (e.g. France and Italy), their approach to public spending and intervention in markets would probably put them to the left of both Democrats and Republicans, the two main US parties.

Local government structure

- Generally the structure of local government appears more robust in Europe than in the USA, with greater dependence on higher tiers of government for funding. This gives central and regional governments in Europe more control over local authorities and brings greater cohesion and direction to public policy. The European Union (EU) also has a binding effect.
- The average US Primary Metropolitan Statistical Area (PMSA) comprises many municipalities, each with its own powers over local taxation and land use planning. In Scandinavia also, the municipalities control taxation and land use planning, with very weak regional planning, but this is not typical in Europe. Even in the most extreme case of France, which has retained the historic *communes* as the basic unit of local government, they are subject to strict planning guidance from the region, the *département* and frequently a *communauté urbain*. Other European countries have evolved larger units of local government. The largest average size is found in England, where most cities are contained within a single local authority and where even the largest conurbations spill over no more than a handful of districts (Merseyside – 5; Greater Manchester – 10; West Midlands – 7). It appears to be generally the case that the smaller and more independent the units of local government, the more there will be competition between them to attract development and thereby encourage sprawling patterns of urban development.

Political and scientific concern for sustainable development

- The impression gained of the USA is that there has been less of a lead in environmental policy from the Federal government and that much of the policy innovation has come from individual states or local municipalities. For example, whilst the USA Federal government has decided not to sign the Kyoto agreement, there is strong 'grass roots' opposition to this decision:

  > 'As of December 2, 2005, 192 US cities representing more than 40 million Americans support Kyoto after Mayor Greg Nickels or Seattle started a nationwide effort to get cities to agree to the protocol'.
  >
  > (http:// en.wikipedia.org/wiki/
  > Kyoto_Protocol#Grassroots_support_in_the_US, cited 18.1.2006)

- Thus there is a great range of political stances towards the environment and urban sprawl in the USA, with some states and some municipalities adopting strongly green and environmentally friendly policies whilst others remain hostile to the environmental agenda. Within Europe, there seems to be a high level of consistency of concern and approach to sustainable urban development both within and between countries. The EU provides a strong lead in environmental policy, which is cascaded down through national governments to regions and local administrations. Some European countries, especially in northern Europe, are amongst the world leaders in developing and implementing environmental policies. Thus it is probably easier to contemplate a European approach to tackling urban sprawl in terms of sustainability than it is to think in terms of a USA-wide approach to urban sprawl.

Economic geography and scale of urban problems

- Gross Domestic Product (GDP) per capita in the USA is around 140% that of the EU average. If we accept transport and housing costs as being approximately comparable between Europe and the USA, the difference in GDP would enable the purchase of more travel or cars and more land or housing space per capita and would encourage urban sprawl.
- Urban areas occupy only about 1% of the total land area of the USA. The overall population density of the USA is 31 persons per km^2, and there is little sense of a shortage of land. The population density of most European countries is many times higher. Urban areas occupy nearly 10% of the total land area of Germany and 7.5% in the UK. In many European countries there is a significant sense of land shortage.

- Few US cities contain a traditional inner core of sought-after middle class housing, whereas many European cities contain large areas of heritage sites and listed buildings, and have a strong tradition of sought-after middle class housing within the central city. They also share a cultural tradition of urbanism, as discussed in Chapter 3.
- Race and racial tensions may also be more significant causes of urban sprawl in the USA than in Europe. 'Racial segregation persists as a central feature of metropolitan housing markets, particularly in those communities with large African-American populations' (Squires, 2002, p. 7).
- The sprawling suburbs around the typical US city are often bigger than their European equivalent; they are growing faster and the divergence in living conditions between suburb and downtown are relatively greater.
- Furthermore, most European countries have had relatively strong planning systems for the best part of a century which simply have not allowed the problem of urban sprawl to get out of control to the extent that it appears to have done in some US cities.
- Another feature of the debate in the USA is that there seems to be a stronger backlash in favour of sprawl than has so far been articulated in Europe.

These differences between the USA and Europe are, in our opinion, sufficient to substantially change the underlying context within which urban sprawl has to be explained, evaluated and controlled. It therefore follows that it is right to have a separate discussion of urban sprawl in Europe, albeit one that learns from the experiences of the USA, but one that develops a unique European theory of urban sprawl.

The development of theory and policy in Europe

Urban sprawl is one of the most important types of land use change in Europe. It is said that sprawl is increasingly damaging to the quality of urban life and brings about major impacts on the environment (e.g. surface sealing, ecosystem fragmentation and increased transport emissions); the social structure of an area (e.g. life style changes and increased spatial social segregation); and the economy (e.g. spatial changes in the demand for development and the location of economic activity). Control of this urban sprawl was one of the earliest reasons for the emergence of modern town planning. As early as 1909, legislation in Britain gave planners an opportunity to determine and manage the pattern and form of urban development. By the end of the 1920s in Britain, there was growing concern and opposition to the unprecedented scale and extent of urban sprawl that seemed to be enveloping every city in the country:

> '[...] there was one aspect of suburban development which caused particu-
> lar public and political concern in the 1930s building boom. This was the
> tendency for arterial roads to be subject to ill-considered ribbon develop-
> ment of cheaper housing extending out well beyond the more continuous
> built-up areas. The practice saved the developers the cost of building proper
> residential roads, but damaged the scenic quality and undermined the effi-
> ciency and safety of main roads by mixing local and through traffic. It was
> disliked even by many of the right-wing opponents of town and country
> planning'.   (Ward, 1994, p. 48)

However, control was ineffective, as between 1922 and 1939 over 340 000 hectares of rural land in England and Wales were converted to urban uses: a 40% increase in the total urban area of the country (Ward, 1994, p. 49).

In the aftermath of World War II, many European governments, both East and West – with several exceptions in Southern Europe – sought to invest heavily in planned urban expansion schemes, either to absorb the overspill from urban renewal programmes or to accommodate population growth. In many cases, these developments took the form of freestanding new towns (especially in Britain and France) or peripheral extensions to existing urban areas. Much of this planned urbanisation, regardless of location and even where they took the form of multi-storey developments, was built at lower densities than those that could be found in the existing urban areas: it was planned urban sprawl.

In the second half of the twentieth century, after the initial phases of post-World War II reconstruction, much of Western Europe experienced long periods of economic growth. With this growth came ever more urbanisa-tion. The speed of change was rapid: for instance, the proportion of urban land in Belgium increased from 16.3% in 1990 to 18.8% in 2002 (a rise of around 15% in 12 years); in France the proportion of urban land increased by 23% over the same period and Denmark saw a similar increase in the decade up to 2000 (Eurostat, Indicators of Sustainable Development, 2006). But whilst some urban areas continued to grow, many, especially the large conurbations of North-West Europe, reached their zenith in the middle of the century and then declined as economic restructuring removed much of the employment from their cores. In Southern Europe, many conurbations continued to grow right up until nearly the end of the century (Leontidou, 1990) and the same might have been the case in Eastern Europe but for the fall of the 'iron curtain' and the massive shutdown of traditional industries following exposure to western competition.

Except in Southern Europe, urban populations typically fell as cleared areas were rebuilt at lower densities and households were moved out to new peripheral social housing estates, expanded towns and new towns. In some countries, notably the UK, economic growth combined with low interest rates to support a boom in speculative housebuilding for suburban owner occupation; the demand coming from households who were car-owners and able to consider living at ever greater distances from the urban core. This was less the case in countries such as the Federal Republic of Germany, where the acute housing shortage led local authorities to favour high density social housing developments at the expense of low density private dwellings (Power, 1993, p. 112). Similarly, in the planned Eastern European economies, sprawl was tightly controlled. In Warsaw, for example, decades of central planning ensured that the tendency towards urban sprawl in the post-war period was relatively weak. In Warsaw, the central city – rather than the peripheral suburbs – remained the more attractive place to live, and it was only after 1978 that the rate of population growth in the suburban ring exceeded that of the central city (Lisowski & Gutry-Korycka, 2002a,b, p. 6, 9).

Throughout the period of the slum clearance programmes, from the 1930s to the 1960s, the inner areas of many Northern and Western European cities were losing population. Until late in the period, this reduction in urban density was perceived as beneficial for it was associated with (though not the direct cause of) improvements in housing conditions and public health. It also provided space for new schools and other amenities. However, the 1970s, across Europe, saw a sea change in urban policy. This outward migration from the central cities was increasingly perceived as problematic, particularly as the local tax base began to decline at the same time as residual (non-migrating, non-sprawling) populations were tending to become disproportionately old, poor and dependent upon local authority services. Governments were becoming concerned about the costs of slum clearance and seeking cheaper alternatives that were less demanding upon public expenditure. Local communities were becoming critical of the slum clearance process and the lack of quality in the replacement housing offered, be it in-situ or in overspill locations. At the same time, there was mounting concern at the destruction of urban heritage in the interests of 'modernisation' as notions of urban conservation began to emerge.

This powerful cocktail of pressures led to the beginnings of a new policy known as urban regeneration. Slum clearance was gradually replaced by area improvement, and attempts were made to reverse urban decline and tackle deprivation through a series of new managerial and fiscal measures. In the Federal Republic of Germany, the 1971 *Städtebauforderungs-gesetz* allowed local authorities to establish inner-city area improvement schemes, within which grants were made available for the renovation of older property. In the UK, Housing Acts in 1969 and 1974 provided a major impetus to a similar shift in policy. In the Netherlands, policy began to shift in favour of urban regeneration from the mid-1970s with Amsterdam and Rotterdam trailblazing a participative approach that has since been emulated in many other localities. At the same time, many governments introduced or radically strengthened policies for the protection of existing built environments of architectural or historic interest. The conservation of urban heritage and the repopulation of visually attractive urban neighbourhoods has become a priority; often with the side effect of gentrifying the area. With increasing globalisation, urban competition has escalated in Europe (Jensen-Butler *et al.*, 1996). In Barcelona, the 1992 Olympics were a strong impetus to urban regeneration, but Athens had to wait for the turn of the millennium in preparation for the 2004 Olympics to even obtain a metro and a new international airport. However, in both instances, this event-led regeneration activity was carried out with at least one eye on improving the image and competitive position of the city (see Chapter 3).

Despite these changes, the general experience of European urban agglomerations in the late twentieth century was continuing suburbanisation and sprawl. At the same time, household size was declining as more young adults and elderly people lived away from their extended families, and as divorce rates rose and the number of single-parent families continued to grow. All of this added to housing demand. Some groups, notably small adult households, were happy to live in the city, but most others sought to live in the suburbs or beyond. A countervailing trend could be seen in international migration into (Western) European cities from less developed countries. A high proportion of such in-migrants settled initially in the inner cores of major cities in Northern Europe, where housing and employment were most readily available. In some cases, these trends became associated with racial tensions and anti-social behaviour, which in turn became drivers of demand for residential sprawl. In Southern Europe, the opposite case was also frequently true, since criminality in the suburbs and beyond is said to have kept people in the inner city. Suburbanisation and sprawl also brought increasing spatial social segregation: social housing estates were allocated to the working class on the basis of need (by definition excluding the middle classes), whilst new suburban private housing developments, frequently built at some distance from social housing areas, excluded those who could not afford their prices. Both types of sprawl tended to exclude a residual older and less able population, and some smaller households – who often remained in the urban core.

Changing industrial structures have also influenced these processes of urban sprawl. A number of trends can be observed: the shrinkage and closure of traditional industries; the movement of production to other regions and countries; the decentralisation of employment to suburban locations; and the development of new forms of employment, especially in the service sector, in city centres and at suburban or exurban locations. Industrial closures and shrinkage had the effect of removing employment and weakening the links between inner urban housing and inner urban workplaces, thereby encouraging the outward migration of those seeking work to suburban locations or to make longer distance moves to other regions. Conversely, these closures also created large tracts of vacant and derelict land with the potential to be reused for other purposes. In practice, these other uses frequently turned out to be housing, thereby providing some assistance with re-urbanisation and slowing the process of sprawl.

By the late 1980s, urban sprawl was also being seen as a serious environmental problem. According to the Brundtland Commission:

'The uncontrolled physical expansion of cities has ... had serious implications for the urban environment and economy. Uncontrolled development makes provision of housing, roads, water supply, sewers and public services prohibitively expensive. Cities are often built on the most productive agricultural land, and unguided growth results in the unnecessary loss of this land'.
    (World Commission on Environment and Development, 1987, p. 240)

Three years later, the European Commission's *Green Paper on the Urban Environment* suggested that strict zoning policies had led to the separation of land use and the development of extensive residential suburbs, which stimulated traffic generation. For this reason the Commission called for town planning strategies that would emphasise mixed use and denser urban development (Commission for the European Communities, 1990, p. 60). The UN Agenda 21 asked that all states promote sustainable patterns of urban development and land use (UNCED, 1992, Ch. 7), and the UK Government's 1994 strategy for sustainable development called for more compact urban development that would use less land and enable reduced energy consumption (Cabinet Office, 1994, p. 161).

By the end of the decade, the control of urban sprawl had become a major consideration of urban policy in most European countries. Furthermore, the European Spatial Development Perspective, produced for the European

Commission in 1999, emphasised the point that:

'Uncontrolled growth results in increased levels of private transport; increased energy consumption; makes infrastructure and services more costly; and has negative effects on the quality of the countryside and the environment. In addition, increasing prosperity in many areas has fuelled the demand for second homes with the result that many locations can now be described as weekend towns .... In many urban areas in the EU, development pressure on areas surrounding cities has become a problem. It is therefore necessary to work together to find sustainable solutions for planning and managing urban growth'.

(European Commission, 1999, pp. 64–65)

Most recently a report jointly commissioned by the European Environment Agency and the European Commission concluded:

'It is clear according to the good governance criteria that the EU has specific obligations and a mandate to act and take a lead role in developing the right frameworks for intervention at all levels, and to pave the way for local action. Policies at all levels including local, national and European need to have an urban dimension to tackle urban sprawl and help to redress the market failures that drive urban sprawl. The provision of new visions for the spatial development of Europe's cities and regions is vital for the creation of a range of integrated mutually reinforcing policy responses'.

(EEA, 2006, p. 48)

But it has to be acknowledged that tackling urban sprawl is a very difficult problem. As Dieleman and Wegener have pointed out, there are presently 'more tendencies towards spatial separation of urban functions than spontaneous tendencies for new forms of multifunctional, mixed-use settlements'; and these pressures encouraging sprawl are not transient phenomena but, as we discuss below in Chapter 9, the outcome of long-term and fundamental changes in social and economic conditions (Dieleman & Wegener 2004, p. 320).

Furthermore, the analysis of theory and policy has also to acknowledge that even within Europe there are subdivisions and groupings of countries that may make it inappropriate to develop a single continent-wide explanation for urban sprawl, or one discussion of consequences or policies. In their analysis of urbanisation and urban growth in Europe, Hall & Hay (1980) identified considerable variability in urban trends over the decades 1950–1970 in the different regions of the continent. In the region they named Atlantic Europe (which they define as Great Britain and Ireland), they found a strong tendency towards decentralisation of population away from urban cores, together with substantial inter-regional shifts in population, similar to the North American model. Northern Europe (Sweden, Norway and Denmark) seemed to be following similar trends but with a time lag of a decade or more. In Western Europe (Belgium, Netherlands, Luxembourg and France) it was difficult to identify any homogenous trend, with the Netherlands and Belgium decentralising and France showing a strong tendency towards centralisation. Similarly in Central Europe (Federal Republic of Germany, Switzerland and Austria) there were contrasting trends with both population and employment decentralising in Switzerland and Austria, whilst in Germany population seemed to be decentralising whilst employment continued to centralise. However, in Southern Europe (Spain, Portugal and Italy), the North American experience was almost completely contradicted, with a strong tendency towards centralisation still being the norm (Hall & Hay, 1980, pp. 226–227). Southern European cities have experienced different growth trajectories from the cities of Northern Europe. According to Leontidou, throughout much of the twentieth century these Southern cities experienced 'urbanisation without industrialisation' and informal job growth, while popular land colonisation expanded the suburbs (Leontidou, 1990, p. 29); in fact,

> 'the break-up of the urbanisation pattern in the north and the continuously distinct urban growth trajectories in the south indicate the structurally different urban impact of industrial restructuring processes'.
>
> (Chorianopoulos, 2002, p. 708)

But there is another region – Eastern Europe, that was not analysed by Hall and Hay, but was included in a study by van den Berg *et al.* (1982) – where the command economies produced yet another pattern of late twentieth-century urban growth.

Hall and Hay's analysis is more than 25 years old, but it does show the variability of the European experience. Indeed a more recent analysis suggests that:

> 'There is evidence of a substantial breakup of the previous regular pattern of decentralisation, which had been spreading from northern to southern European cities and from the largest to the medium-sized ones. During the 1980s there was a significant degree of recentralisation in many northern European cities … Some urban regions continue to decentralise and decline; others are declining but experiencing relative recentralisation. The pattern is that there is now a greater variation in patterns'.
>
> (Cheshire, 1995)

Although these urban trends have evolved still further over the past decade, our project investigated the extent to which the variability is likely to have remained. In fact, the following chapters will document the point that different parts of Europe continue to experience different urban trends.

Housing systems play an important role in determining the causes and extent of urban sprawl in any one country and have some influence on the scope and means of public intervention to control urban sprawl. Balchin (1996) subdivides his study of housing in Europe into four groups of countries. These are:

- countries where the dominant tendency has been to promote private-rented housing (including Germany and Switzerland);
- countries that have strongly promoted social housing (including Netherlands, Sweden, Austria and France);
- countries dominated by owner-occupation (including UK, Ireland, Spain and Italy); and
- countries where the housing system is in transition (including Hungary, Czech Republic, Poland, Slovenia, Croatia).

Not only do housing systems and the urban experience vary across Europe but so do approaches to intervention: the nature of the planning systems. Thornley & Newman (1996) identify five types of legal and administrative governance in Europe and have grouped countries into 'families' according to administrative type. The British family differs from all other forms of government in Europe. Based upon Common Law, the system is characterised by the lack of any written constitution and the doctrine of *ultra vires* (the scope of local government activity is limited to that permitted by statute, in contrast with the doctrine of general competence that is the norm in the rest of Europe). The Napoleonic family, originating in France but permeating much of Southern Europe, aims to provide rules for government and behaviour (even if contravened by informality). There are written national constitutions and sectoral codes of rules for state intervention in urban development, land ownership, so forth. Local administrations, especially the French communes, often have substantial powers enshrined in the constitution and carry considerable political weight, while elsewhere, as in Greece, nation-wide rules for planning and housebuilding make for rigid systems. The Germanic family (Germany, Austria, Switzerland) shares the notion of codification with the Napoleonic family but with even stronger abstract and intellectual foundations. Government in each of these countries is based on a federal system. The Scandinavian family (Denmark, Sweden, Norway, Finland) was historically based upon the old Germanic style of law, but has evolved a more pragmatic style than that of the modern Germanic states. The approach to administration is also a compromise, for whilst local self-government is seen as a cornerstone of local democracy, local government has been reorganised into larger, more efficient units. Finally, the East European family is not so much a grouping but a number of individual states, each in the process of transformation in the post-communist era. Some have reverted to former systems of government, whilst others are evolving new approaches (Thornley & Newman 1996, pp. 28–38).

Thus, any debate about policy responses to urban sprawl must recognise that the scope for intervention, the administrative level and the nature of that intervention will vary considerably between each regional 'family' of European government, each type of planning and housing system, and the nature of local urban trends. Nevertheless, there are some common underlying causes of urban sprawl that can, to a greater or lesser degree, be seen across modern European societies.

Methodology

Much of the existing research into urban sprawl has been carried out in North America and, with few exceptions, much of the literature on the topic comes from that location. However, the European experience of urban sprawl has to be set against different socio-economic and cultural backgrounds, different political settings and different stages of economic development across European countries. Not only is Europe different from North America; many parts of Europe are substantially different from each other. The diversity of history, geography, cultures and socio-economic conditions across European countries and regions is striking. For these reasons Europe justifies its own research and its own body of theory on this topic. This book attempts to make a contribution to the development of that theory. Furthermore, comparison between Europe and North America can help understanding of the processes of urban sprawl in both contexts.

The city is a human biotope, and an important objective of urban planning is the prosperous and healthy life of its citizens, as well as the protection of the environment from speculative pressures, private appropriation of land, entrepreneurial exploitation and profiteering. As has been suggested here, the causes of sprawl are powerful and the consequences complex and difficult to analyse. It is therefore probably unrealistic to think of eliminating sprawl. A more realistic goal for urban planning is to reduce the negative effects of sprawl where possible and to deal with the adverse consequences of sprawl within a perspective of sustainable development. This approach suggests that the major task for planners is to facilitate the integration of physical and social functions, thereby reducing traffic distances, land use and time consumption in the city. Seen from this perspective, the desire to influence and steer the dynamics of urban sprawl provides a powerful legitimating reason and justification for spatial planning.

The high level of diversity across Europe makes it very difficult to formulate a coherent picture, and almost impossible to be comprehensive. Therefore, we decided to identify a small number of important *archetypical perspectives on European sprawl* and use these to inform our views on causes, consequences and policy responses. Our original intention was to use the data gathered from these case studies solely to develop a qualitative model of the processes involved in urban sprawl. However, it very quickly became apparent that this approach would be too restrictive and miss the diversity and plurality of sprawl processes in Europe. We have opted for the richness of detailed explanation that could only be obtained through detailed case studies and through the inputs and views of experts and stakeholders. We have therefore moved to an approach based upon an open framework of modelling and qualitative assessment and inspection. These archetypical perspectives and an assessment of consequences are used as a starting point for discussion and, where possible, to give some more concrete recommendations for managing a 'smart sprawl', that is, a process of urban change which seeks to fulfil the needs of the actors demanding sprawl without inducing problematic consequences.

In preparing this book we set out to avoid a number of methodological traps:

1. stressing generalities and underplaying diversity – which initially was attempted and ended up in banalities;
2. generalising experiences into a model, from insufficient examples of urban development – which would lead to insupportable conclusions and policy recommendations;
3. following a positivistic paradigm of quantitative modelling and forcing qualitative knowledge into quantitative relations;
4. taking a view on sprawl which has a strong scientific focus to the exclusion of the reality of the problems that have to be solved by citizens, planners and administrations;
5. deciding to prioritise either the micro- or the macro-perspective on urban sprawl – which for good reasons can be assumed to be a multi-scale process;

6. opting for single-sector models or over-reductionism of reality to facilitate the functioning of models – which would result in inadequate complexity and over-simplistic models;
7. performing a micro-perspective analysis and later on (reluctantly) adding the meso- and macro-dimensions.

To provide an empirical basis for writing, the experience of urban sprawl was explored through case studies in seven urban agglomerations across Europe. In order to avoid pitfall 2, the criteria of analysis were developed in the light of these cases instead of determining them in advance. To do the latter would have enforced comparability at the cost of adequacy. To avoid pitfall 4, we involved stakeholders from each case study area in our deliberations, through workshops and interviews. This was devised as an open process and yielded the interesting result that it was not possible to generate a meaningful formal Europe-wide dynamic model (even a qualitative one) from this common knowledge base. The reason being that the concepts had to be very broad to represent the different cases adequately, with the consequence that the relationships identified on the basis of these concepts would have been extremely vague or simple (e.g. dominated by linear cause-effect chains). Our original objective of constructing a dynamic qualitative model on this (mainly) macro-level was therefore abandoned (thus avoiding pitfall 6). Instead, this part of the analysis became pure qualitative research with the aim of identifying those characteristics of case-specific phenomena upon which some generalisation might be based. This process yielded the identification of the four archetypical perspectives on urban sprawl presented in Part II of this book, which – in different combinations – help to explain the macro- and meso-level forces shaping urban sprawl. Furthermore, these perspectives give a starting point for the discussion of possible policy interventions.

At the same time, it was clear that there were structural commonalities across most of the case studies with regard to the preferences, behaviour and decisions of actors in the processes of urban sprawl. These more micro-scale concepts were clearly embedded in the macro-scale conditions, thereby avoiding pitfall 5. Here, the need for an adequate mathematical formalisation or model to support our deductions became obvious, because simple rules of interaction, each of them well known or at least plausible, added up to a complex network of interrelations. It became almost impossible to deduce the dynamic consequences of such networks simply by inspection. So the QUAM-Model (QUalitative Attractivity Migration) was established as a mathematical framework that would represent qualitative relationships identified in the different case study regions. Feedbacks of changes in a region on the attractiveness for a specific actor class are a typical example where a quantitative representation is not justified by the object, but only by the necessity generated by the method – here we avoided pitfall 6.

The case studies were located in seven urban regions: Liverpool (UK), Stockholm (S), Vienna (A), Athens (G), Leipzig (D), Warsaw (PL) and Ljubljana (SI) (see Figure 1.2). These areas were chosen to represent a variety of different aspects of urban sprawl. Liverpool, Stockholm, Vienna and Athens have all experienced evolutionary change under market economic systems; whereas Leipzig, Warsaw and Ljubljana all illustrate aspects of the revolutionary change from command to market economies in post-socialist Europe that occurred after the fall of the iron curtain. Stockholm, Vienna, Athens and Warsaw are all capital cities and benefit from additional types of investment that cannot be found in Liverpool or Leipzig. Furthermore, these last two cities illustrate the experience of urban sprawl continuing during periods of sustained economic and population decline. On the basis of causes of urban

Figure 1.2   Case study countries and cities.

sprawl, our case studies have been grouped according to four archetypical perspectives which are clear in chapter titles and are analysed in Chapter 9.

The structure of the book

Chapter 2, Sprawl in Europe: The Comparative Background, provides some empirical evidence on trends, processes and patterns of urban sprawl across Europe and in the seven case study areas in particular.

The second part of the book presents our four archetypical perspectives on European sprawl.

Chapter 3 considers infrastructure-related urban sprawl and the southern European city. The authors explore the passage from illegal expansion, without infrastructure, to contemporary investment-led urban sprawl in Greece. Athens depicts an archetype for this capital investment induced sprawl, particularly that fostered by major infrastructure investment in preparation for the 2004 Summer Olympics, such as the new airport and transport infrastructure in the Mesogeia plain.

Chapter 4 focuses on sprawl in the post-socialist city. Three conurbations have been included, all of which were, in the 1990s, dominated by the rapid transition from a planned to a market economy: Leipzig, Ljubljana and Warsaw. Though very distinct with regard to their starting conditions and the amount of investment during the transition period, some general conclusions about sprawl in these areas are possible.

Chapter 5 explores the phenomenon of sprawl in declining urban areas. Two of our case study areas experienced a substantial net-loss of population during the latter decades of the twentieth century, yet concurrently experienced sprawl: Leipzig and Liverpool. This loss of population brings about specific issues associated with urban sprawl, which are quite distinct from those in areas with growing population and economic power.

Chapter 6 deals with the issue of life-style driven urban sprawl especially with respect to second homes. In a number of European countries, including Sweden and Austria, but also Greece, second homes traditionally represent a major component of the way of living. Moving into second homes in rural areas, especially during summer, is seen as a recreational outlet and also as a way to live in more traditional surroundings. Besides the direct sprawl by the construction of new second homes, the conversion of these homes into permanent housing areas increases pressure on the local environment and facilities. Our case study in Stockholm illustrates such trends. Vienna has high levels of second home ownership too.

The third part of the book deals with a series of theoretical questions.

After the analysis of processes mainly referring to a meso-scale perspective of sprawl where dominating trends at the scale of the whole agglomeration and particular sprawling areas have been considered, individual actors are brought centre stage. The hope is that a meso-scale perspective is capable of integrating the micro-scale processes of individual decision making. However, no criteria exist to decide upon the preference of this approach against its inverse, that is, starting from the micro-perspective and integrating meso- and macro-processes into this. For this reason, we developed a fifth perspective on sprawl with a focus on individual actors, their preferences and mutual influences. This *actor perspective* serves as the main qualitative modelling concept and will be discussed in Chapter 7.

Chapter 8 explores policies for the control of urban sprawl, and considers what should be the aims of future policy in the context of the need for sustainable development.

Finally, Chapter 9 offers some concluding thoughts that seek to contribute to emerging theory about urban sprawl in Europe.

In conclusion, most of the attempts to define urban sprawl have concentrated on urban sprawl as a pattern of urban development, or as a noun. Our interest is more with the idea of urban sprawl as a process: a verb. Hence, for us, the simplest way to understand urban sprawl is that it is a process that will always result in the density gradient (from the central area to the periphery of the city) becoming less steep. This also permits us to distinguish urban sprawl from urban growth.

We have seen in this chapter how the evolution of the industrial city in the nineteenth century created both the social desire for sprawl and the income necessary to make it happen. Variations in local conditions, traditions and built environment led to different forms of sprawl in different countries. In the USA, richer than Europe and with more land, car ownership grew faster, building plots became bigger, and suburbs sprawled further and at lower densities than in Europe. In England, more affluent in the nineteenth and early twentieth century than some of its European neighbours – and with a tradition of living in houses (rather than apartments), supported by a planning ideology and a favourable housing finance system – suburbs grew quickly. In France, Germany and some other central European countries, with highly capitalised building industries, traditions of higher density (walled) towns, apartment dwelling and (in the twentieth century) a planning ideology that favoured high-rise building, sprawling suburbs were slower to develop. In much of Southern Europe almost the opposite occurred. Weaker planning systems, combined with more individualised and undercapitalised building processes, led to less organised patterns of low-rise urban growth around many cities.

In the coming chapters, these differences between individual countries and regions are examined in more detail. Trends in urban sprawl and policy responses are considered, and an attempt is made to identify a number of similarities and differences of experience and to develop some typologies of sprawl (archetypical perspectives on European sprawl). But firstly, in the next chapter, we set the scene with a look at some of the trends affecting European cities today.

Note

1   The *villa suburbanae* wealthy Romans set outside Rome, as well as the Renaissance *palazzos* in Florence and Venice, could be seen as prototypes.

References

Abercrombie, P. (1945) *The Greater London Plan 1944*. London, HMSO, London.

Adams, C. & Watkin, C. (2002) *Greenfields, Brownfields and Housing Development*. Blackwell, Oxford.

Alonso, W. (1964) *Location & Land Use*. Harvard University Press, Cambridge Mass.

Balchin, P. (ed.) (1996) *Housing Policy in Europe*. Routledge, London.

Blakely, E. J. & Snyder, M. G. (1997) *Fortress America. Gated Communities in the United States*. Brookings Institution Press, Washington DC.

Bragg, M. (2003) *The Adventure of English: The Biography of a Language*. Hodder & Stoughton, London.

Braudel, F. (1979) *The Structures of Everyday Life. The Limits of the Possible*. Translation from the French, Fontana Press, London.

Bruegmann, R. (2005) *Sprawl: A Compact History*. University of Chicago Press, Chicago.

Burnett, J. (1986) *A Social History of Housing*. Methuen, London.

Hillier Parker, C. B. (2004) *Policy Evaluation of the Effectiveness of PPG6*. Office of the Deputy Prime Minister, London.

Cabinet Office (1994) *Sustainable Development: The UK Strategy*. HMSO, London.

Chaucer, G. (ca 1345–1400) (2003) *The Canterbury Tales*; Translated into Modern English by Nevill Coghill. Penguin, London.

Cheshire, P. (1995) A new phase of urban development in western europe? The evidence for the 1980s. *Urban Studies* **32**(7): 1045–64.

Chin, N. (2002) Unearthing the roots of urban sprawl: a critical analysis of form, function and methodology, Paper 47, Centre for Advanced Spatial Analysis, University College, London.

Chorianopoulos, I. (2002) Urban restructuring and governance: north-south differences in Europe and the EU URBAN initiative. *Urban Studies* **39**(4): 705–26.

Commission for the European Communities (1990) *European Green Paper on the Urban Environment*. CEC, Brussels.

Commission for the European Communities (1999) *European Spatial Development Perspective*. CEC, Brussels.

Couch, C. (1990) *Urban Renewal: Theory and Practice*. Macmillan, London.

Couch, C. & Karecha, J. (2002) The causes of urban sprawl, Urbs Pandens Working Paper, PIK, Potsdam.

Couch, C., Karecha, J., Nuissl, H. & Rink, D. (2005) Decline and sprawl: an evolving type of urban development – observed in Liverpool and Leipzig. *European Planning Studies* **13**(1): 117–36.

Dieleman, F. & Wegener, M. (2004) Compact city and urban sprawl. *Built Environment* **30**(4): 308–23.

Duany, A., Plater-Zyberk, E. & Speck, J. (2000) *Suburban Nation: the Rise of Sprawl and the Decline of the American Dream*. New York, North Point Press, New York.

Engels, F (1987) *The Condition of the Working Class in England*. Penguin, Harmondsworth, 1844.

Eurostat (2006) Indicators of Sustainable Development. http://epp.eurostat.cec.eu.int/portal/page?_pageid=1996,45323734&_dad=portal&_schema=PORTAL&screen=welcomeref&open=/&product=sdi_mn&depth=2.

European Commission (1999) *European Spatial Development Perspective*. CEC, Brussels.

European Commission (2005) *Urbs Pandens Final Report*. CEC, Brussels.

European Environment Agency (EEA) (2004) *Transport Emissions of Greenhouse Gases*. http://themes.eea.eu.int/Sectors_and_activities/transport/indicators/consequences/TERM02%2C2003.10/index_html.

European Environment Agency (EEA) (2006) *Urban Sprawl in Europe: The Ignored Challenge*. European Environment Agency, Copenhagen.

Ewing, R. (1994) *Characteristics, Causes and Effects of Sprawl: A Literature Review, Environmental and Urban Issues.*, FAU/FIU Joint Center, Washington DC.

Fishman, R. (1987) *Bourgeois Utopias: The Rise and Fall of Suburbia*. Basic Books, New York.

Fothergill, S. & Gudgin, G. (1982) *Unequal Growth: Urban and Regional Change in the United Kingdom*. Heinemann, London.

Galster, G., Hanson, R., Ratcliffe, M. R., Wolman, H., Coleman, S. & Freihage, J. (2001) Wrestling sprawl to the ground: defining and measuring an elusive concept. *Housing Policy Debate* **12**(4): 681–717.

Gauldie, E. (1974) *Cruel Habitations – A History of Working-Class Housing 1780–1918*. George Allen & Unwin, London.

Garreau, J. (1991) *Edge City: Life On The New Frontier*. Anchor Books, New York.

General Accounting Office of the USA (GAO) (1999) Report to Congressional Requesters: *Community development: extent of federal influence on "urban sprawl" is unclear*, Washington DC, GAO/RCED-99-87. http://www.gao.gov/archive/1999/rc99087.pdf#search='origins%20of%20urban%20sprawl'.

Goodall, B. (1972) *The Economics of Urban Areas.* Pergammon Press, Oxford.

Gordon, P. & Richardson, H. (1997) Are compact cities a desirable planning goal? *Journal of the American Planning Association* **63**(1): 95–106.

Gordon, P. & Richardson, H. (2000) *Critiquing Sprawl's Critics.* Policy Analysis No. 365, The Cato Institute Washington DC.

Gutry-Korycka, M. (ed.) (2005) *Urban Sprawl: Warsaw agglomeration.* Warsaw, Warsaw University Press, Warsaw.

Haim, M. (2003) *Expanding Beyond Our Limits.* Peaceworks Monitor Archives. http://peaceworks.missouri.org/monitor/2000/novdec/limits.html

Hall, P. (1975) *Urban and Regional Planning.* Pelican, Harmondsworth.

Hall, P. (1988) *Cities of Tomorrow.* Basil Blackwell, Oxford.

Hall, P. & Hay, D. (1980) *Growth Centres in the European Urban System.* Heinemann, London.

Harvey, D. (1989) *The Condition of Postmodernity.* Blackwell, Oxford.

Harvey, D. (2003) *Paris, Capital of Modernity.* Routledge, London.

Hoggart, K. (ed.) (2005) *The City's Hinterland: Dynamism and Divergence in Europe's Peri-urban Territories.* Ashgate, Aldershot.

Hollier, D. (1992) *Against Architecture: The Writings of Georges Bataille.* MIT Press, Cambridge, Mass.

Howard, E. (1902) *Garden Cities of Tomorrow.* London, Swan Sonnenschein, London.

Isserman, A. (2001) Creating new economic opportunities. The competitive advantage of rural America in the next century, In: *Beyond Agriculture. New Policies for Rural America*, Kansas City, Federal Reserve Bank, Center for the Study of Rural America.

Jackson, K. T. (1985) *Crabbgrass Frontier. The Suburbanization of the United States.* Oxford University Press, New York.

Jarvis, H., Pratt, A. C. & Cheng-Chong Wu, P. (2001) *The Secret Life of Cities. The Social Reproduction of Everyday Life.* Prentice Hall, Harlow.

Jensen-Butler, C., Shakhar, A. & van den Weesep, J. (eds) (1996) *European Cities in Competition.* Avebury, Aldershot.

Kelbaugh, D. (1997) *Common Place: Toward Neighbourhood and Regional Design.* University of Washington Press, Seattle and London.

Kivell, P. (1993) *Land and the City.* Routledge, London.

Le Corbusier, 1935, *La Ville Radieuse*, Boulogne, Editions de l'Architecture d'Aujourd'hui, Boulogne.

Leontidou, L. (1990/2006) *The Mediterranean City in Transition: Social Change and Urban Development.* Cambridge University Press, Cambridge.

Leontidou, L. (1993) Postmodernism and the city: Mediterranean versions. *Urban Studies* **30**(6): 949–65.

Leontidou, L. (2001) Cultural representations of urbanism and experiences of urbanisation in Mediterranean Europe. In: R. King, P. De Mas, & J. M. Beck (eds),

Geography, Environment and Development in the Mediterranean, pp. 83–98. Sussex Academic Press, Brighton.

Leontidou, L. (2006) Urban social movements: from the 'right to the city' to transnational spatialities and *flaneur* activists. *City: Analysis of Urban Trends, Culture, Theory, Policy, Action* **10**(3): 259–68.

Lisowski, A. & Gutry-Korycka, M. (2002a) *Urban Sprawl: Definitions, Trends, Processes and Causes.* Urbs Pandens Working Paper, PIK, Potsdam.

Lisowski, A. & Gutry-Korycka, M. (2002b) *Urban Sprawl: European Patterns, Environmental Degradation and Sustainability – The Warsaw Agglomeration.* Urbs Pandens Working Paper, PIK, Potsdam.

McGregor, D., Simon, D. & Thompson, D. (eds) (2006) *The Peri-urban interface: Approaches to Sustainable Natural and Human Resource Use.* Earthscan, London.

Mumford, L. (1938) *The Culture of Cities.* Harcourt Brace, New York.

Newman, P. & Kenworthy, J. (1999) *Sustainability and Cities: Overcoming Automobile Dependence.* Island Press, Washington DC.

Nystrom, L. (2000) *Quality of Urban Life in Europe in the 21st Century, Swedish Urban Environment Council.* Conference Paper, Stockholm.

Office of the Deputy Prime Minister (ODPM) (2003) *Land Use Change Statistics for England (18).* London, National Statistics, London.

Parkinson, R. (1841) *On the Present Condition of the Labouring Poor in Manchester; with Hints For Improving It.* London.

Peiser, R. (2001) Decomposing Urban Sprawl. *Town Planning Review* **76**(3): 275–298.

Phelps, N. A., Parsons, N., Ballas, D. & Dowling, A. (2006) *Planning and Politics at the Margins of Europe's Capital Cities.* Palgrave, Basingstoke.

Power, A. (1993) *Hovels to High-rise: State Housing in Europe since 1850.* Routledge, London.

Riche, M. F. (2000) America's Diversity and Growth: Signposts for the 21st Century, *Population Bulletin* **55**(2), Population Reference Bureau.

Ruskin, J. (ed.) (1905) *Sesame and Lillies.* Gertrude Buck, Longmans Green, New York.

Schorske, C. E. (1981) *Fin-de-siecle Vienna: Politics and Culture.* Cambridge University Press.

Sennett, R. (1990) *The Conscience of the Eye. The Design and Social Life of Cities.* Alfred A. Knopf, New York.

Simmons, P. A. & Lang, R. E. (2001) *The Urban Turnaround: A Decade-by-Decade Report Card on Postwar Population Change in Older Industrial Cities,* Fannie Mae Foundation. http://www.fanniemaefoundation.org/programs/census_notes_1.shtml.

Squires, G. D. (2002) *Urban Sprawl: Causes, Consequences & Policy Responses.* The Urban Institute Press, Washington DC.

Stone, L. J. (1977) *The Family, Sex and Marriage in England, 1500–1800.* Harper & Row, New York.

Thornley, A. & Newman, P. (1996) *Urban Planning in Europe.* Routledge, London.

UNCED (1992) *Agenda 21: Rio Declaration.* United Nations, New York.

UNHCS (1999) UN Habitat Global Urban Observatory and Statistics Unit, accessed at http://www.unhabitat.org/habrdd/trends/europe.html, 12.1.06.

van den Berg, L. *et al.* (1982) *Urban Europe.* Pergammon, Oxford.

Vienna Case Study Team (2003) *On a Theory of Urban Sprawl and Sprawling.* Urbs Pandens Working Paper, Workpackage One Report, PIK, Potsdam.

Ward, S. V. (1994) *Urban Change and Planning.* Paul Chapman Publishing, London.

World Commission on Environment and Development (The Brundtland Comission) (1987) *Final Report: Our Common Future.* Oxford University Press, Oxford.

Zola, E. (1999) *Pot Luck*, [English translation of 'Pot-Bouille' (1882)]. Oxford University Press, Oxford.

2

Sprawl in European Cities:
The Comparative Background

Diana Reckien and Jay Karecha

Urban trends in Europe

This chapter provides an overview of some of the major trends in urban development and sprawl across Europe before going on to describe the characteristics of each of the case study areas used in this book.

The total population of the 25 states of the European Union (EU) was just over 455 million in 2005, giving an average population density of about 117.5 inhabitants per km^2 (Eurostat, 2005). This can be compared with the USA, which had a population of 296 million in 2005 (US Census Bureau) and a population density of about 31.6 inhabitants per km^2. Looking forward over the next 20 years, it is anticipated that the total EU population will increase only moderately. Because the population is ageing and fertility rates are generally low, even this level of growth is dependent upon inward migration from outside the EU. There is also likely to be some modest internal redistribution of population with some internal migration from east to west (European Commission, 2004). According to UN estimates the proportion of the population of Europe living in urban areas is likely to rise from 73.3% in 2005 to 78.0% in 2025 (United Nations, 2004). There is a continuing drift of existing populations from rural to urban areas, and the majority of new immigrants tend to settle in urban areas, reinforcing existing patterns of urbanisation (European Commission, 1999, p.58). If these trends continue, it is estimated that existing or new urban areas will have to accommodate around 28 million additional inhabitants over the next 20 years. The pressure for urban sprawl will be considerable. Furthermore, according to the European Commission there will be:

'A higher proportion of older people, who will, in contrast with previous generations, be more mobile, prosperous and active. Children and young people will increasingly be from immigrant families and will often be caught "between cultures". As has been the case with the extended family of typical rural society, the "average family" is also on the decline. People living alone, single parents (often financially weak) and childless couples (...comparatively financially strong) are increasingly characterising society in the EU. Different groups make different demands on space; social requirements for land use are becoming more complex'.

(European Commission, 1999, pp. 58–59)

In most European countries strong polycentric urban systems can be seen. In many cases these towns and cities are developing networks, pooling resources and sharing functions with other cities. New and changing economic functions are putting pressure on cities to release more peripheral land for commercial and industrial development. Both the growing number of urban households and the increasing affluence of those households are continually pushing up housing demand, in terms of the number of dwellings and their space requirements. Urban sprawl has become a problem across the European Union. Traffic congestion and pollution have become acute problems in many cities. Natural environments, and the built heritage within and adjacent to cities, are under increasing threat from development and pollution. Growing differences in income and life styles are leading to increasing social tensions and segregation within cities. Many communities in inner urban areas and peripheral social housing estates suffer social and economic deprivation (European Commission, 1999, pp. 64–70).

A question arises as to the extent of urban sprawl in Europe: have all cities experienced similar degrees of sprawl or are there variations in trends between countries or between different types of city? In order to obtain an impression of trends in urban sprawl across Europe, we have analysed data from the European Union's 'Urban Audit' *(http://www.urbanaudit.org)*. The Urban Audit presents socio-economic and environmental data for 258 large and medium sized cities within the European Union and candidate countries. Data is generally provided for both the city and 'larger urban zones' (LUZ). According to the Urban Audit:

'political (local government) boundaries were used to define the city level. In many countries these boundaries are clearly established and well-known. As a result, for most cities the boundary used in the Urban Audit corresponds to the general perception of that city. The larger urban zone

(LUZ) allows a comparison between the city and its surroundings. The goal was to have an area from a significant share of the resident commute into the city, a concept known as the "functional urban region". To ensure a good data availability, the Urban Audit works with administrative boundaries that approximate the functional urban region'.

http://www.urbanaudit.org/help.aspx

By comparing data for 1991 and 2001 for both the city and the LUZ it is possible to obtain an impression of population change and the extent of urban sprawl. However, some caution must be exercised in using and interpreting this data, for the boundaries are political and do not necessarily coincide with functional boundaries. The extent to which a functional city is fully enclosed within its political boundary will vary from city to city and from country to country. For example, in the UK the built up area of Liverpool very evidently extends well beyond the local authority boundary of the City of Liverpool, whereas the boundary of Leeds City Council includes not only the built up area of Leeds but also a number of outlying villages and surrounding countryside. So the comparison between cities regarding the amount of sprawl must be treated with some caution. However, the data on the changing amount of sprawl around each city over time (between 1991 and 2001) is rather more robust and the analysis therefore more reliable. Rather than look at all 258 cities, the data has been sampled. The Urban Audit covers a different number of cities in each country. Unfortunately, the data are not comprehensive, and some countries (Spain and France for example) had to be excluded due to lack of data. For each country, where adequate data is available for city and LUZ populations in 1991 and 2001, the largest, median and smallest cities included in the audit have been selected. Where our case study cities have not been included in this sample, we have added them to our list. London has been excluded from the sample because of the distorting effect of its size compared with other cities.

The allocation of cities and LUZs to European zones in the following sections, follows the classification used by Hall and Hay (1980) in their analysis of patterns of growth and sprawl in the European urban system – with the exception that an Eastern Europe zone has been added. Our analysis makes use of the distinction between urban growth and sprawl mentioned in Chapter one. Growth occurs when the population of the conurbation increases. Sprawl occurs when the percentage of population living in the core city declines relative to the total population of the conurbation (LUZ).

Table 2.1 shows results for Atlantic, Northern and Western Europe. The first column shows the percentage change in total population in each city's LUZ. The second column shows the change in the share of the LUZ's population

Table 2.1 Patterns of growth and sprawl across Atlantic Europe, Northern Europe and Western Europe – selected cities

City	Percentage change in population of the conurbation (LUZ) (%)	Change in the percentage of conurbation population living in the core city (%)
Atlantic Europe		
United Kingdom		
Birmingham	−1.63	−0.5
Liverpool	−5.28	−0.8
Leicester	+3.78	−1.6
Ireland		
Dublin	+14.4	−3.4
Cork	+11.5	−6.0
Limerick	+17.7	−3.0
Northern Europe		
Denmark		
Copenhagen	+5.1	+0.6
Aarhus	+5.8	+1.1
Aalborg	+1.9	+0.7
Sweden		
Stockholm	+11.1	+0.1
Western Europe		
Luxembourg		
Luxembourg	+6.6	−3.1
Belgium		
Brussels	+3.7	−0.7
Gent	+1.3	−2.2
Bruges	+1.5	−1.4
Netherlands		
Amsterdam	+7.1	−1.4
Eindhoven	+8.6	−1.0
Arnhem	+6.5	−0.1

Source: Authors' calculation from EU Urban Audit data.

lying within the LUZ's core city. Where there has been a decline in the proportion of the LUZ's population within the core city, sprawl has occurred.

Nearly all of our selected LUZs from Atlantic Europe, Northern Europe and Western Europe, have increased in population during 1991–2001. Of the seven cities, which are the focus of this book, Stockholm LUZ has experienced high growth (+11.1%), while the Liverpool conurbation has experienced significant decline (−5.3%).

Atlantic Europe includes the UK and Ireland. All the conurbations examined are sprawling, although the rate of sprawling in the UK cities is modest. Birmingham and Liverpool stand out as declining and sprawling at the same

Table 2.2 Patterns of growth and sprawl across Central Europe and Eastern Europe – selected cities

City	Percentage growth in population of the conurbation (LUZ) (%)	Change in the percentage of conurbation population living in the core city (%)
Central Europe		
Germany		
Berlin	+1.4	−2.5
Leipzig	−3.1	−3.7
Bonn	+7.1	−1.5
Weimar	+2.8	−0.6
Austria		
Vienna	+2.8	−1.5
Graz	+0.5	−3.5
Linz	+1.4	−4.3
Eastern Europe		
Poland		
Warsaw	+8.9	−0.1
Czech Republic		
Prague	−1.7	−1.2
Brno	−1.3	−1.0
Usti nad Labem	−0.9	−0.8
Slovakia		
Bratislava	−1.2	−1.3
Kosice	+2.6	−1.5
Banska By..	+0.7	−0.8
Hungary		
Budapest	−5.0	−5.5
Miskolc	−2.4	−2.4
Nyiregyhaza	+3.6	−0.2
Slovenia		
Ljubljana	+3.8	−2.5
Maribor	−3.1	−0.4

Source: Authors' calculation from EU Urban Audit data.

time. It is notable that the three Irish cities show some of the fastest growth rates of any of those in our sample and have quite high rates of sprawl.

The cities of Northern Europe appear to be the most successful in combatting sprawl. This is the only zone in which conurbations are consistently growing but achieving greater compaction at the same time. Against this measure, Aarhus is the most successful city in our sample.

In Western Europe all the conurbations sampled are growing with quite modest rates of sprawl. The Dutch cites, in particular, appear to be combining quite high growth rates with strong restraints on sprawl.

Table 2.3   Patterns of growth and sprawl across Southern Europe – selected cities

City	Percentage growth in population of the conurbation (LUZ) (%)	Change in the percentage of conurbation population living in the core city (%)
Southern Europe		
Greece		
Athens	+26.7	−4.8
Larissa	+4.3	+4.9
Kalamata	−0.2	+6.7
Cyprus		
Nicosia	+14.7	+1.4
Italy		
Rome	−1.6	−5.0
Taranto	−1.7	−4.6
Campobasso	−3.4	+0.7
Portugal		
Lisbon	+4.3	−5.4
Porto	+7.5	−5.7

Source: Authors' calculation from EU Urban Audit data.

Central European and Eastern European LUZs (Table 2.2) have shown mixed patterns in terms of growth or decline, 1991–2001, with eleven of our selected LUZs showing an increase in population, and eight of our selected LUZs declining. Of our case study cities, Warsaw (8.9%), Ljubljana (3.8%) and Vienna (2.8%), have each grown, while Leipzig has declined (−3.1%).

The majority of conurbations in Central Europe are growing steadily and all exhibit some degree of sprawl. The exception is Leipzig, which is a declining conurbation and yet displays the second highest rate of sprawl in the zone. However, it must be remembered that Leipzig and Weimar were formerly in East Germany and between 1946 and 1989 were subject to the same type of socialist political regime as the countries of the Eastern European zone.

There is a mixed pattern of urban development across the Eastern Europe zone. Warsaw is expanding quickly with very little sprawl while, on the other hand, a number of conurbations sampled in the zone are, in a manner similar to Leipzig, declining and sprawling at the same time. Budapest stands out as doing particularly badly in this regard.

Five out of the nine Southern European LUZs (Table 2.3) have experienced growth in population 1991–2001. Four of the nine have declined. The Athens LUZ has experienced a dramatic increase in population (+26.7%).

Southern Europe also presents a variety of experiences. Athens seems to be an exceptional case, perhaps unique, with a very high rate of growth combined with an above average rate of sprawl. Larissa in Greece and Nicosia in Cyprus are also growing quickly, but in these cases growth appears to have been more successfully contained within the core city area. Each of the Italian conurbations sampled are suffering population decline and, in the cases of Rome and Taranto, experiencing significant amounts of sprawl at the same time. The two Portuguese conurbations are growing with quite high rates of sprawl.

Table 2.4 shows the conurbations by type according to their growth and sprawl trends. The conurbations fall into four groups. One small group is managing growth with containment: that is to say, the density of population in the core city is increasing faster than that of the conurbation as a whole. These examples are found in two zones; Northern Europe and parts of Southern Europe under Greek cultural influence. A second small group, comprising only two conurbations, both in Southern Europe, are experiencing decline with containment. They are shrinking inwards with the population of the core city being maintained whilst the outer urban areas decline.

The largest group is growing and sprawling at the same time. This includes conurbations from all zones except Northern Europe, with Western and Central Europe being particularly well represented. Finally, there is a group of conurbations that are both declining and sprawling. Here, the density of population in the core city is falling faster than that of the conurbation as a whole. The majority of this group are located in Eastern Europe, although a number of UK and Italian conurbations are also represented. The size of the conurbation seems, at this level of analysis, to have very little influence on sprawling.

Urban trends in the case study cities

There is a great variety of demographic and economic conditions and trends within the countries of the European Union, which have an impact on urban sprawl. Table 2.5 provides some basic data about the countries we have studied.

There are considerable variations in population density between these countries. The UK and Germany each have population densities more than double those of any other country studied. Poland is close to the EU average with Austria, Greece and Slovenia rather below this figure. Sweden is very sparsely inhabited, with an average density only one-tenth that of Germany or the UK. However, these initial impressions need to be adjusted to take account

Table 2.4 Conurbation types: growth and sprawl

Growth with containment	Growth with sprawl
Aalborg	Amsterdam
Aarhus	Arnhem
Copenhagen	**Athens**
Larissa	Banska Bystrica
Nicosia	**Berlin**
Stockholm	Bonn
	Bruges
	Brussels
	Cork
	Dublin
	Eindhoven
	Gent
	Graz
	Kosice
	Leicester
	Limerick
	Linz
	Lisbon
	Ljubljana
	Luxembourg
	Nyiregyhaza
	Porto
	Vienna
	Warsaw
	Weimar
Campobasso	**Birmingham**
Kalamata	Bratislava
	Brno
	Budapest
	Leipzig
	Liverpool
	Maribor
	Miskolc
	Prague
	Rome
	Taranto
	Usti nad Lebem
Decline with containment	**Decline with sprawl**

Cities with names in italics = small conurbations with a population less than 300 000; **Cities with names in bold** = large conurbations with a population over 1.5 million people.

Table 2.5 Population and economic trends across selected European countries

	Population, 2003	Population density, 2003 (Inhabitants per km²)	Projected increase in population 2005–2020* (%)	Average number of persons per private households (PPH) 2003	Gross Domestic Product per capita, 2003, in Purchasing Power Standards (PPS) EU25=100
European Union (EU25)	454 580 100	117.5	+1.92	2.4	100
Austria	8 102 200	98.5	+3.70	2.4	120.3
Germany	82 536 700	231.2	+0.12	2.1	108.2
Greece	11 006 400	83.7	+2.70	2.6	81.0
Poland	38 218 500	122.2	−2.63	3.1	46.9
Slovenia	1 995 000	99.1	0.00	2.6	75.9
Sweden	8 940 800	21.8	+6.7	2.1**	115.7
United Kingdom	59 328 900	244.3	+5.0	2.3	116.5

Source: Eurostat Yearbook 2005, various tables.
*Authors' calculation from Eurostat data.
** Authors' estimate.

of the fact that in some of these countries, Greece and Sweden and parts of Austria in particular, much of the land is undevelopable. This forces urbanisation into selected areas in which the densities obtained are often similar to those of urbanised areas elsewhere in Europe.

The projected increase in population gives an indication of the extent to which each country has to cope with pressures for additional urbanisation and housebuilding. This pressure is mediated by household size: the lower it is, the more dwellings will be required. Hence Sweden and Germany, with an average household size of 2.1 persons per private household (PPH) must provide 476 dwellings to accommodate every 1000 people, whereas Poland with 3.1 PPH need provide only 323 dwellings. This also affects the type of dwellings required, with smaller households more likely to accept apartment dwelling and urban living, whilst larger households are more likely to have preferences for houses with gardens and suburban locations.

Each country's per capita Gross Domestic product (GDP) gives an indication of its relative purchasing power and therefore its economic capacity to provide the required dwellings and infrastructure, whether through market mechanisms or by means of direct state expenditure. Here the richer countries of Northern and Western Europe are clearly at an advantage.

Thus, whilst both Sweden and Austria have some of the strongest rates of growth in households and demand for dwellings, both are in a strong economic position and have well-established planning systems to control and deal with the problems of urban growth and sprawl. Although household growth in the UK is quite strong, it is also regionally imbalanced with most growth forecast in the south and east of the country. Poland, Germany and Slovenia are each anticipating population decline or only very modest growth, so the pressures for urbanisation should be limited. In contrast, with a population growth rate above the EU average and relatively weak economic and planning capacity, Greece may be facing the most problematic future in terms of accommodating urban growth and controlling urban sprawl. Table 2.6 provides more data on the socio-economic profile of the seven case study areas.

The conurbations fall into three groups. The first group includes Athens and Warsaw, which are experiencing rapid growth in the conurbation combined with a substantial increase in sprawl. The characteristic of this group might be said to be economic growth combined with a relatively weak planning system. The second group comprises Ljubljana, Stockholm and Vienna, which are experiencing growth in the conurbation but more modest increases in sprawl. Here, economic growth is combined with more successful controls over urban sprawl. The third group comprises Leipzig and Liverpool, which are experiencing decline in the conurbation combined with strong controls over (or weak pressure for) urban sprawl. Here, relatively weak urban economies are combined with successful controls over urban sprawl. Nevertheless, Liverpool is still, with Athens, one of the most sprawling cities in the study.

The pressure for urban sprawl is also influenced by other factors including employment structure, income levels (GDP per capita), unemployment, household composition and housing tenure. Again, differences can be seen between these cities.

Leipzig and Ljubljana both lie within regions containing a greater than average ratio of industrial employment than is the norm in Europe today. It may well be that these cities still have to go through further structural economic change in the move towards more service-based economies. Such change is likely to have the opposing effects, experienced in Liverpool in the 1980s, of creating socio-economic and environmental pressures for outward migration whilst at the same time releasing urban land that can be

Table 2.6 Socio-economic profile of selected cities

	Athens	Leipzig	Liverpool	Ljubljana	Stockholm	Vienna	Warsaw
Population, 1991							
a) City	772 072	542 512	475 600	272 650	674 452	1 539 848	1 644 515
b) LUZ	3 072 922[a]	940 822	1 438 000	470 641	1 641 669[b]	2 062 969	2 300 000[c]
Population, 2001							
a) City	789 166	493 052	439 476	270 506	750 348	1 550 123	1 609 780
b) LUZ	3 894 573	912 064	1 362 004	488 364	1 823 210	2 121 704	2 631 902
Economic structure of region[d]	Agr 0.9% Ind 24.1% Ser 75.0%	Agr 2.5% Ind 32.2% Ser 65.3%	Agr 0.7% Ind 26.8% Ser 71.9%	Agr: 8.4% Ind 37.5% Ser 55.8%	Agr: 2.5% Ind 22.5% Ser 74.9%	Agr 4.8% Ind 24.8% Ser 70.3%	Agr 18.5% Ind 24.4% Ser 57.0%
Regional unemployment rate	8.7%	17.6%	4.9%	17.6%	5.7%	4.2%	17.6%
Regional GDP per capita EUR = 100	82.3	73.3	103.3	51.3	114.8	130.7	45.6
Experience of change	Growth of core city and conurbation, substantial sprawl	Decline of core city and conurbation, substantial sprawl	Decline of core city and conurbation, slight sprawl	Slight decline of core city, growth of conurbation, some sprawl	Growth of core city and conurbation, no sprawl	Slight growth of core city and conurbation, some sprawl	Slight decline of core city, growth of conurbation, slight sprawl
Average household Size	2.62	1.81	2.34	2.59	1.62	1.97	2.23
Percentage of households that are 1-person households	31	45	37	28	28[b]	45	38
Percentage of households living in owner occupied dwellings	53	10	53	78	27	23	16

Source: EC Urban Audit. [a] Urbs Pandens Athens team; [b] Stockholm City Council Statistics Year Book, 2006; [c] Authors' estimate; [d] Regional Trends, 2006 Table 2.3
LUZ = Larger Urban Zone – essentially the agglomeration but see The Urban Audit (http://www.urbanaudit.org/) for a precise definition.

re-used for residential purposes. The high proportion of agricultural employment in Poland is also likely to be sharply reduced in future, creating pressures for rural to urban migration that will lead to urban growth and sprawl.

There is a significant difference in the wealth and income of these cities. Vienna and Stockholm are affluent cities with high levels of GDP per capita and low unemployment rates; Liverpool too (despite the poverty of the city) is in a relatively prosperous region. In these cities the market demand for additional housing space may be more stimulated than the other four cities that lie in less affluent regions.

The core cities of Leipzig, Stockholm and Vienna all have an average household size below 2.0 combined with more than 40% of households comprising only one person. These are populations for whom high levels of urbanity (the compact city) are likely to prove acceptable. At the other extreme, the core cities of Athens and Ljubljana each have an average household size above 2.5 and very low proportions of single person households (only 28% in Ljubljana). These populations are more likely to seek suburban living environments. Tenure also plays a part, as sprawl tends to be associated with owner occupation. In the core cities of Athens, Liverpool and Ljubljana the majority of households are owner occupiers, in sharp contrast with the other cities studied.

Each of the case study cities is now described in more depth.

Athens

Athens is the capital of Greece and the country's economic and administrative centre. In 2001, about 30% of the population of Greece lived in the Athens conurbation. There is a sharp contrast between the very intensely developed and densely populated core city of Athens and the low density of development found in the surrounding urban region. Athens is an ageing city: inhabitants under 16 have decreased both in relative and absolute terms. On the other hand, the economic activity rate is high (64%) and the city has proved an attractive destination for immigrants (17% of the population are non-EU nationals). Athens was never a highly industrialised city and today its economic base is heavily service-oriented. More than two out of three jobs are in the tertiary sector, with finance, insurance and real estate being particularly strong. Nevertheless, the unemployment rate was around 9% in 2001 (Urban Audit, 2006).

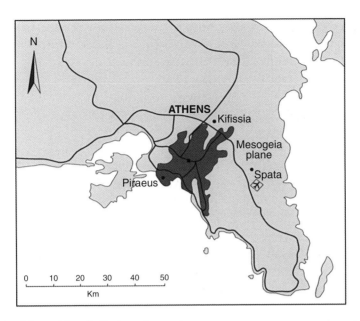

Figure 2.1   Athens. Lines indicate major roads.

Throughout the second half of the twentieth century, Athens experienced heavy environmental problems, especially traffic-related air pollution. In 1995, Athens had some of the highest pollution levels of any large European city according to the European Environment Agency (2001). These environmental problems put a major strain on the inhabitants and their health as well as on the planning authorities to cope with the problem.

Over recent years, the whole of Greece has been eligible for funding as an EU Objective 1 priority region, as well as through the Cohesion Fund. Athens has benefited through the construction of major infrastructure such as a new airport, a new underground metro system and a series of new highways. Much of the city's infrastructure was significantly upgraded for the Olympic Games, held in Athens in 2004. These investments have had an important influence on urban sprawl.

Culturally, the city features important ancient monuments, such as the Acropolis. It has a lively cultural scene, particularly in theatre, with many national and international festivals. The most recent new construction is the Athens Concert Hall, and in the future, a new Acropolis museum, a new Opera house and a Museum of Modern Art are to be built. In the years prior to the Olympic Games in 2004, a 'Cultural Olympiad' was held to reinforce the cultural significance of the games.

The Athens conurbation is governed by two tiers of local government, made up of municipalities and prefectures. There are over 90 municipalities, one of which is the City of Athens: this surrounds the historic centre and includes the traditional business and retail centre of the city. There are also four prefectures within the conurbation. In an effort to build an all-encompassing metropolitan authority, a supra-prefectural authority has been created, covering most of the conurbation.

Despite recent changes and a trend towards de-centralisation of authority, the municipalities and prefectures of Athens do not hold significant powers. The municipalities are responsible for services such as recreational and cultural amenities, minor infrastructure, limited social welfare services, parks and sanitation, and have a limited right to levy property taxes. However, the central government authorities and a large number of sectoral service agencies still handle planning, development, environmental issues, and other major areas such as transport and sanitation.

The historical experience of sprawl in Athens can be seen as a series of waves of development. The first big wave started in the early 1920s, when many thousands of refugees from Asia Minor set up homes outside the existing built up area of Athens. A second wave of inward migration occurred when population flowed from rural Greece towards the capital in search of an escape from rural poverty. They too settled on cheap peripheral land at the edge of the city. From the early 1980s and well into the 1990s, urban sprawl was fuelled by a wave of out-migration of middle class residents from Athens seeking relief from the city's infamous pollution problems. They built new settlements and converted second homes into permanent dwellings.

Today in Greater Athens, the hotspots of urban sprawl are to the East of the agglomeration, on the Mesogeia plain, where investment in the new airport, motorway and suburban railway infrastructure have opened up the area for urbanisation. Until the early 1980s, Mesogeia had remained a relatively agricultural area served by a few small scattered towns. The only urban sprawl was some ribbon development along the main arteries into Athens and a few isolated developments that had 'leapfrogged' beyond the urban fringe. Today the area is rapidly expanding with heavy investment in new housing, industrial and commercial developments.

Leipzig

Leipzig is situated in the Free State of Saxony in Eastern Germany. It lies at the heart of the densely populated Leipzig-Halle urban region. The population of the city stood at just under half a million in 2001, but the agglomeration has been in decline since 1989 – mainly due to a falling birth-rate and heavy out-migration to other regions.

Historically, for many hundreds of years, Leipzig has been known as an important mercantile city. The Leipzig Trade Fairs have been internationally known since medieval times. Together with the neighbouring city of Halle, the area experienced heavy industrialisation in the first part of the twentieth century, which gave the region its distinctive character. The chemical industry and open-cast mining (for power generation) were the most important industrial sectors. The economy flourished, but the natural environment and landscape suffered.

During the socialist regime, industry continued to be an important part of the city's economy but after German re-unification, and the structural adjustments forced upon the area by the transition to a market economy, much of this industry collapsed. Between 1989 and 1995 the number of jobs in industry fell by 70%, whilst since 1989 more than 50000 jobs have been created in banks, insurance companies and private services. Today the economy of the city has moved from one dominated by industry, to one more dependent on services. These rapid structural changes have led to high levels of unemployment. Nevertheless, in recent years the city has seen some new investment in the manufacturing industry, notably in the car industry, engineering, media and communication technology.

Today the regeneration of the city is clearly visible and it is regaining its historic role as a city of trade fairs and music – and a role as financial centre in Eastern Germany. The city is also an important educational centre with the University of Leipzig being the second oldest in Germany. The city offers a variety of cultural events and activities, most notably the Neues Gewandhaus concert hall, the Leipzig Opera House, theatres, variety halls, art galleries and museums, together with high quality parks, sport and leisure facilities. Following the district reform in 1992, Leipzig is divided into 10 municipal boroughs and 63 smaller municipal districts. The council is made up of 71 members, who are elected every 5 years.

Situated in the eastern part of Germany, the former GDR, Leipzig was almost ignorant of the problem of urban sprawl until the Berlin wall came down. Since 1989, the city has experienced several phases of sprawl. The first phase was mainly induced by commercial sprawl immediately after the opening of the German–German border. Thousands of investors came, developed land and erected buildings to exploit the business possibilities and take advantage of the new market. From about 1992 until 1997 there was a period of rapid

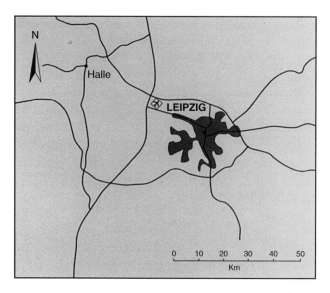

Figure 2.2   Leipzig. Lines indicate major roads.

peripheral residential development as households forsook the poor quality inner-city housing in favour of newly built suburban housing containing modern amenities. Restitution problems and lack of funding had severely limited the rate at which inner-city housing could be improved or replaced with modern apartments.

After 1997 the trend of moving towards the suburbs started to decline. Restitution claims began to be resolved and investment started to flow into the urban regeneration process. New retail and leisure facilities increased the competitiveness of the inner city against the suburbs. Only the development of single-family houses continued to sprawl into the countryside. Since then, suburbanisation around Leipzig slowed dramatically. However, the development free-for-all of the 1990s has left an oversupply of dwellings and commercial premises, both in the inner city and in suburban locations.

Liverpool

During the nineteenth and early part of the twentieth century, Liverpool was the second most important port in England. The population of the conurbation peaked at over 1.8 million in the mid-twentieth century, but since the 1960s changing patterns of trade and the introduction of new technologies reduced employment in the port and port-related industries. Structural changes in industrial demand and lack of competitiveness led to further reductions in the local manufacturing sector, whilst processes of

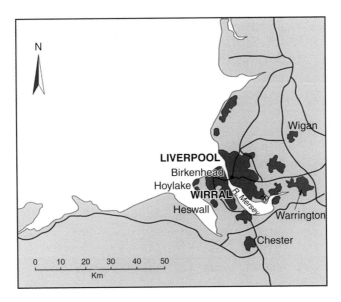

Figure 2.3 Liverpool and Wirral. Lines indicate major roads.

concentration and centralisation saw the loss of tertiary sector jobs. By 2001, the population of the conurbation was a little over 1.4 million and the proportion living in Liverpool, the core city, had fallen from about 43% in 1961 to only 33% in 2001. However, in the last decade, a combination of stronger restrictions on peripheral development and the implementation of powerful urban regeneration programmes have brought this decline under control. There are now clear indications of recovery in the local economy, and some stabilisation in population change. Today, the very great majority of housing development occurs within the existing urban area.

Liverpool's economy today is service orientated, with a fifth of those employed in Liverpool working in the banking and finance sector and a further fifth in distribution. Only one job in eight is in the manufacturing industry. The public service, health and education sectors are the largest employers. However, despite recent improvements in economic performance, Liverpool remains one of the most deprived cities in the UK. Merseyside was granted EU Objective 1 priority status in 1993, which was renewed in 1999.

The city has a significant higher education sector, with over 40 000 students at its three universities. In recent years the city centre has benefited from major redevelopment projects that have improved its environment and amenities. Liverpool has more museums and galleries of national status and more 'listed buildings' than any other area outside London. The Pier head was granted UNESCO 'world heritage' status in 2005. Liverpool has also played an important role in the history of contemporary music and was the home of Merseybeat and the birthplace of the Beatles. Leisure and cultural industries are also growing in importance and the city has been designated European Capital of Culture, 2008.

Liverpool forms part of the Merseyside County Area, a conurbation which is made up of five local authorities – the City of Liverpool and the boroughs of Sefton, Knowsley, St. Helens and Wirral. The City of Liverpool is made up of 30 wards, represented by 90 elected councillors, and is responsible for a wide range of services including: planning and regeneration, waste collection and disposal, schools and nurseries, social housing, road maintenance, parks and gardens and social services.

Wirral, which has been the focus of closer investigation in our project study, lies opposite Liverpool on the west bank of the Mersey. It had a population of around 312 000 people in 2001. The commercial and civic heart of Wirral is in Birkenhead, which lies directly across the Mersey from Liverpool, and to which it is connected by road and railway tunnels. The majority of economic activity is to be found in Birkenhead and along the Mersey shore. Employment has historically been based around the docks and dock-related industries such as ship-building and food processing. Today, these traditional industries have declined, giving way to a more diverse and service-orientated economy.

Urban sprawl in Wirral is an established and mature phenomenon. Over the last 100 years the settlements of (sprawling) west Wirral have developed, firstly as a result of the railways, and more recently as a result of the growth in car ownership. The causes of sprawl in Wirral are much the same today as they were in the past. Outer Wirral is perceived as offering 'a better quality of life', as being quieter, lower in crime, with better amenities and accessibility to the countryside and coast. It can also be shown that households are purchasing housing in outer Wirral as an investment. However, in recent years, the combination of strong 'green-belt' policies in outer Wirral with 'urban regeneration' policies in inner Wirral has dramatically reduced the rate of urban sprawl.

The 'problems' caused by sprawl in Wirral include spatial social segregation, a decentralised urban form which generates high numbers of car journeys and the loss of rural land. On the other hand, urban sprawl in Wirral has provided a good quality of life for those in outer Wirral. There are problems of urban deprivation and social exclusion in parts of inner Wirral, but there is evidence that recent programmes of urban regeneration have had some success.

Ljubljana

The city of Ljubljana is strategically located at the crossroads between Central Europe, the Mediterranean and South-East Europe. The most intensive period of growth in modern times was from 1948 to 1991, when the population of the city rose from 123 000 to 273 000 inhabitants, mainly due to industrialisation and immigration from other parts of Slovenia and other former Yugoslav republics. After Slovenia's independence in 1991, Ljubljana became one of the smallest capital cities in Europe.

Ljubljana is one of Central and Eastern Europe's most economically successful cities. The economy of the city is highly dependent upon producer and consumer services: trade, transport, business and finances, and public administration. The urban region generates 35% of the country's GDP. Unemployment increased during the transitional period, but is below the country's average.

From the 1950s to the end of 1994, the city of Ljubljana was administratively divided into five municipalities/communes. The local government reforms in Slovenia in the 1990s transformed the capital city of Ljubljana administratively and spatially. The territory was reduced from 902 to 272 km^2 and consisted of only one administrative unit – the City Municipality of Ljubljana – and nine surrounding municipalities.

Urban sprawl in Ljubljana has been seen most visibly in the post-socialist years. In the 1990s, a population decline was observed for the first time in the city of Ljubljana (and the agglomeration) showing the shift from urbanisation to counter-urbanisation. Recently, there has been a decline of population in the core city of Ljubljana, stagnation in the agglomeration, but population growth in other municipalities in the urban region.

One of the most important historical reasons for urban sprawl was the existence of a number of small rural settlements and secondary employment centres in Ljubljana, which had the capacity to accommodate a growing number of commuters from the central city. This residential pattern (i.e. self-built owner-occupied single family houses in rural settlements) was supported by the socialist housing policies between 1960–1990 (i.e. 'urbanisation of countryside'). The private ownership of land and public subsidies for owner-occupied single-family houses, relatively good provision of roads and infrastructure, and the quality of landscape all contributed to urban sprawl.

The changes after 1991 accelerated urban sprawl. The privatisation of housing, 1994 local government reforms, the system for local tax revenues,

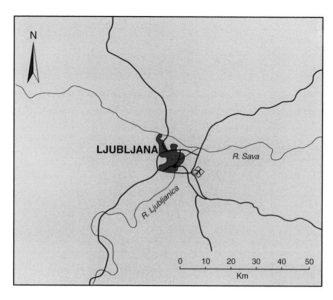

Figure 2.4   Ljubljana. Strong lines indicate major roads.

deferred planning regulations, higher incomes and intergenerational equity, increased car ownership, highway investments and changing lifestyles were all influential.

The city provides a high quality of life, but in the past decade the effects of urban sprawl can be seen in increases in air and noise pollution. Other important consequences of sprawl include increased land consumption, surface sealing and ecosystem fragmentation, environmental pollution and the loss of local identity. Spatial social differentiation is still low, but conflicts are increasing between the traditional population and the new residents.

Stockholm

Stockholm is the capital city of Sweden, located on 15 islands and the mainland where Lake Mälaren enters the Baltic Sea. Around one-fifth of the population of Sweden lives in the conurbation, whose population has grown steadily by about 1% annually over the last decade. The modest population growth anticipated in the country in the coming years is almost entirely fuelled by immigration, and therefore likely to be concentrated in Stockholm and the other major cities. During the twentieth century, the built-up area of Stockholm County has expanded faster than the increase in population. This process, however, has slowed over the last two decades as policy has shifted in favour of concentration in already developed areas.

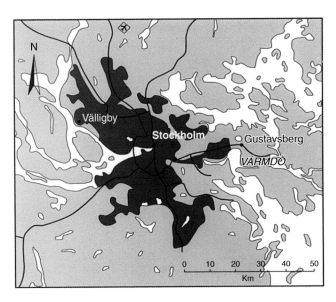

Figure 2.5   Stockholm and Värmdö. Lines indicate major roads.

The region also provides one-fifth of total employment and almost a quarter of the gross national product. The economy of Stockholm is growing faster than that of the rest of Sweden. The local economy is very much based on the service and telecom industries; electronics play an essential role, with the suburban borough of Kista being among the world's most important IT hubs. One characteristic feature is the high knowledge content in the production sector. Most of the capacity for higher education and research in the region is located in the centre and north of Stockholm.

Problems characteristic of many large cities also exist in Stockholm. Although unemployment in the core city was only 3% in 2001, there are higher levels of unemployment among specific social groups and housing segregation has increased in recent years.

Stockholm is home to many cultural institutions including the Royal Opera, the Stockholm Philharmonic Orchestra, the Royal Dramatic Theatre, more than 60 museums and 70 halls for performances and musical events. A New Modern Art Museum was built on the island of Skeppsholmen. In 1998, Stockholm was the European Capital of Culture, hosting more than 1000 cultural events.

The region comprises 26 municipalities with common interests in the fields of employment, housing, leisure activities and transport under the direction of a regional planning authority. Swedish municipalities enjoy extensive local governance responsibilities. Stockholm City Council is responsible for schools, childcare, social services, city planning, local infrastructure (streets, parks, lighting), building permits, health and environment protection. The city is divided into 12 boroughs, each run by a District Council with resources from the City Council.

Stockholm has a very popular inner city as Stockholmers clearly favour a dense and walkable environment. The city centre serves as the 'living room' for the whole region. However, this demand has pushed prices up and forced low income groups outwards, especially towards the public housing in the suburbs. The recent growth of Stockholm has not meant that sprawl, defined as an increase in land use, has accelerated. Stockholm is situated in a landscape with plenty of water, which has affected the physical enlargement, as well as the regional planning, of the city. Over the last twenty years, much of the new development has taken the form of conversion or expansion of existing premises or the re-use of vacant and derelict land. The rising intensity and cost of living in the city is one of the reasons why summerhouses in the area around Stockholm are increasingly being used as permanent accommodation.

The population of Värmdö, situated to the eastern fringe of Stockholm, has increased by 50% over the last 10 years and it is expected to double over the next 20 to 30 years. As the fastest growing municipality in Sweden, it provides an interesting case for the study of urban sprawl. Värmdö is partly on the mainland, but much of it comprises islands in Stockholm's archipelago in the Baltic Sea. There are currently around 30 000 permanent residents, but in summer this number is increased by a holiday population living in about 15 000 summerhouses. About 1000 summerhouses a year are transformed into permanent dwellings and this transformation increases the population by about 500 persons a year. Although surface sealing does not increase so rapidly, there are still adverse effects through increases in traffic and pressure for new and expanded infrastructure in the new areas of permanent living. This is leading to problems with water supply, sewage, social service provision, traffic and public transport.

Vienna

Vienna is Austria's capital and its economic and cultural centre. The city has a population of 1.6 million within a conurbation of 2.2 million. Following a decrease during much of the Cold War period, the city's population has been

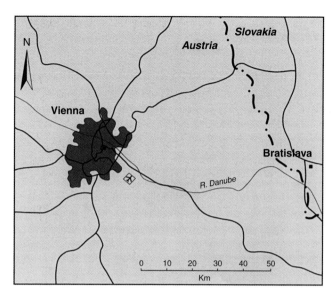

Figure 2.6   Vienna. Strong lines indicate major roads.

rising over the past two decades. The reasons lie in increasing immigration and an improvement in the birth rate.

Since 1989, the local economy has benefited from the opening of the borders to Eastern European countries, especially the Czech Republic, Slovakia and Hungary. Although Vienna still has a significant industrial sector (including electrical engineering, consumer electronics, food, transport, mechanical engineering and metal-processing) manufacturing employment has decreased and now accounts for only 12% of all employment. Service employment is increasing and high-quality public and private services are well represented. City tourism is also playing an increasing role in the city's economy, with the majority of visitors coming from outside Austria.

The city is home to five universities and three arts and music academies. Additionally, there are a number of colleges (*Fachhochschulen*) and non-university research institutions, such as the Academy of Sciences. The city hosts 30 000 students. Due to its history, Vienna has a rich cultural heritage and an internationally renowned tradition in music, literature and art. There are opera houses, concert halls, theatres, museums and festivals, many of them of international reputation. The city centre has UNESCO 'World Heritage' status.

The Austrian constitution guarantees municipalities the right to self government and a right to levy taxes. Vienna has a city council which is elected for a
period of five years. Each of the 23 districts within the city has a district par-
liament, which is also directly elected. The city administration has extensive
responsibilities including city planning, and the provision of infrastructure
and services (e.g. kindergartens, schools, waste and water management).

The first developments around Vienna that are regarded as sprawl started
in the 1960s. They were induced by business activities and followed by residents, which over the years built up to become a dense urban structure to the
south of the city. Vienna and its surrounding areas are extremely interwoven,
especially with regard to the labour market, which has increasingly become
a single regional travel-to-work area. Nearly 12% of persons employed in
Vienna live in the surrounding areas of Lower Austria, and 20% of persons
employed in the surrounding areas of Lower Austria live in Vienna.

As in Stockholm, the central city has become a much sought-after residential location offering a very dense but high quality living environment and
vibrant cultural life. There are, however, inner urban areas beyond the central
city that display a number of social and economic problems.

The opening of the borders to the east has made the suburbs to the south-
east and north-east of the city more attractive and therefore vulnerable
to urban sprawl. A planned improvement of the traffic infrastructure will
give a further impulse to development. With a rising population, improved
accessibility and cheaper prices on the periphery there are considerable
pressures for both residential and commercial urban sprawl. The proximity of this development to the border with the state of Lower Austria brings
about various problems, including competition for development and difficulties in coordinating planning processes. They exacerbate the impact of
these pressures for urban sprawl. As in Sweden, there is some conversion
of former summerhouses to permanent homes, especially amongst retired
people.

Warsaw

Warsaw, the capital of Poland, is located in Mazowieckie province, in East-
Central Poland. The city of Warsaw has a population of about 1.6 million
inhabitants (in 2000) which is about 4% of the total population of Poland.
The city of Warsaw covers an area of 512 km^2 and is divided into 18 districts.
The conurbation includes more than 2.5 million people in a sprawling
agglomeration that stretches up to 40 km from the city centre.

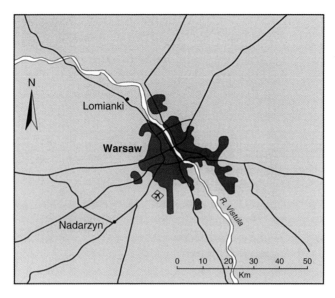

Figure 2.7   Warsaw. Lines indicate major roads.

The city has had a turbulent history throughout the twentieth century. Virtually destroyed during World War II, the city was rebuilt under the post-war socialist regime during the 1960s and 1970s and is now a UNESCO 'World Heritage' site.

Warsaw today boasts a developing service sector economy, including first class universities and cultural facilities. There is a strong commercial sector, although manufacturing suffered badly after the opening up of the economy to western market forces after 1989.

The central city remains a popular residential location, and environmental conditions in central Warsaw are good compared with many other cities. Despite often stated preferences for a house with garden, there has been only limited out-migration from Warsaw to the suburban zones. In recent years, the rate of growth of the suburban population is below that of previous decades. However, changes such as the gradual improvement of the urban and regional transportation system and rising real incomes are likely to stimulate urban sprawl in the future.

Problems caused by sprawl mainly relate to the development of previously greenfield land on the periphery whilst there are still around 100 km^2 (20% of the total area of the city) available for redevelopment within the existing urban area.

Warsaw experienced urban sprawl during the 1950–2000 period, with an increasing share of its population located in suburban areas of the city. Łomianki and Nadarzyn, two suburban communities, are the focus for a more detailed study of Warsaw. Here, the well-educated and wealthy households predominate among newcomers. Residents' views on urban sprawl are mixed. Disadvantages are seen in higher land prices, further burdens on the local infrastructure, rising crime rates, a growing differentiation in lifestyles and the disappearance of local ties. But, on the other hand, sprawl has brought investment, construction work, more spatial order and a more aesthetically pleasing urban form.

Conclusions

The population structure of Europe is changing: growth is slow and heavily dependent upon in-migration, and households are getting smaller. These changes are increasing the proportion of the population living in urban areas. At the same time, these urban areas are decreasing in density. Increased affluence, more owner occupation, increasing social tensions and the search for 'quietude' encourage demand for urban sprawl, especially among families.

A few cities, notably in Northern Europe, are coping well with these pressures and have strong planning systems that are able to achieve 'contained growth' without sprawl. Some cities in South-Eastern Europe are also facing similar patterns of development, but probably as a result of historic and cultural pressures rather than as a result of planning policies. But elsewhere in Europe, sprawl – whether accompanying growth or decline– remains a problem.

The context for change varies considerably between each of our case study cities. Athens is something of a special case, where sprawl has historically been fuelled by waves of in-migration, urban environmental pressures and, more recently, heavy investment in infrastructure at the periphery of the city. The cities of Eastern Europe illustrate the impact of transition from socialist to free-market economies, with its effect on local economies, social patterns and planning systems. Liverpool and Leipzig show the pressures for suburbanisation and sprawl even when the local economy and population are in decline. Stockholm and Vienna have strong planning systems with well-developed patterns of urban living, but their very affluence creates pressure for sprawl, particularly through the acquisition and occupation of second homes. Each of these different situations is investigated in more detail in the next four chapters.

Appendix: Patterns of growth and sprawl across European cities

City	Total resident population, 1991		Total resident population, 2001		City population as a % of LUZ population, 1991 (%)	City population as a % of LUZ population, 2001 (%)	Population change 1991–2001 (%)	Change in % of LUZ population in the core city 1991–2001 (%)
	City	LUZ	City	LUZ				
Birmingham	1 004 500	2 374 300	977 087	2 335 652	42.3	41.8	−1.63	−0.5
Liverpool	475 600	1 438 000	439 476	1 362 004	33.1	32.3	−5.28	−0.8
Leicester	281 500	728 600	279 915	756 139	38.6	37.0	+3.78	−1.6
Dublin	478 389	1 341 661	495 781	1 535 496	35.7	32.3	+14.4	−3.4
Cork	127 253	279 487	123 062	311 479	45.5	39.5	+11.5	−6.0
Limerick	52 083	200 833	54 023	236 334	25.9	22.9	+17.7	−3.0
Copenhagen	464 773	1 718 805	499 148	1 806 667	27.0	27.6	+5.1	+0.6
Aarhus	264 136	605 447	286 668	640 637	43.6	44.7	+5.8	+1.1
Aalborg	155 664	485 787	161 661	494 833	32.0	32.7	+1.9	+0.7
Stockholm	674 452	1 641 669	750 348	1 823 210	41.1	41.2	+11.1	+0.1
Berlin	3 465 748	4 866 047	3 388 434	4 935 524	71.2	68.7	+1.4	−2.5
Leipzig	542 512	940 822	493 052	912 064	57.7	54.0	−3.1	−3.7
Bonn	298 227	820 858	306 016	879 240	36.3	34.8	+7.1	−1.5
Weimar	62 750	149 736	63 522	153 868	41.9	41.3	+2.8	−0.6
Vienna	1 539 848	2 062 969	1 550 123	1 823 210	74.6	73.1	+2.8	−1.5
Graz	237 810	355 858	226 244	357 548	66.8	63.3	+0.5	−3.5
Linz	203 044	517 043	183 504	524 444	39.3	35.0	+1.4	−4.3
Warsaw	1 644 515	2 416 600*	1 609 780	2 631 902	61.2	61.1	+8.9	−0.1
Prague	1 214 174	1 976 178	1 169 106	1 941 803	61.4	60.2	−1.7	−1.2
Brno	388 296	738 869	376 172	729 510	52.6	51.6	−1.3	−1.0
Usti n L	98 178	246 197	95 436	243 878	39.9	39.1	−0.9	−0.8
Bratislava	442 197	606 351	428 672	599 015	72.9	71.6	−1.2	−1.3
Kosice	235 160	334 452	236 093	343 092	70.3	68.8	+2.6	−1.5

Continued

Appendix: Continued

City	Total resident population, 1991		Total resident population, 2001		City population as a % of LUZ population, 1991 (%)	City population as a % of LUZ population, 2001 (%)	Population change 1991–2001 (%)	Change in % of LUZ population in the core city 1991–2001 (%)
	City	LUZ	City	LUZ				
Banska By..	83 400	111 244	83 056	111 984	75.0	74.2	+0.7	−0.8
Budapest	2 016 458	2 583 635	1 777 921	2 453 315	78.0	72.5	−5.0	−5.5
Miskolc	195 433	288 769	184 125	281 867	67.7	65.3	−2.4	−2.4
Nyiregyhaza	115 089	214 200	118 795	221 927	53.7	53.5	+3.6	−0.2
Ljubljana	272 650	470 641	270 506	488 364	57.9	55.4	+3.8	−2.5
Maribor	119 828	320 800	114 891	310 743	37.4	37.0	−3.1	−0.4
Athens	772 072	3 072 922*	789 166	3 894 573	25.1	20.3	+26.7	−4.8
Larissa	114 334	270 612	132 779	282 156	42.2	47.1	+4.3	+4.9
Kalamata	50 260	166 964	61 373	166 556	30.1	36.8	−0.2	+6.7
Nicosia	171 600	238 600	200 686	273 642	71.9	73.3	+14.7	+1.4
Rome	2 775 250	3 761 067	2 546 804	3 700 424	73.8	68.8	−1.6	−5.0
Taranto	232 334	589 576	202 033	579 806	39.4	34.8	−1.7	−4.6
Campobasso	50 941	238 958	50 762	230 749	21.3	22.0	−3.4	+0.7
Lisbon	663 394	2 266 202	564 657	2 363 470	29.3	23.9	+4.3	−5.4
Porto	302 472	1 013 220	263 131	1 089 118	29.9	24.2	+7.5	−5.7
Luxembourg	75 833	128 140	76 688	136 625	59.2	56.1	+6.6	−3.1
Brussels	950 045	1 687 200	973 565	1 750 328	56.3	55.6	+3.7	−0.7
Gent	230 246	390 861	224 685	395 986	58.9	56.7	+1.3	−2.2
Bruges	117 063	163 066	116 559	165 575	71.8	70.4	+1.5	−1.4
Amsterdam	702 444	1 232 488	734 594	1 320 137	57.0	55.6	+7.1	−1.4
Eindhoven	192 895	657 401	202 397	714 157	29.3	28.3	+8.6	−1.0
Arnhem	131 703	653 907	139 329	696 162	20.1	20.0	+6.5	−0.1

Source: Authors' calculation from EU Urban Audit data.

* Authors' estimate.

References

European Commission (1999) *European Spatial Development Perspective.* EC, Brussels.

European Commission (2004) *The Social Situation in the European Union.* EC, Brussels.

European Commission, EUROSTAT (2006) http://epp.eurostat.ec.europa.eu/

European Commission (2006) Europe in figures – Eurostat yearbook 2005, http://epp.eurostat.ec.europa.eu/portal/page?_pageid=1334,49092079,1334_49092702&_dad=portal&_schema=PORTAL

European Environment Agency (2001) http://www.eea.europa.eu/

Hall, P. & Hay, D. (1980) Growth Centres in the European Urban System, Heinemann Educ.

Stockholm City Council (2006) Stockholm City Council Statistics Year Book, http://www.stockholm.se/Extern/Templates/Page.aspx?id=115120

United Nations (2004) World Population Prospects: The 2004 Revision http://esa.un.org/unpp/p2k0data.asp

Urban Audit (2006) http://www.urbanaudit.org/

Part II

Types of Urban Sprawl in Europe

3

Infrastructure-related Urban Sprawl: Mega-events and Hybrid Peri-urban Landscapes in Southern Europe

Lila Leontidou, Alex Afouxenidis, Elias Kourliouros and Emmanuel Marmaras[1]

Introduction: theory and method

Urban cultures affect urban sprawl in a fundamental manner. This comes to the foreground as we turn to the only South European city in our project, Greater Athens, as a case study in the broader area of Mediterranean Europe. This chapter will focus on the unrelenting urbanism of Southern Europeans, combined with their pragmatic attraction to urban infrastructure; in contrast with anti-urban geographical imaginations of Anglo-Scandinavian cultures, which drive Northern versions of lifestyle-driven urban sprawl (Leontidou, 2001). In Southern Europe, grassroots and top-down interventions (from the local, metropolitan, national and EU levels) clash or reinforce each other in the crystallisation of urban-oriented material cultures and the creation of compact cities. Around them, sprawl has been traditionally initiated by popular strata, but recently a broader class basis is creating post-suburbanism as defined in recent research (Phelps *et al.*, 2006). In URBS PANDENS we have studied hybrid peri-urban landscapes on the rural–urban fringe of the capital of Greece in order to investigate how the expansion, or lack of it, of infrastructure beyond the urban agglomeration of Athens relates to urban sprawl and how this compares with other cities of Mediterranean Europe.

It has been established in previous research that Athens belongs to a 'Mediterranean' city type, with immense diversity within it, but with many differences from North European cities (Leontidou, 1990). We will here resume the argument against some taken-for-granted assumptions in urban studies, by bringing the diversity of urban cultures to the foreground in approaching European cities. The structure and dynamics of Mediterranean European cities are not adequately understood or explained through traditional spatial analysis. It is still posited that Southern Europe lags behind the North and it is maintained that lack of wealth here obstructs choices for sprawl (Bruegmann, 2005, p. 10, 77). This ignores a long history of spontaneous popular suburbs and illegal sprawl. These cities definitely do not conform to Alonso-type models of urban land use based on rent-paying ability, rational behaviour of urban actors and land rent/distance curves (Vickerman, 1984), nor to the 'life cycle' model of urbanisation- suburbanisation- disurbanisation- reurbanisation (Van den Berg *et al.*, 1982). These Anglo-centric models distort the characteristics of Euro-Mediterranean urban development and are inappropriate for Athens, and for many other Mediterranean cities for that matter (Leontidou, 1990; 2005). The focus of this chapter is on the transition from a past of urbanisation, popular suburbanisation and sprawl without basic infrastructure in Southern Europe, to a present of infrastructure-driven urban sprawl on the occasion of mega-events, which several South European cities have hosted: Lisbon, Seville, Barcelona, Rome, Genoa and many more. The spotlight is on Athens and its 2004 Olympics as a turning point between two models of urban sprawl, both related to infrastructure, first attracting, now following it.

The variety of cities included in our project offers a formidable opportunity for understanding urban development in Athens, as well as Barcelona and cities on the Spanish coasts, Italian cities from Genoa through Rome to Naples, cities on the Adriatic coast, and of course Greek cities. These will all be contrasted with urban agglomerations in other European regions and especially the North. In this chapter we will contrast cultures of Northern anti-urbanism where pastoral geographical imaginations result in *life style-led* urban sprawl on the one hand, and Southern urbanism where cities are magnets of culture and people, and urban sprawl is *infrastructure-related*, on the other.

This chapter is based upon qualitative research including personal observation, historical urban studies, expert interviews with local authorities, building enterprises and NGOs using a 'snowball sampling' method, and census data analysis, in order to understand urban sprawl in Attica and locate it in the broader Mediterranean context. We will return to the concept of the 'metropolitan periphery' – a concept from earlier research (Leontidou, 1990) which is even more useful now that Athens has acquired its own satellite towns – and combine it with the more recent concept of post-suburbanisation, whereby the exurbs are transforming. This will be approached through a study of infrastructure expansion on the occasion of the Athens Olympics.

'Astyphilia' and popular spontaneous suburbanisation until the 1970s

Positive geographical imaginations for urban life as an antidote and a shield from rural poverty and insecurity formed the basic undercurrents of spontaneous urban sprawl and informal popular settlements springing up around all South European cities. We have shown elsewhere that Mediterranean societies share cultures of urbanism, and this even has a name in Greek, *astyphilia*, that is, 'friendliness to the city'. This contrasts with anti-urbanism, which developed after the industrial revolution in Northern Europe and Anglo-American cultures in particular (Williams, 1973; White & White, 1977). Schorske (1998, pp. 43–9) traces the process whereby Europe switched from a view of the 'city as virtue' in the Enlightenment, to the 'city as vice' after the industrial revolution. In previous research, we have explored this antithesis in *space rather than time*, arguing that anti-urbanism has not taken root in Mediterranean Europe and contrasting North/South representations of cities during the twentieth century (Leontidou, 2001).

The Anglo-American culture of life style-led urban sprawl is exemplified by the flight of the elites beyond city limits because of their attraction to pastoral lifestyles near the countryside as an alternative to, and as a means to counteract, the ills and perils of urban living. The nature/city dualism saturates Northern European and American literature (Williams, 1973) and it was no wonder that the affluent classes left urban squalor and congestion in order to breathe the country air in their everyday lives. The tradition of urban sprawl or satellite suburbs created in the search for a rural idyll and a lifestyle in pastoral surroundings, also suburbanised Swedish and other Nordic cities. The Burgess zonal hypothesis of concentric urban growth and the Alonso model stress the proverbial 'preferences' of affluent populations for the city edges, and this view has saturated urban studies and still operates as an assumption within the field (as in Bruegmann, 2005).

'Preferences' in North Europe did indeed have their material manifestations. These geographical imaginations fed Northern urban planning policy for green belts, suburbs, new towns and health legislation, which created topologies of land use zoning and satellite settlements. Land use in the countryside and peri-urban land was tightly controlled and regulated. It would be unthinkable to see popular invasions of the urban fringe in Britain or the USA, as these were inhabited by elites and affluent populations. Seaside shacks and shanties like 'plot-lands' in Peacehaven in Britain (Hardy & Ward, 1984), and illegal building, were effectively controlled and in fact suppressed at birth (Leontidou, 1990, pp. 247–8). Containment in green belts and strictly safeguarded suburbs, or sometimes gated communities, did not preclude urban sprawl outward from the large agglomerations. This followed the highways in the USA, while in England controlled expansion beyond the green belts brought the limits of the city outward, to the 'New Towns' and satellite settlements.

These Anglo-American models are easily contrasted with the Mediterranean tradition of compact cityscapes and informal urban development or sprawl toward spontaneous popular suburbs. Urban residents of Mediterranean Europe have not been seeking rural utopia. The urban sprawl *vs* containment interplay in Greece, Italy and Spain has involved populations inspired by geographical imaginations of urbanity rather than any sort of rural idyll. For historical reasons of socio-economic development, rurality in a great part of Mediterranean Europe has been synonymous with economic backwardness, migration, poverty and insecurity; whereas urbanity, on the contrary, has been synonymous with economic prosperity, better job opportunities and social amenities or infrastructure linked to a higher quality of life (Craglia *et al.*, 2004). Popular spontaneous urbanisation created suburbanisation in parallel with constant gentrification of the inner city by the more affluent classes. Those who could afford it clung to the inner city, and exercised only loose control over peripheral urban land. Even today, some Southern countries have no land registration systems. In Greece, land registration was initiated in the 1990s, but the process remained incomplete due to squandering of available EU funding. Popular squatting on the urban fringe was tacitly accepted, but also occasionally penalised. Speculative building, and *spontaneous urbanisation* more generally, (Leontidou, 1990) created popular suburbs built illegally by people seeking urbanity in the Mediterranean.

The pastoral representations and ideology that have fed mainstream spatialisations and planning trajectories in the developed North European cities and regions, have never acquired a stronghold among South European localities striving to survive by sending vast numbers of their younger population as migrants to Northern Europe and the USA. These migrants left behind their backward rural home-regions, where insecurity was both political (civil war) and economic (unemployment, bandits and usurping). This rural exodus escalated from the first postwar decades and included both external and internal migration. Large masses of rural populations moved to cities in search of jobs, social infrastructure and amenities for a better living. Migrants could not afford to inhabit the central city, but they tried to build their settlements as close as possible to it. Their *astyphilia* was pragmatic and related to survival strategies. They followed infrastructural developments and sought employment in the urban economy, entering the informal sector.

Urban sprawl was thus caused by the urban poor who wanted to *approach* the city, rather than move away from its squalor, as Anglo-American suburbanites tended to. Governments turned a blind eye, and the urban poor were tacitly allowed to create their unauthorised spontaneous popular sub-urbs (Leontidou, 1990; Beja Horta, 2004). The contrast with British and North European planning and green belt policy can hardly be over-emphasised. The Mediterranean model kept its homogeneity on the urban fringes with respect to spontaneous popular settlement, despite the several types of land-lordism in Southern Europe (private, large and small, state, church) (Fried, 1973, p. 115). Small plots were bought rather than invaded; these were semi-squatters rather than squatters. Usually, large properties were subdivided by landlords and speculative entrepreneurs and were sold to migrants, who built in violation of the building code and planning legislation which forbade resi-dential building on 'agricultural' plots outside the city plan. This process was aided by lawyers, notaries and engineers in its 'technical' aspects. Popular suburbs were quite close to the centre, so that cities were thus kept com-pact (Marmaras, 1996). They did not sprawl to the extent of Anglo-American ones. The *afthereta* (illegal houses) of Athens and the *borgate* (poor neigh-bourhoods) already mushrooming in the Roman urban fringe in the early 1900s, were at a small distance from the inner city. Iberian cities, espe-cially Barcelona and Lisbon, also sprawled outward through spontaneous urbanisation at relatively short distances, around 20 km. (Leontidou, 1990).

In most Mediterranean cities, the limits of the city were defined by popu-lar land colonisation until at least the mid-1970s. This kind of sprawl was related to the survival strategies of internal migrants, peasants migrating to Athens, as well as popular strata and working-class groups. It was also related to infrastructure, which was sought but denied to the settlers. Illegal settlements by the working class preceded infrastructure provision. Semi-squatters *first followed infrastructure, and then attracted it.* They settled as close as possible to roads, electricity posts and water pipes, and 'stole' from them if they could. Otherwise, they were served by trucks bringing water to the community, by petrol lamps and fireplaces. Infrastructure arrived much later, if at all, long after piecemeal ex-post-facto 'legalisation' integrated some communities into the city plan.

Popular strata and speculators were the main pressure groups for infras-tructure expansion as follows. Landowners sold some 'agricultural' plots dispersed throughout each area, where it was illegal to build, in anticipa-tion of popular pressure for infrastructure expansion and the consequent appreciation of the rest of their property (Leontidou, 1990). The government often 'gave in', tacitly allowing squatting by its ambivalent policy.[2] There are even references to illegal dwellings built with subsidies from the state in Rome (Fried, 1973, p. 29, 120). Communities without infrastructure emerged overnight, especially in periods of political instability when the police were occupied elsewhere.

Table 3.1   Urbanization in Greece & major cities: population in 1951–2001

Year of population census	Greater Athens	Rest of Attica	Greece	Greater Thessalonica	Primacy indices	
					Athens as a % of Greece	Thessalonica as a % of Athens
1951	1 378 586	177 443	7 632 801	297 223	18.06	21.56
1961	1 852 709	205 265	8 388 553	380 732	22.09	20.55
1971	2 548 065	249 784	8 768 641	557 360	28.97	21.87
1981	3 038 245	331 180	9 740 417	706 180	31.08	23.24
1991	3 072 922	450 486	10 259 900	749 048	29.95	24.38
2001	3 187 734	574 076	10 964 020	794 327	29.07	24.92

Sources: Leontidou, 1990, p. 104; 1996, p. 246; updated from National Statistical Service of Greece (ESYE) censuses for 1991–2001.

This process has been especially interesting in our case study, Greater Athens. Lacking a colonial background and by-passed by the industrial revolution, Greece retained a largely rural settlement pattern until the inter-war period. However, Athens grew rapidly; today its population has risen to 3 475 000 people and it is ranked as the 98th city in the world.[3] During the last census (2001), the Prefecture of Attica contained 3 761 810 inhabitants, or 34.31% of the population of Greece. Attica tripled its population in the course of the post-war period (Table 3.1), while its two cores, Athens and Piraeus (sectors 601 and 701 respectively on Figure 3.1), lost some of their inhabitants in the 1980s and 1990s but remained very dense, with 745 514 and 175 697 inhabitants respectively in 2001. There is usually a slight underestimation of population in the capital of Greece, because first-generation migrants usually move to their places of origin of during census periods in order to ensure their viability as Municipalities by retaining funding from the centre.

The distribution of population has been always uneven, and influenced by segregation, filtering and the formation of social enclaves. The popular western suburbs of Athens and Piraeus grew without any technical infrastructure; while in the eastern and northern sectors of the city, transport was already important in the creation of suburbs in the nineteenth century. Among them, the bourgeois suburb of Kifissia in the north east of the conurbation (part of sector 203 on Figure 3.1), was created by the railroad company (Leontidou, 1989) and is now being transformed by malls and economic activity to a post-suburban locality (Phelps *et al.*, 2006). On the other side, to the south west, the Athens–Piraeus railroad attracted clusters of industry, which created the first instances of infrastructure-driven urbanisation in the nineteenth century (Leontidou, 1989) – but distances were short and we really can not use

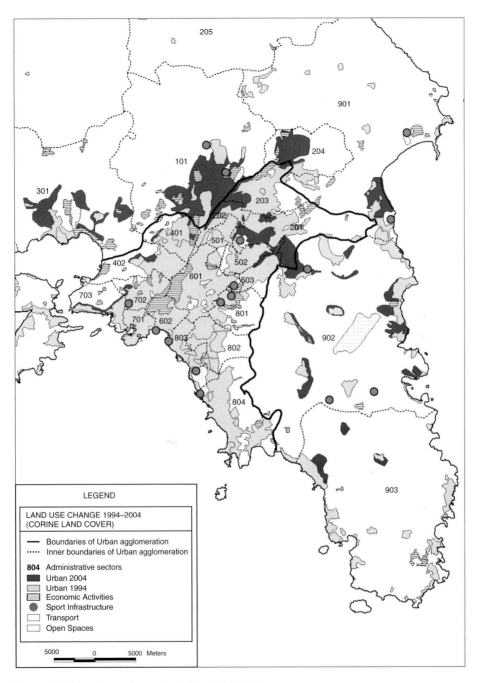

Figure 3.1   Land use change in Attica 1984–2004.

the term 'sprawl' in the context of the compact city. Then, during the inter-war period, suburbs emerged spontaneously when refugees arrived from Asia Minor. Their settlements surrounded the city, first by the initiative of the League of Nations, then by popular land invasions and illegal housing. In inter-war Athens, the lack of infrastructure did not deter people from sprawling the city outward. The only interesting case studies of infrastructure planned before settling, besides Kifissia in the nineteenth century, emerged in the inter-war period: Ekali (part of sector 203 on Figure 3.1), Psychiko and Philothei (part of sector 502 on Figure 3.1), Nea Smyrna (part of sector 803 on Figure 3.1), and a few other 'garden cities' (Leontidou, 1989, pp. 215–16; Karydis, 2006, pp. 265–9). The late 1920s also saw water infrastructure intalled, and the building of the Marathon dam in North Attica (part of sector 901 on Figure 3.1; Biris, 1966; Kaika, 2005).

In the years of increased rural to urban migration during the civil war and throughout the post-war period, Athens emerged as a modern city without infrastructure around its popular suburbs. Migrants kept arriving to find informal work in an incubator of economic growth which had few industries, but was an important metropolitan centre offering many informal work opportunities (Leontidou, 1990). Migration to Athens has established the basic axes of spatial segregation since the 1920s: inside/outside the official city plan was a duality echoed not only between the inner city and the outskirts, but also between the east and west of the agglomeration, concentrating middle and working classes respectively. The migrants building spontaneously, combined with the inefficient planning system in Greece, have produced urban environments with severe infrastructure deficiencies during the twentieth century, and hybrid landscapes of urban-rural features on the urban fringes.

Two central features of the mode of production in the authorised housing sector were 'self-building' (*aftostegasi*) – under the responsibility and supervision of each family – on the one hand, and exchange-arrangements (*antiparochi*) – with entrepreneurs building on land provided by the family in exchange for some flats – on the other (Marmaras, 1989, pp. 63–64). Illegal additions consisted of converting balconies to rooms and glass houses in Athens apartment buildings (Leontidou, 1990). Illegalities within the approved city plans further increased densities, congestion and air pollution. In general, Mediterranean cities are compact, with high-rise buildings and illegal additions on terraces and basements giving the middle classes extra space. Rooftop additions create supplementary dwellings for exploitation, as in Roman apartment buildings (Fried, 1973, p. 59); the adjunction of *áticos* and *sobre-áticos*, illegal room extensions retreating from the facade gain Barcelona residents some height. Illegality within the city plan has been most obvious in the case of Naples (Allum, 1973, pp. 36–9, 296–7). Elsewhere in the south, illegality has been more 'democratically' spread, and a whole population was well trained in contravening regulations and devising informal strategies of living and working (Leontidou, 1990).

All these processes, even if they comply with the nationwide building code (ΓΟΚ), defy planning in the sense of organised rather than individualised urban development. In Greece, urbanisation has not been preceded by legislation for spatial allocation, land use and settlement formation, as elsewhere in Europe. Institutional change and laws have been *consequences* of urban sprawl, rather than causes or preconditions. Urban sprawl has resulted sometimes in spontaneous urban expansion followed by ex-post-facto 'legalisation' of settlements, and at other times in the passing of legislation. After the refugee inflow, the whole planning apparatus was based on the Legislative Decree (LD) of 1923 'about town plans of the State' (*Government Gazette* 228, 1923; Leontidou, 1989; Marmaras, 2002, p. 188; Karydis, 2006, pp. 289–96). This was restricted to 'legalised' areas and did not regulate illegality, land consumption, loss of agricultural land, forest fires – which have been often attributed to arson – or the destruction of natural habitats. No legislation for land policy was passed for half a century after the 1923 LD, during a period of inter-war dictatorship and German occupation, post-war right-wing governance followed by a coup d' etat and a military dictatorship in 1967–74.

From the inter-war period to the first post-war decades, Athens thus grew by illegal self-built housing sprawling onto cheap suburban land. Spontaneous urbanisation and urban sprawl escalated from the 1950s until the time of the dictatorship. Settlements without water and sewage systems and without any approved street layouts – not to mention public transport and social amenities – mushroomed in the urban periphery. When most of these settlements were 'legalised' by the military junta in the early 1970s, fines were paid but no infrastructure was installed. Given the location of spontaneous settlements, it was sometimes impossible to extend infrastructure to the most unlikely places, such as steep slopes of hills and ravines. Infrastructure deficiencies and the nature of landscapes of illegal settlements, such as Perama on the west (Figure 3.2), drove planners to exasperation and led to environmental deterioration, social exclusion and vulnerability of residents.

Squatters and residents of popular suburbs kept undermining any effort at planning legislation, and state planning officials were reluctant to implement it by force because of the fear of the political cost for the party at office (Kourliouros, 1995, pp. 729–4; 1997). It was only after the entrance of Greece to the EU in 1981 that laws were amended and European programmes

Figure 3.2   Illegal settlements at Perama outside Athens in 2003.

and frameworks such as the Integrated Mediterranean Programmes began to make some difference. By the early 1980s internal migration to Athens had slowed, and by the 1990s it had stabilised (Leontidou, 1990). Illegal urban sprawl continued, though in a different context, as we will discuss in the next section.

Modernism and urban land policy after EU accession

Greece joined the EU in 1981, the year when the primacy of Greater Athens peaked (Table 3.1), and the city contained one-third of the Greek population. After this, primacy receded (Leontidou, 2005); however, population in the Attica prefecture (in a sense the broader metropolitan region of Greater Athens) kept growing, and Athens is still today the greatest single population and employment concentration in Greece. By 1981, the period of spontaneous suburbanisation had already ended, but sprawl through illegal building continued in a new speculative – rather than popular – guise. Middle class households sought better living conditions outside the congested and polluted city and created several types of sprawl in Attica around Athens, individually or through their cooperatives. Entrepreneurs also decentralised, initially supported by the military government. Modernism, or rather 'selective modernisation' (Headrick, cited by Kaika, 2005, p. 110), did not preclude the reproduction of Mediterranean urban structures, especially the central location of affluent classes and constant gentrification, though enclaves of poverty and minorities were appearing at some central downgraded locations (Leontidou, 1990).

Land policy emerged in Greece in the mid-1970s, after the dictatorship and in anticipation of EU accession. The post-dictatorial period of conservatism (1974–81) brought about some planning innovations while economic recession was gaining momentum. Planning legislation included regulations on plot exploitation sizes and land use. The new Constitution of 1975 provided land policy with constitutional backing by the article 24, and the first ministry with planning responsibilities was founded – the Ministry of Regional Planning, Housing and the Environment (Law 1032/1980). In legislative terms, Law 360/1976 'about regional planning and the environment' appeared in the official *Government Gazette* (151, 1976), and the notorious 'ekistic' Law 947/1979 'about urban areas' has become the most contested item of land policy on sprawling areas (*Government Gazette* 169, 1979). It introduced the idea of the future inhabitants' contribution of land or money: a portion of their plot should be contributed to the public authority toward the development of infrastructure and the creation of open spaces (parks, squares, fields for sports, etc.) and public utility installations (hospitals, schools, churches, nursery schools, etc.).[4] However, the introduction of these planning innovations was prevented by the reaction of the landowners against the money and land contribution specified in Law 947 and at least one Minister was removed in the process.

After EC accession (1981), the socialist party elected to office, PASOK, attempted State-driven modernisation reforms of the planning system, such as citizens' participation,[5] decentralisation in decision-making processes, empowerment of local authorities in urban planning, etc. In 1983, the new Law 1337 'for the extension of town plans, urban development and relevant regulations' (*Government Gazette* 33, 1983) was passed. Its philosophy was similar to that of Law 947, but it also introduced some more innovative provisions.[6] In the context of the implementation of this law, the Ministry of Regional Planning, Housing and the Environment prepared structure plans for the extension of all the towns of the country, actually planning for urban sprawl. It started by launching the programme 'Enterprise of Urban Reconstruction' (ΕΠΑ) in the mid-1980s and ratified the Structure Plan of Athens in the mid-1980s (Law 1515/1985). Numerous plans had existed in the past, but none of them were ratified by law so as to form an actual basis for undertaking strategic action.[7] This multiplicity of plans and proposals for Athens

Table 3.2 Population growth of small towns and villages in the Mesogeia plain, 1961–2001

Municipalities	1961	1971	1981	1991	2001
Koropi	7862	9367	12 893	16 813	25 325
Markopoulo	5046	5399	9388	10 499	15 608
Spata	5409	5814	6398	7796	10 203
Pallini			5475	10 908	16 679
Paiania	5032	6111	7285	9727	13 013

Source: Adapted from ESYE census data by C. Rondos.

was supposed to become organised and finally implemented through ΕΠΑ. However, in reality, neither ΕΠΑ nor the Athens structure plan were that successful; though they signalled a beginning of land policy and planning urban sprawl, the population would not support them.

The Athens Structure Plan channelled sprawl towards East Attica, to the Mesogeia plain, which extends eastwards from the Athens conurbation (sector 902 in Figure 3.1). It is physically separated from the conurbation by a natural barrier, the Hymettus mountain, but it is still accessible by a couple of transport axes (Athinon–Lavriou and Mesogeion–Rafina avenues) connecting the conurbation with the plain's main urban settlements (Figure 3.1). Until the early 1980s, Mesogeia remained a relatively agricultural area (mainly olive groves and vineyards) with scattered villages and small towns across it (Koropi, Markopoulo, Spata, Pallini, Paiania, etc.). As shown in Table 3.2, since the 1970s, all major urban settlements in the Mesogeia plain have exhibited marked population increases.

The beginnings of infrastructure-driven urban sprawl in Attica can be attributed to industrial parks, which started with industrial location planning (Wassenhoven *et al.*, 1988; Vliamos *et al.*, 1992). During the 1980s, there was a broader shift toward planning in Greece, which attempted to bring itself into line with European standards in view of EU accession (Kourliouros, 1995, chapter 3). After Greece joined the EU in 1981, development planning took off with the 'Mediterranean Integrated Programmes' in 1984–86, which included Attica. In the wake of the Single European Act, Greece was an 'Objective 4' region, and was funded for regional development as well as peripheral urban infrastructure. In this 'developmental' context, the ratified Structure Plan of Athens in the mid-1980s (Law 1515/85) proposed the creation of a number of industrial parks, scattered across the region of Attica along major transport axes, in areas with

existing industrial agglomerations. A couple of industrial parks were proposed at inner-city locations (Eleonas area and Peristeri in sectors 602 and
402 respectively in Figure 3.1); another set of parks was proposed in the
northern suburbs of the Athenian conurbation (Metamorphosis, Avlona in
sectors 202 and 205 respectively in Figure 3.1); five parks were proposed
in Thriasio Pedio (a western peri-urban area with heavily polluting manufacturing plants in sector 301 in Figure 3.1), two parks in the Mesogeia
plain (Paiania and Koropi) and one in the southern edge of the plain, near
the city of Lavrion (part of sector 903 in Figure 3.1).[8] Development programmes for Attica since that period have had a bearing on the creation
of infrastructure and post-suburban sprawl at the turn of the millennium.
They were followed by population growth as a consequence – but also a
cause, in a self-perpetuating spiral – of industrial re-location, which initiated
infrastructure-driven urban sprawl, transforming East Attica from a rural to
a hybrid landscape.

The Mesogeia plain has been seen as a potential development location in
all Athens Structure Plans, but has only recently grown into an area of
spillover for the agglomeration, a post-suburban plain for industrial decentralisation. This has intensified the process of commuting, which is a
very interesting cause and consequence of urban sprawl. The iterative process operates here, as population follows economic activity and vice versa,
mediated by commuting, which depends especially on the accessibility
afforded to various urban areas by the transport infrastructure provided and
by rates of car ownership. Mesogeia is a post-suburban locality but is as
yet far from 'suffering' the full consequences of urban sprawl. The hybrid
landscape of different types of sprawl throughout Attica is more complex
than the landscape of spontaneous popular suburbanisation predominant
around Athens and Piraeus. Types of sprawl emerging can be classified as
follows:

Successive layers of spontaneous urban sprawl, 1922–1970
Sprawl was first created by workers and popular strata in the inter-war period,
seeking affordable housing as close as possible to industry and urban infrastructure, rather than by middle classes or elites escaping urban squalor. We
have amply discussed the process of *fragmented* popular semi-squatting,
especially during 1922–1970 around Athens (Leontidou, 1990), especially in
the west and north (sectors 702, 703, 401, 402, 101 in Figure 3.1). As population in illegal settlements kept growing, increasing political pressures
for 'inclusion' and 'legalisation' of these nuclei led to successive relocations of the borderline inside/outside the city, outwards. Illegal building
was stopped by the dictators (1967–74), through the alternation of force
(demolitions) and consent ('legalisations' – Leontidou, 1990). Pressures for

infrastructure provision instigated by landowners were less successful. There are still communities in Attica without technical infrastructure, water and sewage systems. These are of lesser interest to investors, and the public sector did not fund such networks until the early 1980s, and then only within the Athens basin. The illegal urban sprawl problem has been reproduced along expanding zones around the city, in Attica, for different and more diverse social classes.

Middle class suburbanisation, 1980s and 1990s

Later, the booming speculative building sector, also fuelled by the military junta, caused the intensification of urban congestion and the proverbial 'nefos' – the air pollution cloud over Athens. This, along with the permissive building code, led to a wave of middle class and elite suburbanisation during the 1980s, evident in Figure 3.3. On the north east of the agglomeration and along the southern coasts, middle class suburbs grew at high densities and quite close to the city centre while, at the same time, western popular suburbs, as well the Athens and Piraeus cores – a zone in the capital reaching from west to east – lost population (Figure 3.3). This continued during the 1990s too, but with a resumption of the development of Western Athens (Figure 3.3).

Athens does not have any gated communities. Exclusive areas have been created, of course, especially when masses of refugees entered the city in the inter-war period. The most interesting case is Psychico, where the building code was used as a mechanism of segregation in the inter-war period (Leontidou, 1989). However, bourgeois suburbs were very close to the city and soon became dense with multi-storey apartment buildings, encouraged by the dictators. It was not sprawl, but an expansion of the compact city nucleus sectorally outward, which has caused today's severe congestion problem.

Leapfrogging urban sprawl

We have already referred to the first leapfrog development in modern Athens, Kifissia in the nineteenth century (part of sector 203 in Figure 3.1). There are many cases in which urban sprawl (legal or illegal) leapfrogged to places located away from the conurbation but still within commuting distance from it, and these fall into four categories: (a) sprawl attached to pre-existing villages away from the city (Paiania, Koropi, etc. sprawling outward within sector 902 in Figure 3.1); (b) new developments by cooperatives on new land (discussed below); (c) a less marginal phenomenon has been leapfrogging urban sprawl around 'green villages', or along seashore towns servicing second or resort middle class housing demands, which then became

(a)

Figure 3.3a Population change in Attica, 1981–1991. Dark circles: Population increase. White circles: Population decrease.

permanent residences; finally another type (d) has been related to 'action planning' legislation or to technological parks, which, however, has rarely been successful.

Housing cooperatives
None of the above types of urban sprawl found in the Mesogeia plain have been planned. The same holds for the creation of new settlements by interest groups. Since the inter-war period, *housing cooperatives* have purchased cheap land, have subdivided it into plots, and have developed it into settlements. Sometimes planners stepped in, as in Nea Smyrna (an inter-war refugee settlement, part of sector 803 in Figure 3.1) or Helioupolis in the south of Athens (part of sector 802 in Figure 3.1). In the post-war period, some characteristic examples of this sub-type of leapfrogging urban sprawl have

(b)

Figure 3.3b   Population change in Attica, 1991–2001.

included the settlements of cooperatives of judges in Schinias, of University staff, the 'Hippokrateios politia' (a housing cooperative of medical doctors), and the 'Kallitechneioupoli' (a housing cooperative of artists).

The metropolitan periphery
Industries first appeared in the Athens metropolitan periphery on the border between North Attica and Beotia (on the north of sector 205 in Figure 3.1). This suburban and peri-urban manufacturing growth initially took place spontaneously, in clusters near major transport arteries (Leontidou, 1981; 1990; chapter 5; Kourliouros 1995; 1997) in a pattern resembling the sectoral industrial location model (Bale, 1988, chapter 8). The first sprawl thus consisted of new peri-urban industrial spaces outside Attica: along the Athens–Lamia national highway (Oinofyta, Halkida) in the north, along the Athens–Korinthos highway (Elefsina, Megara, Agioi Theodoroi, Korinthos) in the south west. However, there were similar developments within Attica,

eastwards in the Mesogeia plain (Paiania, Pallini, Spata, Koropi, Markopoulo, Lavrion, sectors 903 and 903 in Figure 3.1). Peri-urban growth was initiated by both the creation and the relocations of new plants. An extended survey in 1987–88 revealed that more than 40% of surveyed plants at two major peri-urban localities were, as a matter of fact, relocations (Wassenhoven *et al.*, 1988). More than 70% of the relocated plants moved to the metropolitan periphery from inner-city sites (Athens and Piraeus; Kourliouros, 1995, p. 212). Post-suburban hybrid landscapes emerged from the coexistence of rural/ urban, of the residential/ commercial/ industrial, and other land uses.

In general, urban sprawl in Attica until the turn of the millennium was secondary to popular suburbanisation around Athens, as is evident in Figure 3.3. Within the agglomeration, middle class suburbs grew at higher rates than working class ones. The Athens and Piraeus cores, along with a zone in the capital reaching from west to east, lost population. By contrast, the population of the metropolitan periphery all around the agglomeration grew (Figure 3.3). Mesogeia gained 26 207 inhabitants in the 1980s and 38 737 in the 1990s from physical change and migration. In other words, sprawl and peri-urban transformation were kept at relatively low levels in the rest of Attica until the end of the past millennium, combining mostly 'ribbon' and 'leapfrogging' types. Ribbon urban sprawl was observed along the main avenues, whereas leapfrogging urban sprawl tended to pop-up in settlements by cooperatives, but also in seashore resort towns or in green villages. A further type, that of organised urban development, planned according to legislation as outlined previously, has been marginal and very rare. The agricultural character of Mesogeia, with vineyards and olives, was not destroyed at the time, though the ecological footprint of Athens expanded enormously (Kaika, 2005, p. 190), with the densification of the compact city. The Marathon lake in northwest Attica reached its lowest level in 1951, and Yliki in Beotia on the northwest had to be tapped by 1958. However, by the 1980s this too proved inadequate, when major works for the Mornos dam and reservoir – further to the northwest, beyond Beotia – were completed, after the merging of the water and sewage authorities to one company, EYDAP, by Law 1068/1980 (Kaika, 2005, p. 133).

Toward the entrepreneurial city and post-Olympic landscapes

European urban cultures in the past millennium were full of antitheses: South *vs* North meant *astyphilia vs* pastoral preferences, compact *vs* sprawling cities, the attraction of the inner city *vs* the suburbs for affluent

residents. In the present millennium, however, dualisms are being deconstructed. Population movements, especially in the post-socialist era, indicate
a revival of inner-city living rather than urban sprawl, not only in the South,
but also in the North of Europe. *Re-urbanisation* and *gentrification* are
enhanced by organised urban regeneration due to urban competition, which
brings about the commodification of the city, or 'city marketing' or 'selling
places' (Kearns & Philo, 1993; Jensen-Butler *et al.*, 1996; Bailly *et al.*, 1996).
The invention of neoliberal strategies for visibility and urban entrepreneurship push aside the welfare state, reform and redistributive planning. Urban
governance switches all the way round from urban planning to city design,
from comprehensive reforms to selective local interventions, from delib-
erative to communicative planning, from welfare planning for residents to
urban decoration for global tourism and hyper-mobile transnational capital
(see also: Taylor, 1999; chapter 8; Campbell & Fainstein, 2003; Beriatos *et al.*,
2004). New strategies of multilevel urban governance and competition set
in motion new processes after the end of bipolarity.

Cities of north and south, west and east Europe, shift to new modes of
urban regulation, from public urban reform to the entrepreneurial city of
public–private partnerships – (Newman & Thornley, 1996; Bailly *et al.*,
1996; Craglia *et al.*, 2004). This constitutes a 'New Political Culture' or the
'New Urban Politics' (Cox, 1995; Clark *et al.*, 1998; Beriatos *et al.*, 2004)
enhancing the cultural economy of cities after the loss of their industrial
economy (Scott, 2000; Hall, 2000), or representing them as commodities
in an ongoing economic–noneconomic debate (Kourliouros, 2003). Mediterranean Europe, which has not experienced much of an industrial revolution,
slides easily from spontaneous urbanisation to urban entrepreneurialism,
postmodernism and urban competition (Leontidou, 1993; 1995). Northern
cities are influenced in an important way, as they even speak of 'Mediterraneanisation', which was first named in Liverpool, but was also enacted in
many other inner cities around the globe – central Baltimore, Glasgow, the
Melbourne and London waterfronts, the Graz island, 'reconquered' cities
such as Lyon, Strasbourg, Copenhagen, Melbourne and others (Leontidou,
2001).

Values for central living in Mediterranean urban Europe are combined with
a rural second home for days of leisure. Throughout the Mediterranean and
a lot of continental Europe, second-home access has been important in the
creation of compact cities: already in the early 1980s, between 8 and 20% of
urban residents had access to a rural second home (White, 1984; Leontidou,
1990), and the rate has gone up considerably since then, with the spread of residential tourism of North–South migrants lining the Mediterranean shores
(Leontidou & Marmaras, 2001). In Southern Europe, holiday homes may be

located at the place of origin of migrants to cities, but they are also built outward from the urban agglomerations. This is exactly where sprawl – or rather leapfrog development – often appears. As it is, Mediterranean sprawl increasingly involves a sort of seasonal family life pattern, fragmenting time between work and leisure, commuting and suburban living, or between first and second home, within the year and the week. Such seasonal sprawl creates traffic jams during weekends and holidays, when everybody wants to leave the city – Athens, Rome, Barcelona – and then come back at the same time. Later on, the second home may become a main home, as has happened already in the Attica region and is discussed below. This type of sprawl contrasts with controlled suburbanisation in British cities and the urban sprawl beyond them by affluent classes. It also contrasts with Anglo-American patterns of ribbon development of main homes in the remote suburbs, which inspired Doxiadis' 'Ecumenopolis' and Gottman's Megalopolis (Martinotti, 1999).

The present wave of infrastructure-driven urban sprawl in Attica belongs to the entrepreneurial city model where the Olympic bid and actual works were planned, constructed and supervised by a multitude of fragmented agents of state and local authorities and, in parallel, by large economic enterprises and public–private partnerships (Beriatos *et al.*, 2004). The 2004 Olympics created a new set of urban dynamics as the building of the Olympic infrastructure, the new airport, motorways and extended suburban railway system created a new wave of urban sprawl. Increasingly, population and industry followed new infrastructure created in anticipation of the 2004 Olympics: *infrastructure-led urban sprawl* in Attica replaced the previous model of sprawl without prior infrastructure provision around Athens.

Transport works were at the epicentre, starting with the major project of the new international airport of Athens (El. Venizelos, Map 3.1 in the centre of sector 902). In the 1980s an extended area in the heartland of the Mesogeia plain, Spata, was selected as its location and the properties included in it were expropriated despite local mobilisation to the contrary.[9] But the major infrastructure-driven development in Spata accelerated when Athens won its bid to host the 2004 Olympic Games. A lot of works then started in the Mesogeia plain, attracting labour and population. The airport started operating in 2001 almost simultaneously with an inner-city major infrastructural work, the Attico Metro, long overdue since the first proposal, 40 years before it was opened to circulation (Smith & Assoc., 1963). Two further major transport works intensified urban sprawl: the suburban railway, *proastiakos*, now reaching as far as Korinth and rendering it an Athens satellite town; and the completion of the Attica highway, also discussed over more than three decades in the Athens Master Plans as Stavrou–Elefsinas

Figure 3.4   Urban sprawl in Attica: aereal view of the Mesogeia plain in 2005.

Avenue, and is now completed as 'Attiki Odos'. In the third year of its operation, 2007, it is already causing ribbon development. Sprawl is now visible
in immediate sight, especially from the air as El. Venizelos aircraft take off
(Figure 3.4).

However, infrastructure provision was limited to transport, and of course
sports centres to host the Olympics (Figure 3.1). By contrast, drainage
and sewage have not been provided, and East Attica is still not served by
such networks. Environmental degradation relates with this, as well as
deforestation and consequent soil erosion from flooding. The inadequate
stormwater drainage system causes frequent flooding to both the city and
the peri-urban areas with resulting large-scale destruction. Deforestation
and soil erosion are also caused by frequent forest fires in Eastern Attica.
The year 2004 was an exception, probably because of the increased security measures taken for the Olympic Games. Every year, summer fires have
destroyed forests and agricultural land. In many cases, they are attributed
to arson aiming at freeing public land for private settlement development.
Overbuilding causes surface sealing. This is a consequence of illegal urban
sprawl and the lack of structured planning and programmes for urban
growth.

The lack of a land registry system results in illegal development and mixed land uses, which in turn creates further hybridity of landscapes and has made the uncontrolled and unsustainable change of peri-urban land use possible and quite profitable for the landed interests/developers coalition. Environmental problems resulting from this include the consumption of agricultural and forest land, air pollution in the areas of sprawl by industry and transport (airport) and water pollution. All these developments have transformed the past agricultural character of the Mesogeia plain into a *hybrid urban* one – a transformation in which large-scale transport infrastructure investment has played a pivotal and catalytic role. The following types of sprawl are new and can be added to the typology developed in the previous period:

Ribbon development and post-suburbia
In the first post-war decades, ribbon development was based on building regulations for areas outside the city plan which controlled agricultural land by forbidding other uses, but allowed the development of several urban uses (housing, industrial, commercial, tourist, etc.) along transport axes, provided that the plots had a minimum size by type of use. This created the most obvious case of *infrastructure-driven* urban sprawl, ribbon development along the highways. The actors initiating this type of urban sprawl were various decentralising land-intensive and transport-dependent urban activities such as branch plants, warehouses, commercial exhibitions and superstores, forming 'clusters' or 'districts' of similar activities. In such ribbon developments, no regulations for land use control (or zoning arrangements) exist. Housing developments have usually accompanied the formation of such 'districts' resulting in highly diversified land use patterns and hybrid landscapes. Through time these ribbons have tended to get interconnected into grids that have formed densely built-up post-suburban clusters, in which case ecosystem fragmentation and surface sealing beyond and along each highway have been the resulting environmental problems.

In the new millennium, a new type of ribbon development has begun, with new settlements around roads and works in the aftermath of the 2004 Olympic games.[10] The Olympic works are now surrounded by hybrid landscapes in Attica, especially to the east and north. Their dispersal defies the Mediterranean compact city tradition, but it is combined with abandonment.

Second homes and their conversion into main ones
A special case of ribbon development along coasts emerges as transport links the periphery with the inner city. Second homes in Attica and along the coasts leading outward from it, are turning into main homes in the familiar

Greek pattern of expansion without infrastructure provision. Increasingly, with the extension of transport to former remote areas, sprawl intensifies with the conversion of second homes into main ones, especially on the east coast – Artemis (Loutsa), Rafina, Schinias, Nea Makri, etc. (coasts of sectors 901 and 902 in Map 3.1). These are not only middle-class resorts: during the past decade, a lot of workers from Western Athens have been building their summer homes in places like Loutsa.[11] Now, as generations move apart to inhabit new dwellings, these summer homes turn into main homes; but they still lack sewage infrastructure.

The phenomenon of conversion has spread since the Athens Olympics 2004. The highway and the suburban railway have enormously expanded the areas ripe for urban sprawl – but the cost of commuting with the new public transport system is considerable and inaccessible for the low-income groups, as is the cost for private cars through the new toll highways and bridges. This means that commuters will belong to the middle and upper classes, provided that new drainage and sewage networks are created: at present, the only infrastructure driving this sprawl is transport.

Residential tourism and European suburbanites
The Athens Olympics 2004 seem to have initiated the settlement of Attica coasts by Europeans. This belongs to a recent wave of residential tourism by North–South migrants all along the Mediterranean coasts and especially in Spain (Leontidou & Marmaras, 2001). Since the eighteenth and, mainly, the nineteenth century, affluent Europeans have moved to villas on the Mediterranean coasts seasonally, but it was only very recently that this important version of migration escalated and lost its seasonality. As European integration proceeded, and especially after the Maastricht Treaty, affluent populations migrated beyond city and, indeed, national boundaries, toward the Mediterranean in migratory waves which are increasingly important for the whole of Europe.

Athens has attracted residential tourists to islands in the past, who, unlike those settling in Spain, were not mainly pensioners (Leontidou & Marmaras, 2001). However, after the 2004 Olympics British, German and Austrian migrants, of whom the majority are pensioners, are reported to have bought houses on the coasts around Nea Makri and other areas of second homes.[12] Their presence has been important in new housing, about 30% of which is reported to have been lent or bought by foreigners living in a kind of suburbia very far from their cities of origin. International investors foresee about one million residential tourists in the near future in Greece, and have started to construct housing for them.

Post-Olympic leapfrogging

The Olympic Village has been another case of leapfrogging over still undeveloped land, and is becoming a remote but very upgraded housing complex for workers (in sector 101 of Figure 3.1). It has been a gated community for avoidance of trespassing, until the lottery decided about its inhabitants among AOEK (Workers' Housing Organisation) beneficiaries. As many as 25 000 families rushed to take part in the lottery of October 2004 for 2290 homes, and there were some racist incidents when foreign workers won houses. These estates have not been surrounded by sprawling squatters. However, sprawl by other population groups for different reasons has emerged next to the major Olympic infrastructural works and in other niches of the periphery of Athens. There is also a densification of what used to be disadvantaged neighbourhoods in the western suburbs.

Satellite towns

During the new millennium, Athens is acquiring its own satellite towns. Chalkida to the north was the first, developing after industrial growth in the metropolitan periphery. This has now gone further, to Levadia, where new activities – including the recent establishment of a university department – have increased the town's attractiveness to students, staff and service labour. To the south, Korinth has benefited since the Olympics from commuting via the new suburban railway, which links it directly to the new Athens airport via the inner city.

The nature of urban sprawl in the Mesogeia plain during the present decade has several attributes of post-suburbia: it has been industrial and commercial more than just residential. This can be also deduced from the nature of population change in the area. Local authorities estimate a population rise of 30–40% during the first few years of the new millennium, especially since the transport infrastructure works. However, despite the high estimates, it seems questionable whether population will rise as sharply as speculative building in the area. It has been suggested that there is now an oversupply of new development, exceeding demand.[13] Nevertheless, building goes on and every year 5000–7000 new buildings are added in the Mesogeia plain, and these will increase, given the planned urbanisation of 425.km^2 in various Mesogeia localities,[14] which is leading to appreciation of property values.[15] The demand by Europeans will also attract more entrepreneurial interest and more sprawl.

The structure of population growth in Mesogeia provides interesting evidence of the difference from the typical suburbia of North and West European cities sprawling outward. There is some evidence that migration over the last two decades does not involve any major relocation of families toward the Mesogeia plain. The number of small households increased substantially before the turn of the millennium, probably pointing to young male migrants especially, who have settled in Mesogeia in search of agricultural, service or construction work. The number of households in Mesogeia increased from 15 800 in 1981 to 37 117 in 2001 (+134.9%), and the average household size fell from 3.33 in 1981 to 3.16 in 1991 and, dramatically, to only 1.34 in 2001. Couples with more than one child decreased proportionately, although they still represent the majority in all census years. This throws light on a very important aspect of social exclusion and segregation, as it means sprawl should be attributed less to the typical suburban families who have created sprawl in other cities, but rather to specific economic activities and their workers, mostly migrants. In fact, Albanian and Kurdish migrants have moved to East Attica as well as the West, in order to find affordable housing, work in the Olympic construction sites, and also find informal work in Mesogeia. It is interesting that they were not housed in shacks typical of Third World peri-urban settlements, but in market niches around villages and towns. This, however, was the state of affairs before the Olympics were staged in 2004. Since then, relocations of Greeks as well as other Europeans to the coasts have changed migration dynamics.

Mega-events and Mediterranean urban futures

The first years of urban sprawl in Attica were associated with the growth of industrial parks on the one hand, and second homes on the other; but the vineyards and olive groves were largely left in place until the end of the twentieth century – at least to a considerable extent. Now these are fragmented and crossed by large transport works such as the international airport of Spata, the 'Attiki Odos' highway, the metro and the suburban railway, or infrastructural works for Olympic games. As we turn to post-Olympic urban futures, interesting comparisons can be drawn between Barcelona and Athens with respect to the place of Mediterranean cities in urban competition for the attraction of mega-events, ways of hosting them and then taking advantage of their effects. In all cities there is a balance between two types of works: those promoting built heritage and tradition with local spatial references in the inner city, and those promoting innovative design by celebrities, with broader spatial references and global aspirations. This combination 'glocalises' the cities (according to one approach, Beriatos *et al.*, 2004), while at the same time enhancing the hybridity of the cityscapes, according to our model. Euro-Mediterranean cityscapes have had their own distinctive traditions for a very long period, something that is now pushed to the foreground to the point of 'Mediterraneanisation' of Northern cities. In the context of urban competition, entrepreneurialism and the commodification of cities, Spain provided three star examples in 1992, hosting international events with massive corporate mobilisation: Barcelona for the Olympics, Madrid as the 'European City of Culture', and Seville of EXPO 92 (Garcia, 1993; Leontidou, 1995).

The case of Athens differs from those of Spanish cities in several crucial respects, which render the discussion about the international role of Athens (Economou *et al.*, 2001; Marmaras, 2003) rather secondary in this context. Though Barcelona opted for compact design and developed the Olympic Village within the city, combining it with redevelopment of old industrial sites along the waterfront (Marshall, 2000), it sprawled henceforth in two directions: along the B30 highway on the west and over the hills (Bruegmann, 2005) and along the coast with the densification of residential tourism (Leontidou & Marmaras, 2001). Athens spilled over the hill of Hymettus, too, and started to experience residential tourism, though it followed nothing like the Spanish compact Olympic City policy. In its case, the fragmentation of Olympic works and their scattering all over Attica has been of central importance for urban sprawl. While in several cities during the present millennium, sprawl coincides with planned gentrification, this has not been so in Athens – where gentrification has been left to private actors and is well under way – because it was reproduced traditionally. Though it is not planned, it is still revitalising the better areas and is then triggered in other neighbourhoods next to new metro stations. Unlike other South European cities sharing geographical imaginations of urbanism and the compact city cultural tradition – Spanish cities, Lisbon, Genoa and others, who renovated their cores and ports – Athens did not take advantage of this mega-event to revitalise its central declining areas (Beriatos *et al.*, 2004). Renovation in Elaionas started two years later on occasion of a football stadium. The Olympics left the Greeks with a multitude of works, scattered in North and East Attica (Figure 3.1). Unfortunately, some are now ghost landscapes and waste deposit dumps, with the contested Marathon rowing lake being the worst and saddest case, because it destroyed an ecosystem without any positive effect. There were mobilisations at the time, but environmental NGOs are weak in Greece (Afouxenidis, 2006), and decisions had been taken. In all, Athens did not valorise its Olympic heritage and has missed a formidable opportunity. Other South European cities have been upgraded, renovated, renewed and constantly reurbanised on the occasion of mega-events. Some have missed the chance.

However, Athens compares positively with other cities when some postmodern versions of sprawl are considered, among them residential tourism, which bursts toward the southern coasts and islands of Europe. As it spreads from the South of France to Italy and Spain and now Greece, we can perceive the Mediterranean seasonal life patterns influencing and indeed penetrating the Northern places of origin. Residential tourism is another type of 'Mediterraneanisation' which affects Northern European populations, who buy properties along Mediterranean coasts and islands and stay there for maybe half of the year, or longer (Leontidou & Marmaras, 2001). This is a sort of long-distance sprawl, as removed from cities as the French Riviera is removed from Paris, or British cities, for that matter (Nelson, 2001). Although residential tourists to Greece rather prefer islands, such a pattern of cosmopolitan sprawl has already affected Attica, where Europeans as well as local populations line the coasts and nearby islands. This is not likely to turn into the major wave which has changed the face of Costa Blanca from Barcelona to Alicante, via Benidorm and further, in Spain.

The diversity of Southern exurban landscapes is complicated by such differences as those between Barcelona and Athens, combined with Mediterranean particularities pointing to urban futures of sprawl and post-suburbia caused by diverse and intertwined socio-economic, political and cultural forces. This sprawl may often locate much further from the cities than hitherto imagined, with consequences as ambivalent as the contradiction of positive lifestyles and negative environmental effects.

Notes

1 Many thanks to: Dr Costas Rondos (Assistant Professor of Quantitave Methods in Social Sciences at the University of the Aegean) for documentation of population, employment and land use change in Greece; Dr Thomas Hadzichristos (Surveying Engineer and Geographer) and Ms Dora Manta (Surveying Engineer) for mapping; Mr Kyriakos Tourkomenis (Geographer and Regionalist) for documentation and interviews; Mr Panayiotis Pongas (Engineer) for material on the Athens Olympics; and Ms Maro Evangelidou, Architect and Planner of ORSA (Organisation of the Athens Master Plan), for acting as a stakeholder and advisor to the team.

2 Evangelidou (2003) calls it 'bilingual' control, because it was introduced in policy or legislation, but was not actually implemented. She also notes the 'bilingual' policy in favour of the compact city and implementation against this and in favour of sprawl.

3 See database http://www.citypopulation.de. It is noteworthy that other Mediterranean cities like Barcelona, Rome and Napoli have similar population levels and similarities in their sprawl dynamics with Athens, though Napoli is different from the other cities in many ways.

4 The contribution in land was equivalent to 40% of the private land and 30% of the private land in cases where the system of development zones (ZEΠ and ZAA) would be implemented, with comprehensive planning and development practices (Marmaras, 2002).

5 Instead of bridging the 'gap of trust' between state and citizens, the planning reforms tended to widen it. As relevant analyses have shown, however, citizens' participation in the planning process has not been substantial since the crucial decisions are still made by the central government (Ministry of Environment and Planning). Christophilopoulos (1990) has coined the term 'pseudo-participation'. Broad urban strata tend cumulatively to be repelled by state-initiated urban-industrial planning attempts, and anti-industrial mentalities have predominated in Greater Athens (Leontidou, 1981; Kourliouros, 2001).

6 For example, the timely planning of the urban surroundings and outskirts, the determination of a higher plot ratio in all the new urban extensions, equal to 0:80 – except for some cases where for social purposes the plot ratio could be bigger than 0:80 – and the gradation in the calculation of the contribution in money and land of the land owners in accordance to the size of their properties.

7 Manufacturing activity was a special concern: a preparatory study carried out by the Ministry of Environment and Planning in the context of the Structure Plan (Hatzisocratis, 1983), identified the major problems of Athenian manufacturing, calculated the future needs for industrial space and proposed the creation of a spatially balanced system of industrial and handicraft parks within and around the Athenian conurbation (with Kourliouros).

8 Kourliouros, 1995, p. 252; in the context of the industrial parks' initiative, the Ministry of the Environment funded the National Technical University of Athens in order to study the whole issue in a comparative perspective, evaluating international experiences, and to prepare a pilot-project for the organisation and planning of two major industrial parks, Koropi-Vari and Metamorphosis (Wassenhoven *et al.*, 1988). Ministry officials used this as a guideline for other studies of industrial parks appointed to private planning offices. The state's planning machinery was evidently set in motion, but anti-industrial ideology prevailed (Kourliouros, 1997; 2001).

9 This local mobilisation had an economic goal: higher prices for the expropriated properties.

10 The Attica highway and the Spata airport; see presentation by journalist Gryllakis on NET, 20.02.2005, who thinks that 1 in 5 inhabitants of the Athens centre will live or have a second home in Mesogeia in the next 10–15 years.

11 Interview with the mayor.

12 Estate agent interviewed by journalist Gryllakis in NET on 1.1.2007. Foreign residents of Attica were also interviewed, stating that buying a house is preferable to building because of its lower cost compared with their countries, also referring to building costs in Attica as low.

13 Estate agent interviewed in 20.02.2005.

14 Communities included in the plan are around the towns of Pallini, Gerakas, Rafina, Pikermi, Marcopoulo, Spata, Paiania, Artemida, Koropi, Kalyvia,

Keratea: Gryllakis on NET, 20.02.2005. More extensions took place throughout 2006.
15   According to the estate agent interviewed in 20.02.2005, prices range between 1000 and 1800 Ł per m^2 in the communities in question.

References

Afouxenidis, A. (2006, in Greek) Facets of civil society in Greece: the example of environmental and anti-racist NGOs. *Episteme & Koinonia* **16**: 163–78.

Allum, P. (1973) *Politics and Society in Post-war Negles*. Cambridge U.P.

Apostolopoulos Y., Loukissas P. & Leontidou L. (eds) (2001) *Mediterranean Tourism: Facets of Socio-economic Development and Cultural Change*. Routledge, London.

Bailly, A., Jensen-Butler, C. & Leontidou, L. (1996) Changing cities: restructuring, marginality and policies in urban Europe. *European Urban and Regional Studies* **3**(2): 161–76.

Bale, J. (1988) *The Location of Manufacturing Industry: Conceptual Frameworks in Geography*. Oliver & Boyd, Edinburgh.

Beauregard, R. A. & Body-Gendrot, S. (eds) (1999) *The Urban Moment. Cosmopolitan Essays on the Late-20th-Century City*. Sage, London.

Beja Horta, A. P. (2004) *Contested Citizenship: Immigration Politics and Grassroots Migrants' Organizations in Post-Colonial Portugal*. Center for Migration Studies (CMS), New York.

Beriatos, E. & Gospodini, A. (2004) "Glocalising" urban landscapes: Athens and the 2004 Olympics. *Cities* **21**(3): 187–202.

Biris, C. (1966, in Greek) *Athens – From the 19th to the 20th Century*. Foundation of Town Planning and History of Athens, Athens.

Bruegman, R. (2005) *Sprawl: A Compact History*. University of Chicago Press, Chicago & London.

Campbell, S. & Fainstein, S. (eds) (2003) *Readings in Planning Theory*. Blackwell, Oxford.

Christophilopoulos, D. (1990, in Greek) *Urban and Regional Planning: A Technical Process or a Social Science?* Sakkoulas, Athens.

Clark, T. N. & Hoffmann-Martinot, V. (1998) *The New Political Culture*. West View Press, Boulder CO.

Cox, K. (1995) Globalization, competition and the politics of local economic development. *Urban Studies* **32**(2): 213–24.

Craglia, M., Leontidou, L., Nuvolati, G. & Schweikart, J. (2004) Towards the development of quality of life indicators in the 'digital' city, *Environment & Planning B: Planning and Design* **31**(1): 51–64.

Economou, D., Getimis, P., Demathas, Z., Petrakos, G. & Pyrgiotis, J. (2001, in Greek) *The international role of Athens*. YPEHODE, ORSA & Thessaly University Editions, Volos.

Evangelidou, M. (2003, in Greek). The Odyssey of 'illegal building' in Greece. Comments on occasion of an interesting day conference in the 'Ombundsman'. *Geographies* **6**: 95–100.

Fried, R. C. (1973) *Planning the Eternal City: Roman Politics and Planning since World War II*. Yale University Press, London.

Garcia, S. (1993) Local economic policies and social citizenship in Spanish cities. *Antipode* **25**(2): 191–205.

Government Gazette (*Efimerida tis Kyverniseos* in Greek) no. 228, 1923; no. 151, 1976; no. 169, 1979; no. 33, 1983.

Hall, P. (2000) Creative cities and economic development. *Urban Studies* **37**(4): 639–49.

Hardy, D. & Ward, C. (1984) *Arcadia For All: The Legacy of a Makeshift Landscape*. Mansell, London.

Jensen-Butler, C., Shakhar, A. & van den Weesep, J. (eds) (1996) *European Cities in Competition*. Avebury, Aldershot.

Kaika, M. (2005). *City of Flows: Modernity, Nature and the City*. Routledge, London.

Karydis, D. (2006, in Greek) *The Seven Books of Town Planning*. Athens: Papasotiriou.

King, R. De Mas, P. & Beck, J. M. (eds) (2001) *Geography, Environment and Development in the Mediterranean*. Sussex Academic Press, Brighton.

Kearns, G. and Philo, C. (eds) (1993) *Selling Places: The City as Cultural Capital, Past and Present*. Pergamon Press, Oxford.

Kourliouros, E. (1995) *Industrial Space in Contemporary Athens: The Development and Transformation of a Southern European Metropolis*. Unpublished PhD thesis, London School of Economics and Political Science, Department of Geography.

Kourliouros, E. (1997) Planning Industrial Location in Greater Athens: the interaction between deindustrialization and anti-industrialism during the 1980s. *European Planning Studies* **5**(4): 435–60.

Kourliouros, E. (2001, in Greek) *Itineraries in Theories of Space: Economic Geographies of Production and Development*. Hellenica Grammata, Athens.

Kourliouros, E. (2003) Reflections on the economic-noneconomic debate: a radical geographical perspective from the European South. *Antipode* **35**(4): 781–99.

Leontidou, L. (1981, in Greek) *Employment in Greater Athens 1960–2000, and the Prospects of Development of Economic Activities in the Hellenicon Airport Site*: DEPOS, Athens.

Leontidou, L. (1989/2001, 2nd edn/in Greek) *Cities of Silence: Working-class Space in Athens and Piraeus, 1909–1940*. ETVA (Cultural Technological Foundation of the Hellenic Bank of Industrial Development) and Themelio, Athens.

Leontidou, L. (1990/2006, 2nd edn) *The Mediterranean City in Transition: Social Change and Urban Development*. Cambridge University Press, Cambridge.

Leontidou, L. (1993) Postmodernism and the city: Mediterranean versions, *Urban Studies* **30**(6): 949–65.

Leontidou, L. (1995) Repolarization in the Mediterranean: Spanish and Greek cities in neoliberal Europe, *European Planning Studies* **3**(2): 155–72.

Leontidou, L. (2001) Cultural representations of urbanism and experiences of urbanisation in Mediterranean Europe. In R. King, P. De Mas, & J. M. Beck (eds), *Geography, environment and development in the Mediterranean*, Sussex Academic Press, Brighton, pp. 83–98.

Leontidou, L. (2005 in Greek) *Ageographitos Chora [Geographically illiterate land]: Hellenic Idols in the Epistemological Pathways of European Geography.* Hellenica Grammata, Athens.

Leontidou, L. & Marmaras, E. (2001) From tourists to migrants: international residential tourism and the 'littoralization' of Europe. In: Y. Apostolopoulos, P. Loukissas, & L. Leontidou (eds), *Mediterranean tourism: Facets of socio-economic development and cultural change*, Routledge, London, pp. 257–67.

Marmaras, E. (1989) The privately-built multi-storey apartment building: the case of inter-war Athens. *Planning Perspectives* **4**: 45–78.

Marmaras, E. (1996) From the policy of Town Planning to that of Urban Compactness: Athens during the first half of the twentieth century, International Planning History Society and ETIPOP (eds), Proceedings on *The Planning of Capital Cities*, pp. 459–74.

Marmaras, E. (2002, in Greek) *Planning and Urban Space: Theoretical Approaches and Facets of Greek Urban Geography.* Athens: Hellenika Grammata.

Marmaras, E. (2003, in Greek) Seeking the strategic role of post-Olympic Athens. *Architektones* **39**, 55–59.

Marshall, T. (2000) Urban planning and governance: Is there a Barcelona model? *International Planning Studies* **5**(3): 299–319.

Martinotti, G. (1999) A city for whom? Transients and public life in the second-generation metropolis. In: R. A. Beauregard, & S. Body-Gendrot, (eds), *The Urban Moment. Cosmopolitan Essays on the Late-20th-Century City*, London, Sage, pp. 155–84.

McGregor, D., Simon, D. & Thompson, D. (eds) (2006) *The Peri-urban Interface: Approaches to Sustainable Natural and Human Resource Use.* Earthscan, London.

Nelson, M. (2001) *Queen Victoria and the discovery of the Riviera.* I. B. Tauris, London.

Newman, P. & Thornley, A. (1996) *Urban Planning in Europe: International Competition, National Systems and Planning Projects.* Routledge, London.

Phelps, N. A., Parsons, N., Ballas, D. & Dowling, A. (2006) *Planning and Politics at the Margins of Europe's Capital Cities.* Palgrave, Basingstoke.

Schorske, C. E. (1998) *Thinking with History: Explorations in the Passage to Modernism.* Princeton University Press, New Jersey.

Scott, A. J. (2000) *The Cultural Economy of Cities.* Sage, London.

Smith, W. & Assoc. (1963) *Athens Basin Transportation Survey and Study.* Ministry of Public Works, Athens.

Taylor, N. (1999) *Urban Planning Theory Since 1945.* Sage, London.

van den Berg, L., Drewett, R., Klaasen, L. H., Rossi, A. & Vijverberg, C. H. T. (1982) *Urban Europe: A Study of Growth and Decline.* Pergamon Press, Oxford.

Vickerman, R. W. (1984) *Urban Economics: Analysis and Policy.* Philip Allan, Oxford.

Vliamos, S., Georgoulis, D. & Kourliouros, E. (1992, in Greek) *Industrial Parks: Institutions, Theory and Planning Methodology.* Papazisis & Hellenic Bank of Industrial Development, Athens.

Wassenhoven, L., Georgoulis, D., Kourliouros, E. *et al.* (1988) *Planning and Organi-zation of Industrial Parks in Attica Prefecture: Koropi-Vari and Metamorphosis Industrial Parks.* Research report, (7 Volumes), NTUA/Ministry of Environment, Spatial Planning and Public Works, Athens.

White, M. & White, L. (1977) *The Intellectual Versus the City: From Thomas Jefferson to Frank Lloyd Wright.* Oxford University Press, Oxford.

White, P. (1984) *The West European City: A Social Geography.* Longman, London.

Williams, R. (1973) *The Country and the City.* Chatto and Windus, London.

4

Sprawl in the Post-Socialist City: The Changing Economic and Institutional Context of Central and Eastern European Cities

Nataša Pichler-Milanovič,
Małgorzata Gutry-Korycka and Dieter Rink

Socialist cities in Central and Eastern Europe

The processes of urban sprawl are very *heterogeneous* across Europe, much more than in the US, which roots in the diverse history and cultures of European nations and calls for a European perspective on sprawl. In definitions based around morphological form, urban sprawl is generally measured as a deviation from the compact city form, such as suburban growth, ribbon or leap-frogged development. Definitions based on land use tend to associate sprawl with the spatial segregation of land uses, and with the extensive mono-functional use of land for single-family residential development, free-standing shopping malls, industrial or office parks and large recreational areas (e.g. golf courses, theme parks, etc.)

The URBS PANDENS project has included three case study cities from Central and Eastern Europe that were dominated in the 1990s by the transformation process to democratic society and a market economy. These cities are experiencing major transitions in terms of the economy, policy and institutions: Leipzig (Germany), Ljubljana (Slovenia) and Warsaw (Poland). Despite some significant differences between these cities, similarities with specific respect of post-socialist transformation can also be observed. Though very distinct with regard to their starting conditions at the end of 1980s, and the amount of investment during the transition period in 1990s, some general conclusions on patterns, causes and consequences of urban sprawl in these cities are possible.

The historical and political legacies of city development after World War II in Central and Eastern Europe show that the urbanisation processes in socialist countries differed from those in capitalist countries. The differences between the socialist and capitalist urban development were the most significant at the intra-urban level. The socialist model of housing development and urban planning, the centralised planned economic system and the non-existence of (urban) land markets are the most important features that have shaped a distinctive structure of socialist cities, significantly different from capitalist cities in Western Europe. Socialism has left its most lasting imprint on the inner-city periphery, where large housing estates were built, and also in the central city areas, dominated by deteriorating historic buildings.

In the 1980s, some analyses of internal structure and socio-spatial differentiation of socialist cities were based on the effects of provision and distribution of housing among different social groups in particular city localities (see Enyedi, 1992; Kennedy & Smith, 1989, etc.). According to Musil (1993) the analysis of the housing system, housing policy and urban planning in former socialist countries were more adequate than the analysis of land markets, as key factors explaining the pattern and dynamics of residential segregation in capitalist cities. Hence, the residential differentiation in socialist cities did not generally show the extremes of social class segregation, as a consequence of egalitarian principles of 'equality'. The suburbanisation process did not play an important role before 1985 in shaping the growth patterns of socialist cities as in the capitalist countries. As a result the socialist cities were more compact than capitalist ones. The industrial development of former socialist cities were infamous for their legacies of poor environmental quality, which is a major determinant now in both attracting and retaining economic activity and high quality labour force in the city.

Therefore the development of socialist cities was in many aspects unique, which also means that cities in Central and Eastern Europe had great similarities to each other at the beginning of the transformation period in early 1990s.

By 2000, the population of Central and Eastern Europe had reached 125 million with 60% in urban areas. The region has experienced the most rapid post- World War II growth in total and in urban population of any region in Europe, but with large differences between the countries. More than half of the urban population in Central and Eastern Europe live in cities with

Table 4.1 Growth of urban population in Central and Eastern Europe 1950–1990

Country	1950 000	%	1970 000	%	1990 000	%
East Germany	13 040	72.0	12 592	73.8	15 759	76.8
Poland	9 605	39.0	17 088	52.3	12 310	61.3
Czechoslovakia	6 354	51.5	8 942	62.3	11 836	75.7
Hungary	3 553	38.6	4 992	48.2	6 295	59.5
Romania	3 713	23.4	8 335	40.9	11 723	50.6
Bulgaria	2 001	27.5	4 510	52.9	5 967	66.4
Yugoslavia	3 269	21.9	7 385	35.9	11 125	46.5
Albania	250	20.5	800	37.4	1 135	35.5
Total	**41 785**	**39.4**	**64 644**	**51.2**	**83 920**	**60.0**

Sources: Hamilton, 1979; Hamilton *et al.*, 2005.

less than 100 000 inhabitants, while cities with 100 000 or more inhabitants contain a quarter of the region's population. In Estonia and Latvia, as in Bulgaria and Hungary, the high concentration of population is particularly visible in and around national capitals. The capital cities of Poland (Warsaw), Romania (Buchurest), and the Czech Republic (Prague), Lithuania (Vilnius), Slovakia (Bratislava), Slovenia (Ljubljana), Albania (Tirana) concentrate far lower proportions of their national population (UNECE, 1997; UNCHS, 2001).

Transition reforms in Central and Eastern Europe

The dramatic changes since 1989 – the collapse of communist power, the break-up of the Soviet Union, Czechoslovakia and Yugoslavia and the end of the Cold War – have reconfigured Central and Eastern Europe. The countries have undergone a political, economic and institutional transformation from various forms of socialist structures towards democratic and market-economy systems. Political, economic and geo-strategic reforms have lead to important structural changes in Central and Eastern Europe, characterised by re-orientation of trade to EU markets, price liberalisation, economic and therefore industrial re-structuring, shift from industrial to service economy, transformation of enterprises, privatisation, foreign direct investments (FDI), a shift from supply to the demand-oriented economy and, finally, the membership of international organisations and associations – especially the EU.

Therefore, urban sprawl in Central and Eastern European cities can also be interpreted as a consequence of the process of *transformation* or structural adjustment as a shift to democratic societies and market-based economies (e.g. privatisation, restitution, decentralisation, individual choices), and *internationalisation* or functional (re)integration in the global processes (i.e. taking 'western' values such as new shopping centres, type and standard of houses, golf courses, theme parks, etc.), but mainly influenced (at first) by American values and way of life.

In this respect, the pressures of the world economy, particularly in terms of city competition for attracting capital investment, are just as applicable in Central and Eastern Europe as elsewhere in the world (Enyedi, 1998; Hamilton *et al.*, 2005; Keivani *et al.*, 2001; Marcuse & van Kempen, 2000). Secondly, the accession of some Central and Eastern European countries to fully-fledged membership of the European Union (EU) in 2004 and 2007 represents a completely new phase of institutional development. The systematic process of EU enlargement and integration, *Europeanisation* – or rather *'EU-isation'* – of values, standards, norms and policies can thus be interpreted as a specific 'mode' of globalisation of Central and Eastern Europe in a particular macro-regional context.

In the early 1990s it was assumed that transformation from a centrally-managed socialist economy within the context of a single (communist) party system, towards a market economy and a civil, democratic society, would project cities in Central and Eastern Europe rather uniformly along a linear trajectory. This would, in turn, result in their convergence through time towards the spatial-structural and functional characteristics of cities in advanced market economies, or at least with those in Western Europe. Such thinking, however, was not only naïve in retrospect, but was often based on a lack of understanding of the 'power of the past' to differentiate city trends. To varying degrees contemporary developments in, and the characteristics of, cities in Central and Eastern Europe, are also *path dependent* on their pre-socialist as well as their socialist legacies.

During the 1990s, the paths of city development and change between those in Central, South-East and East Europe appeared to be diverging significantly. This occurred in different ways, to different degrees and on different levels. *Central Europe* has re-emerged as a distinctive sub-region embracing the Czech Republic, Hungary, Poland, Slovakia and Slovenia (or more precisely *Central-East Europe*). Although former East Germany became part of re-unified Germany and the European Union (EU) in 1990, it is also in some respects part of this sub-region. As a result of this *sub-regionalisation* some territories can be differentiated according to their distinctive features and trends in city transition and development, including patterns of urban sprawl

(see Hamilton *et al.*, 2005):

- Cities in former *East Germany* which became integrated overnight into the German market economy and the EU (including Leipzig). 'Shock therapy' has radically altered East German cities as a result, although the regeneration and reintegration of Berlin is a special case since it has been acquiring the capital city functions of a reunified Germany within the EU, while also lying close to the frontier with Poland.
- Cities in the 'fast track' reforming states in *Central Europe*, and new EU member states, that is, Czech Republic, Hungary, Poland and Slovenia. These cities have been experiencing varying degrees of commodification of production factors and productive capacities, and have been amongst the cities in the region most exposed to globalisation and EU-isation influences through flows of capital, information, people, technology and trade.

The transformation process was the most dramatic in countries with the most radical reforms, such as former East Germany, Poland, Czech Republic and Hungary, but not in Slovenia. The differences, such as the speed of transformation processes, the domination of private ownership, or the role of (foreign) capital are also evident among post-socialist cities. Such cities are more firmly on a path of converging cities in market economies, as a result of de-industrialisation or industrial restructuring, the growth of producer and consumer services, the implementation of diversified foreign investment and the emergence of small firms and entrepreneurship within the context of reorganisation of production systems. Indeed, capital cities in these states have been playing the leading role in achieving a major shift in economic trends from recession and decline in the early-to-mid 1990s to significant economic growth in the mid-to-late 1990s, some more recently than others.

In the 1990s *intra-city transitions* with regards to urban sprawl was influenced particularly by decentralisation and local government reforms, property restitution and privatisation, physical upgrading of the built environment, changes in land use patterns and capital investments. These transitions of urban pattern are mostly a product of demographic decline, social diversification and restructuring of urban activities. Changes in property ownership, public administration and finance, transport and energy costs, employment and housing costs and opportunities have raised questions about the competitiveness and sustainability of Central and Eastern European cities, and their roles in social, economic and political affairs within and beyond Europe (Pichler-Milanović, 2001).

City transformation in Central and Eastern Europe is most notably associated with de-industrialisation, commercialisation of the historic core,
revitalisation of some inner-city areas, and residential and commercial suburbanisation in the outer city ('urban sprawl'). The process of housing
rehabilitation and revitalisation of the historical cores can be observed in
combination with growing tourism and demand for space in central locations for expanding retail and office activities. Reconstruction of historically
important buildings and sites is another activity seen as a way of preserving
cultural heritage, showing respect for tradition and is part of a growing awareness about environmental quality. The development of offices, multipurpose
commercial centres and leisure facilities, through refurbishment of existing
buildings or new infill development, and the gentrification promoted by the
private or public sector, are prevailing interventions in inner-city areas.

The most significant changes in the land use pattern of the post-socialist
cities in Central and Eastern Europe are similar now to those identified in
other European cities (see Kivell, 1993):

- growth of the urban fringe (suburbanisation and desurbanisation);
- reurbanisation and revitalisation of the central city areas;
- growth of need for infrastructure, especially transport and telecommuni-
  cations;
- growth and decline of particular urban nodes due to relocation of industry
  from city centres, and establishment of commercial zones and shopping
  centres at the city periphery.

While the high density of built-up land and the preservation of historical heritage in some Central and Eastern European cities may constrain
the possibilities for new development, the largely post-war reconstructed
inner-city areas of Warsaw and Berlin – with their numerous vacant open
spaces – are open for new possibilities. However, disputes about restitution
and unresolved ownership rights have up to now limited more intensive
(re)development in the central parts of Warsaw, while Berlin (and Leipzig) is
booming due to the *Investitionsvorranggesetz* ('priority of investment law'),
that enables the political authorities to grant land in the city centre to high
capital investors, and merely remunerate the former owners (see Couch *et al.*,
2005).

Restitution with land and property market price deregulation had a significant impact upon the urban form of post-socialist cities. However, effects
have mainly been visible in the historic core of cities, since the peripheral
urban areas were mainly characterised by prefabricated housing estates and
have been subject to privatisation. These processes, with high demand for

office and retail space in the central city areas, have led to a large housing price differentiation between the central and peripheral locations.

The characterisation of urban transformation at the city periphery that was first comprehensively observed in Prague (see Sýkora, 1998, 1999) as in other Central and Eastern European cities since 1990 are the following:

- residential suburbanisation takes several forms, such as speculatively built multi-dwelling houses for sale (e.g. low rise, row, or sale of plots of land for single-family housing construction), transition of existing suburban villages with 'in-fill' of new single family – usually detached – housing developments. Residential suburbanisation contributes to a reversal of the traditional socio-spatial pattern of the socialist city with the socio-economic status of population declining with distance from the centre;
- commercial development has a more significant impact on the transformation of outer city areas than housing construction (e.g. concentration in complexes built along major highways – 'ribbon' development – and important transport intersections and also around rail and subway stations). An important proportion of retailing moves to the suburban zone (e.g. out-of-town shopping centres), there is also creation of suburban business parks and office complexes (e.g. near to the airport). This is largely due to greater personal mobility with the rise in car ownership;
- speculative industrial and warehousing development, with high potential for development of industrial premises, are usually developed at the major junctions on the motorway network.

Suburbanisation is also adding another ring to the existing spatial structure of the city.

The patterns of urban sprawl in post-socialist cities

Residential

As a consequence of several decades of strong political, institutional and economic regulation during the socialist period, the Central and Eastern European cities underwent significant changes in their spatial organisation that were most evident in the intra-urban structure of particular cities. Medieval historic core and inner-city areas built at the end of nineteenth century, with the exception of modest high-rise office development, were dominated by a deteriorating building stock nationalised in the 1950s and badly maintained until the 1990s. High-density housing estates were constructed at the city periphery, while high quality low-rise housing estates for the political end economic elites were located in the green belt. Self-built detached family houses were built in suburban settlements (villages) lacking sufficient infrastructure, and largely inhabited by lower socio-economic groups.

Until 1990, the housing stock in the Central and Eastern European capital cities (with the exception of Sofia and Ljubljana), was dominated by the public rental sector, although the owner-occupied sector was always substantial, in the form of single private family houses or owner-occupied flats in cooperative or condominium multi-family buildings. At this time, because of growing economic problems, public sector housing construction, which in 1980 accounted for between 40 and 60% of new housing production in most Eastern European countries – and even up to 85% in Baltic countries (Tsenkova, 2005; Pichler-Milanović, 2001) – began to decline, dropping significantly in the early 1990s. Comparative data from the 1990s (UN, 2001) shows that the Czech Republic, Slovak Republic and Bulgaria still managed to maintain a significant public housing supply with more than 20% of total housing stock, followed by Poland, Slovenia, Lithuania and Estonia with about 10%. However, recent evidence suggests a further decline of public supply in this sector, to come close to Latvia – the extreme example – with 68% of dwellings completed by the public sector in 1990 dropping to 0% at the end of 1990s (Donner, 2006; Tsenkova, 2005).

Residential suburbanisation has occurred in some socialist cities (e.g. Ljubljana, Budapest, etc.) since the 1970s, predominately in the form of 'satellite' dormitory neighbourhoods or in the existing suburban villages. Since the late 1980s these processes have become more profound, and in the 1990s were followed by industrial and commercial suburbanisation mainly along motorways and access roads.

The socialist legacies of housing development, architectural design and urban planning strategies are reflected in transformation of land use patterns and morphological structure of post-socialist cities. Political and economic reforms in the 1990s have had important effects on city transformation in Central and Eastern Europe. In the urban context the reintroduction of land and housing markets in post-socialist cities have been the main effects of transition reforms (Pichler-Milanović, 1994; 2001). A sophisticated system of property prices has developed reflecting the location, quality, size, accessibility and level of service in particular city areas. Property prices in capital cities are often 30–50 % higher than in other cities. Price increase is the most significant in attractive inner-city locations and some residential areas at the city outskirts, showing the sharp difference between the city centre and peripheral areas (see also Struyk, 1996; Hegedüs *et al.*, 1996; Pichler-Milanović, 2001).

Under the previous socialist systems, housing policy had been aimed at guaranteeing all citizens equal opportunity of access to housing. Although this goal was never entirely achieved in any of the former socialist countries, a varying but continuous supply of housing was nonetheless maintained through the provision of low-cost prefabricated high-density housing estates. A substantial amount of the funds required for the construction of these large housing estates was secured through various forms of public financing and state subsidies.

While the changes introduced in the political and economic systems of former socialist countries have had profound effects on the social and economic situation of their populations, the provision of housing has become one of the spheres to which little or no serious attention has been addressed in the majority of Central and Eastern European countries. With regard to housing, the most important changes include the withdrawal of direct state financing of new housing construction, the privatisation of the previous public housing stock, and the restitution of housing to private owners that had been nationalised during socialist times.

The rapid privatisation of public rented housing in the 1990s has substantially increased home ownership in most of the former socialist countries (with the exception of East Germany, Poland and the Czech Republic, which implemented a different model of housing privatisation) with levels ranging from 85–90%, well above the EU average of 62% (Tsenkova, 2005).

The privatisation of the housing sector was one of the most import political decisions at the beginning of the 1990s in Slovenia (and Hungary) in support of private property rights and a market economy. This privatisation induced a major increase in housing prices, both for rent and buying. In contrast, the construction of new multi-dwelling housing decreased in the city of Ljubljana in the 1990s, despite some of the highest housing costs in Central Europe in the inner city (Pichler-Milanović, 2001; 2005).

With the exception of the former East Germany, the sharp decrease in the level of house construction is characteristic of all Central and Eastern European countries. The liberalisation of the labour market as a consequence of the liberalisation of the economy has meant new opportunities for labour mobility and migration. Due to a lack of suitable alternative housing policies to match the new macro-economic situation, labour mobility and positive migration have, however, been seriously restricted by growing constraints on the housing market.

Commercial

The most important common feature that has influenced property development in all post-socialist capital cities, especially in the first phase of transformation (i.e. until 1995), was the general lack of premises for commercial use contrasting with a rapidly growing demand for modern offices and retail space.

Commercial development constitutes an important force that has substantially contributed to a massive reorganisation of land use patterns in the Central and Eastern European cities in the post-socialist era. Such development has been recognised as a tool of local economic regeneration and growth, and has often been supported by central government policies as well as by local entrepreneurially-oriented politicians. Local governments in most of the former socialist countries have facilitated real estate and commercial property development using land in their ownership, together with development grants, through easing planning control and land use regulation.

In the second half of the 1990s, the focus for development moved towards certain inner-city districts and peripheral areas, as a result of structural changes and differentiation in commercial market demand, together with scarcity of available land left in the city centre. There was rising demand for retail, warehousing and light industry, together with demand for larger scale office space (e.g. now ranging from 1 000–15 000 m^2, where previously there had been only up to 500 m^2) (Sýkora, 1998; Hamilton, 2005). Figure 4.1 shows a retail development, typical of this commercial revolution, at Nadarzyn near Warsaw.

Foreign investments have been particularly evident in trade and advance services, (e.g. financing, real estate, marketing, media), while foreign developers have become very influential actors in the commercial property development process, most notably in office and retail premises. In most of the Central and Eastern European cities, due to a relative lack of financial and technical know-how at the local level, foreign developers/investors have increasingly dominated the development of the best quality office space.

Currently, foreign retailers have become a very significant force in all Central and Eastern European capital cities and large regional centres, either by acquiring existing operations or by establishing joint ventures with local

Figure 4.1   Janki-Nadarzyn shopping megacentre.

partners. The out-of-town sector has been the most active one, predominantly financed by foreign firms. The domestic retail sector has also been expanding quickly, but most often in downtown locations or residential neighbourhoods and on a smaller scale.

The reduction of industrial uses after 1990, with respect to the number of employees and industrial land occupancy, is significant for most of the cities. In some of the capital cities such as Prague, Budapest and Ljubljana there was virtually no demand for speculative industrial and warehousing development in the 1990s (Sýkora, 1998; Dimitrovska, 2005). In Warsaw, on the contrary, the demand for new industrial space is very strong. There is a strong belief that rapid modernisation and increasing direct foreign investment in industrial development will help Warsaw remain one of the largest industrial concentrations in Poland and in Central Europe (Węcławowicz, 2005).

The restructuring of the industrial sector has had little impact on the property market. Privatisation of outdated industrial premises and complexes, often in poor condition, has resulted in their lease and sale to multiple private owners, making the subsequent management and maintenance of infrastructure sometimes very difficult. Large, underused (existing or planned) industrial and warehouse zones have been released for other uses, most often for commercial investments and housing. Currently, these former industrial areas are often seen to represent a problem in the image of major parts of the inner city, but they also represent a potential land resource for the future. Brownfield restructuring for industrial uses is very rare.

Industrial investment is moving out of the inner-city areas, to greenfield locations around motorway junctions just outside the administrative city boundary or even beyond, to agglomerations of smaller towns,or to other regions. Other important locations for new industrial and warehousing development have developed near to major airport sites. There has also been a tendency for the development of combined light industrial, retail and warehousing zones (e.g. as Warsaw Industrial Centre, 36 000 m^2).

Transport and infrastructure

Increasing efforts to develop international transport and telecommunication networks have been a common characteristic of most of the post-socialist countries. Priority has been given to the construction of multi-modal transport corridors, to improve connection between national transport networks and those of neighbouring EU countries, and to facilitate compliance with higher environmental standards in transport development.

In the last decade, three main shifts could be observed, determining the role and structure of transport: the shift from railway to road transport, the shift from public to private and individual transport and the shift from domestic to international transport. Until the early 1990s, railway transport played a dominant role in former socialist countries, its share being much higher than in EU countries. Since that time, however, the volume of rail transport has decreased dramatically in the Central and Eastern European countries; in 1994 it was less than 50% of the 1990 level, while road transport was on the increase (Vision Planet, 2000). While the projects of the Trans-European Transport (TEN) network in EU member countries are principally focused on modernisation and development of high-speed railway networks (80% of the financing is devoted to this objective), in the Central and Eastern European accession countries, 52% of the financing requirement is devoted to motorway construction, while the share for railways is only 36%.

The shift from public to private and individual transport is closely connected with the shift from rail to road. The subsidies to public transport are decreasing, while the number of private cars is increasing dramatically in all post-socialist countries. Apart from environmental and energy efficiency consequences, the public–private shift has additional social consequences, as with the decline in public transport, some groups, especially children and elderly people, are increasingly left deprived of the means of mobility. The decline of public transport is beginning to have serious consequences in the surrounding rural areas of cities and within larger urban agglomerations.

The shift from domestic to international transport is closely connected to the structural change of the economy. Within international transport, another important shift has taken place. Both in freight and passenger transport, the share of transport to and from Western European market economies has increased significantly, while the intensity of transport connections between Central and Eastern European countries has decreased. However, in more recent years, trade and transport between neighbouring countries has begun to rise again, resulting in a more balanced structure of economic and transport relations.

The concentration of investments in transport in most of the capital cities has focused on the construction of ring roads and motorways for better connection of the city road systems with newly built motorways. The building and refurbishment of petrol stations and parking facilities (e.g. underground and multi-storey garages) can also be observed. Traffic congestion has rapidly become a common problem in all post-socialist cities.

At present, with regard to infrastructure development, one of the main tasks is the interconnection of the electricity, oil and gas pipeline systems of the two halves of Central Europe, which were separated from each other in the past, in order to ensure the diversification of energy sources and security (Vision Planet, 2000).

The causes of urban sprawl in the post-socialist cities

The case study post-socialist cities were located in several countries: Leipzig (Germany), Warsaw (Poland) and Ljubljana (Slovenia). These areas were chosen to represent similarities in different aspects of urban sprawl, through the revolutionary change from command to market economies in post-socialist Europe that occurred after the fall of the Berlin Wall in 1989 and dismantling of the overall 'iron curtain'.

The most important causes of urban sprawl in the post-socialist case study cities are as follows:

- **economic restructuring** (deindustrialisation, unemployment, growth of SMEs capital investments, lack of space in the inner city, income growth and differentiation);
- **demographic change** (low natural increase, population decline, aging, outmigrations, decline in the size of households, societal differentiation);

- **land policy and property rights** (lack of institutions, instruments and rules of planning, inexperienced planning authorities in the 1990s, lack of development control, problems of restitution and privatisation of property, competition between local authorities for investors, conversion of agricultural land, and 'greenfield' development, lack of building land for single family houses in cities);
- **Quality of life** (consumption and new life style patterns, preference for single family detached house with a garden near green areas, increased motorisation, shopping and leisure patterns).

Leipzig

Leipzig is situated in the Free State of Saxony in Eastern Germany. Together with the city of Halle (population around 270 000), Leipzig (population around 500 000) has historically been at the heart of one of the largest industrialised regions in Central Europe. The population of Leipzig has been in decline since the early 1960s, a process that accelerated with the building of new social housing estates on the periphery of the city in the 1970s. Through the last two decades of the GDR, residential areas continued to decay and urban infrastructure became ever more worn. As everywhere in the former East Germany, the economic and societal transformation of the 1990s imposed difficult structural changes on the region. Today, industry is no longer the region's leading economic force but the growing service sector has by no means made up for the tremendous loss of jobs in industry. Leipzig has lost almost one fifth of its inhabitants between 1990–2000; approximately half due to migration to more prosperous regions in West Germany, and half due to suburbanisation and urban sprawl. These trends have given Leipzig the peculiar character of a massively *sprawling though declining* (e.g. 'dwindling') urban region (Nuissl & Rink, 2005).

In the first part of the 1990s Leipzig experienced a period of heavy urban sprawl that was induced by a set of incentives that largely stemmed from the institutional framework. Urban sprawl began almost immediately after the fall of the Berlin Wall, with shopping malls appearing in the suburban areas, followed by new industrial and low density multi-dwelling housing estates. Compared with the decaying inner city under restitution, this new suburban housing is very attractive to many inner-city inhabitants. The federal housing and tax policies have provided strong incentives for urban sprawl, the most famous of which is a subsidy for the acquisition of property by private households ('*Eigenheimzulage*') the vast majority of which are built on greenfield sites, triggering a building boom, frequently incompatible with the idea

Table 4.2   Urban sprawl in Leipzig

<1989	1989–1992	1992–1997	>1997
During the socialist period Leipzig did not experience urban sprawl until the fall of the Berlin wall	Commercial sprawl occurred immediately after the German reunification in 1990. Number of investors came to Leipzig, developing land and constructing new buildings to explore the business opportunities and take advantage of the new market	Residential sprawl was induced mainly due to the lack of good quality inner city housing. New multi-dwelling buildings at the city periphery of Leipzig were erected to serve the wishes of many people	The suburbanisation trend started to decline after 1997 due to innercity revitalisation, resolving of restitution claims, property market development, and provision of new retail and leisure facilities. Urban sprawl turned into provision of single family houses. But due to oversupply of dwellings many premises are left empty. The property prices declined both in the inner city as well as on the periphery of Leipzig

Peculiarities of urban sprawl in Leipzig:

– The context of post-socialist transformation, decline and 'catch-up' development.
– Urban sprawl was almost completely induced by investors from outside Leipzig and massively supported by public funding and incentives (e.g. infrastructure, housing, etc.).
– High speed sprawl (in the first part of 1990s) with a sudden end (at the end of 1990s) due to oversupply of housing and shopping facilities.
– The best example of extensive and top down urban sprawl in Central and Eastern Europe.

of sustainable land use and of limited relevance to an urban region with a shrinking economy and decreasing population (see Chapter 7 in this book). In addition, demand was governed by low quality housing in the inner-city areas that was exacerbated through unresolved property rights at that time. The latter made renovation and reconstruction almost impossible, thus lower and middle-income residents looked for alternative housing with higher quality standards.

After 2000, residential suburbanisation in Leipzig has fallen to very low levels and there are very few peripheral development projects planned or under construction in either the retail or the residential sector. Today, Leipzig is experiencing significant urban sprawl only in the commercial and industrial sector oriented towards the enabling of economic growth, and consequently city competitiveness. As a result, local authorities often compete for investments, meaning that investors have a strong bargaining and decision making power over these new developments, for example the new BMW plant.

Warsaw

Warsaw, the capital of Poland, is located in Mazowieckie province, in central-east Poland. The city of Warsaw has a population of about 1.6 million inhabitants (2000) that is only about 4% of the total population of Poland. The city of Warsaw covers an area of 512 km^2 and is divided into 18 districts. The urban region includes more than 2.5 million people in a sprawling agglomeration that stretches up to 40 km from the city centre.

The central city remains a popular residential location. The city does not yet appear to suffer some of the inner city social, economic and environmental problems that characterise many other European cities. Despite the common (verbal) preferences for a house with a garden no major population flows from the city of Warsaw to the suburbs have been observed. In recent years, the rate of growth of the suburban population is below that of previous decades. But the gradual elimination of present constraints such as the hardships of daily commuting due to inadequate and inefficient metropolitan transport, the high costs of a single family house with a garden in comparison with the average salary and the improvement of living conditions in the suburbs, will hence stimulate urban sprawl in Warsaw in the near future.

In the 1990s, the ring of Warsaw agglomeration became an attractive place for new jobs and residences as a result of market and institutional reforms, such as transformation of the economy, shift in location of economic activities, bringing back the land rent, decentralisation of decision making, local government and fiscal policy reforms as well as the income differentiation. At the local level, the suburbs are becoming very attractive locations for the investors. In the case study suburban communities (Łomianki and Nadarzyn) north and south from the city of Warsaw, well-educated and wealthy people predominate among newcomers.

In Warsaw, in the 1990s, the growth rate of new dwellings was highest at the city periphery ring when compared to the inner city. Similarly to Leipzig, the very first years of the 1990s saw an intensive construction of new buildings, hardly governed by any planning processes and often built without planning or building permission. There is, however, a rather limited extent of residential sprawl around Warsaw due to relatively low propensity of people to move, especially due to high costs of new dwellings in relation to income. The only significant new development in the 1990s occurred in the form of owner-occupied single-family detached houses at the city periphery and in surrounding rural and urbanised settlements. This contributed to residential sprawl. Figure 4.2 shows the rapid pace of change in Lomianki, one of the main 'hot spots' of sprawl north of the city of Warsaw.

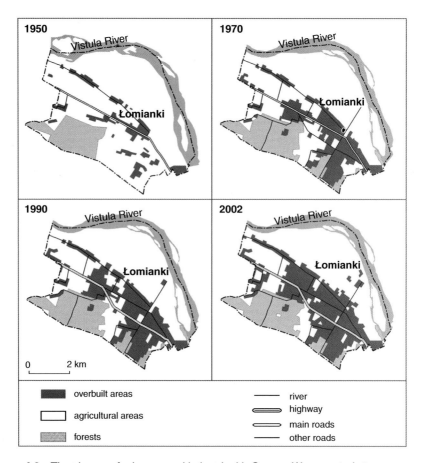

Figure 4.2   The phases of urban sprawl in Łomianki. *Source*: Warsaw study team

Main problems caused by sprawl in Warsaw agglomeration concern the conversion of open land to urban uses ('greenfield' development) in the suburbs while at the same time there is vacant land within the central city. Built-up areas occupy 50% of the total area of Warsaw. Open land for investment in the central city is still estimated to about 100 km^2 (20% of the total area of the city). The central city of Warsaw suffers from a lack of coordination in the urban management and still unregulated land ownership relations (Gutry-Korycka, 2005).

Ljubljana

At the end of the 1980s, a population decline was observed for the first time in the city of Ljubljana and its agglomeration, showing the shift

Table 4.3 Urban sprawl in Warsaw

<1991	1990–1995	1995–2000	>2000
During the socialist period Warsaw did not experience urban sprawl due provision of housing, jobs and services in the city of Warsaw, and low investments in infrastructure in suburban areas and surrounding villages	Sights of commercial sprawl due to deindustrialisation and growth of small and medium sizes enterprises (SMEs) in suburban areas. Availability of private and unregulated land at lower prices in suburban and rural areas.	Residential suburbanisation due to preferences of wealthy people for single family houses and middle class for new multi-dwelling low density houses in the suburbs with a good access to central Warsaw (urban railway or main road). In the case-study suburban communities (Łomianki and Nadarzyn) well-educated and wealthy people predominate among newcomers.	New trends in urban development of Warsaw will induce sub-urbanisation and urban sprawl in the future: – office and commercial property development and densification of central Warsaw; – improvement of metropolitan transport and roads; – further increase of property prices and higher residential density in central Warsaw; – income growth and differentiation.

Peculiarities of urban sprawl in Warsaw:

– Weak evidence of socio-economic and environmental problems in inner-city Warsaw.
– Large areas of accessible open space in the inner city.
– Difficulties of daily commuting due to inefficient metropolitan transport and roads.
– Deferred urban sprawl.

from (sub)urbanisation to disurbanisation. The data from the last Censuses (1991–2002) show a decline of population in Ljubljana urban settlement (city proper), the City Municipality (inner city), an overall stagnation, but population growth in suburban municipalities, and other municipalities in Ljubljana's urban region. The most important historical (or cultural) reasons for urban sprawl in an urban region is the existing settlement pattern, that is, large numbers of small (rural) settlements and secondary employment centres (small towns), as well as the high share of 'deagrarised' population, living in rural settlements.[1] They are usually employed in nearby urban settlements and commute daily from their private, predominantly self-built family detached houses constructed on their own land.[2] The close accessibility of urban settlements (as employment, services and education centres), owner-ship of private land (inter-generation inheritance or purchase), availability

Figure 4.3 Pijava Gorica: new housing sprawling into the countryside near Ljubljana.

of detached single-family houses (self-built or inherited), and overall quality of life in rural areas were the most important 'pull' factors, first for 'urbanisation of the countryside' in 1960s and 1970s, and than from 1980s for the process of suburbanisation.

The predominant (traditional) residential pattern of self-built owner-occupied single family houses in smaller settlements was also supported by socialist housing policies (1960–1990).[3] Private ownership of land and availability of (public) subsidies for construction of owner-occupied single-family houses, relatively good provision of roads and communal infrastructure in rural areas, and high quality of landscape all contributed to residential sprawl until the 1990s.

After 1991, the most important causes of urban sprawl could be found in transition reforms, that is, the privatisation of housing (1991–1995), restructuring and privatisation of enterprises, and local government reforms after 1994. The system of local tax revenues, deferred planning regulations and control, higher incomes and inter-generational equity, increased investments in motorways and car ownership, as well as the new lifestyle patterns have also been important causes of sprawl since 1995. The city of Ljubljana and its agglomeration also provide a high quality of living environment with low crime levels (Pichler-Milanović, 2001; 2005).

After 2000, the urban sprawl in Ljubljana's urban region was further encouraged with low availability of urban land for sale and high property prices, low

Figure 4.4   Iska Loka: an individual free-standing family house, dispersed sprawl near Ljubljana.

number of non-profit rented dwellings in the inner city of Ljubljana, competition of local authorities for residents (new 'suburbanites') and investors with the provision of lower land development tax. Improvement of roads and completion of motorways has induced multiple commuting patterns for work, education, shopping and leisure purposes, but not on a larger scale as in Leipzig.

The consequences of urban sprawl in post-socialist cities

Ecosystem fragmentation

The industrial pasts of former socialist cities were infamous for their legacies of poor environmental quality, which is a major determinant in both attracting and retaining economic activity and high quality labour force in the city. In the 1990s the energy consumption increased in Central and Eastern European cities for heating, due to higher number of dwellings and transport, due to increase in the number of motor vehicles. Traffic congestion due to daily commuting represents one of the most important city problems, especially with regards to increase in air and noise pollution.

Loss of agricultural land and forests (including areas of natural beauty) to urban uses has occurred due to residential, commercial and recreation

Table 4.4   Urban sprawl in Ljubljana

<1991	1991–1995	1995–2000	>2000
Urbanisation of the countryside since 1960s and suburbanisation in 1980s due to availability of private land and construction subsidies for single family houses in suburban and rural settlements.	Residential sprawl due to privatisation of public rented housing, restitution of property and deferred supply of new multi-dwelling housing in inner-city areas. Increase of new single family (detached and row) houses built without any subsidies in suburban municipalities.	Commercial sprawl due to privatisation of social enterprises, growth of SMEs, de-industrialisation, FDI, new enterprise zones and shopping centres at the greenfield sites, and expansion of motorways. Recycling of urban land for new multi-dwelling buildings in inner-city area. Residential sprawl still dominant in the form of newly built single family detached houses, low density row and multi-dwelling houses for purchasing at lower prices than in inner city of Ljubljana. Introduction of mortgages.	Mixed type of new development and urban sprawl patterns: new office, technological and science parks, commercial zones, new shopping and leisure facilities, recreation areas, mixed type of housing developments.

Peculiarities of urban sprawl in Ljubljana:

– Urbanisation of the countryside from 1960s onwards with the provision of public subsidies for construction of single family detached houses in suburban and rural areas.
– Relatively small size of the inner-city of Ljubljana and a number of small settlements in agglomeration and the urban region (i.e. approx. 1 000) within 30 min accessibility from the city centre.
– Transition reforms in 1990s (privatisation, restitution, local government reforms, deindustrialisation, etc.).
– High levels of housing ownership (e.g. from 67% to 90% after privatisation of housing in the first part of 1990s).
– Higher land and property prices in the innercity of Ljubljana than in suburban municipalities.
– Accessibility and good quality of roads and motorways.
– Rather sustainable patterns of urban sprawl.

developments and transport infrastructure at the city periphery. Surface sealing is a consequence of decline of agricultural activities in rural areas, through conversion of agricultural land and building activities on open (greenfield) land.

Ecosystem fragmentation is mostly caused by development of new transport infrastructure (motorways). Unplanned (or poorly planned) sprawl at the edge of the existing settlements cuts off the green areas, and therefore disconnects the network of 'eco-corridors' important for the migration of some animal species. The increase of concentration of heavy metals in

Table 4.5 Characteristics of the City of Ljubljana and its urban region

Administrative and functional classification of the city of Ljubljana	Area (km²)	Population (1991)	Population (2002)	Density (Pop. per km²)	Annual population change (%) 1961–71	1971–81	1981–91	1991–02
Ljubljana Urban Settlement (NUTS 7)	147	267 008	257 338	1 750	2.86	2.09	0.25	−0.34
Ljubljana City Municipality (NUTS 5)	272	272 637	264 269	972	2.84	1.90	0.41	−0.28
Ljubljana Agglomeration	902	321 607	321 235	356	2.44	1.86	0.54	−0.01
Ljubljana Urban Region (NUTS 3)	2 555	463 802	485 843	190	2.10	1.84	0.67	0.43
Metropolitan Region (or FUA)	4 990	617 892	646 868	130	1.63	1.58	0.66	0.42

Inner-city: Ljubljana urban settlement ('city proper');
Administrative city (>1994): Ljubljana City Municipality;
Administrative city (1955–1994): Ljubljana agglomeration (5 communes);
Ljubljana Urban Region ('statistical' NUTS 3 region) (>2000);
Metropolitan region (FUA): Ljubljana Urban Region and municipalities within NUTS 4 of Kranj (6) and Škofja Loka (4) in Gorenjska NUTS 3 Region, and NUTS 4 Koèevje (4) and Ribnica (2) in South-East NUTS 3 region.
Source: Statistical Yearbook of the City of Ljubljana (various years); Statistical office of the Republic of Slovenia (various years).

the soil threatens the quality of (underground) drinking water reserves and first-class agricultural land, due to the pressure caused by low-density houses (with individual sewerages), large scale commercial zones, but mainly due to increased transport activities.

Urban sprawl also acts in a way contrary to the principles of sustainable development by contributing to an accelerated reduction of agricultural area and natural ecosystems. Loss of the 'local identity' of rural settlements can be also considered as a negative impact of urban sprawl. The new settlement pattern as well as architectural diversity of new residential and commercial buildings significantly changes the rural landscape. The new developments often ignore natural factors (i.e. geomorphology, forest edge, streams, etc.) as well as traditional settlement patterns and size. The traditional distinction between 'urban–rural–natural' landscapes is often not visible any more (i.e. 'placelessness'). Most significant changes appear along main roads, which attract various types of development of highly diverse appearances – that is, car retail shops, McDonalds and Chinese restaurants, large shopping centres, businesses premises, large petrol stations, so forth.

But the evaluation of the environmental impact of urban sprawl is ambiguous. The case study cities of Warsaw and Ljubljana, for example, are characterised by satisfied environmental quality (i.e. diversified system of green areas, preserved fragments of natural vegetation). The contamination of air is lower than in most highly urbanised areas in Europe. The inhabitants of the Warsaw agglomeration suffer from low quality drinking water combined with the lack of a developed sewage system or organised waste management system, especially in suburban areas. In Ljubljana, the risk of environmental pollution mainly comes from transport activities and inadequate local sewage systems in rural settlements.

In Leipzig, new roads, industrial estates and settlements are very dense along the corridor Halle-Leipzig. Land use development at the urban periphery in the 1990s was enormous (mainly on agricultural land) in comparison with Ljubljana and especially with Warsaw, with deferred urban sprawl development due to lack of appropriate infrastructure and investments.

Economic costs

Since 1989, the restructuring of international economy and also the weakening of national boundaries have been challenging post-socialist cities. City competitiveness is very much dependent on the strength of the economies and, consequently, political stability in Central and Eastern Europe. Transformation reforms and EU accession requirements have had an important impact on the competitiveness of large and capital cities as centres of political, administrative, commercial, financial, technological, scientific and cultural activities.

City competitiveness emphasises the effects of city transformation on supply and demand constraints for economic development and property and labour markets. The evidence of patterns, processes and changes in international integration of post-socialist cities is mostly visible through trade flows and foreign direct investment, which became a key force in shaping the evolution of globalising trends with decisions and activities of (multi)national firms and investors. Internationalisation has also had a profound impact on the labour market. The growing number of Western employees working in (some) Central and Eastern European cities (e.g. 50 000 in Prague) is an important force on the property market, demanding new or renovated up-market housing and thus contributing to changes in the built environment. Improved city accessibility and transport infrastructure is reflected in the number of large-scale projects undertaken in Central and Eastern European urban areas (e.g. upgrading of airport facilities, motorways, ports, intra-city transport, etc.).

In the urban form, this means demand for space for new warehouses, shopping and leisure centres, industrial, offices and science parks, infrastructure and other urban land uses to increase local employment, value added activities, accessibility, budget revenue, so forth. This demand will further increase the amount of the built-up land and, consequently, the overall cost of land development and consumption. High economic costs are related to, not only increased construction activity and provision of infrastructure at the city periphery, but also to oversupply and under-utilisation of the social and technical infrastructure in declining parts of the inner city. Large investments are seen in motorways, but not in rail infrastructure or in a efficient public transport system.

In the Leipzig-Halle conurbation, oversupply of built-up land and facilities during the 1990s at the city periphery has produced vacancies and decline in property prices with a 'saturated' market coupled with uncertain economic conditions after 2000. In the inner city of Ljubljana, the overall increase of property prices from 1995 and the extremely high price-to-income ratio has produced 'speculative' urban land banks, unaffordable housing and a higher loans-to-income ratio. The more extensive urban sprawl process seems to be inevitable in the Warsaw agglomeration in the near future, but the question is whether it can be planned and managed on sustainable principles to avoid the negative consequences of urban sprawl as seen in Leipzig or in Ljubljana?

Although the inhabitants see more negative consequences of urban sprawl than positive ones, they perceive them as common and inevitable. The emerging processes of globalisation and city competition advantage some areas and disadvantage others, creating uneven economic and social development both between and within cities. Emerging economic reforms such as demand for global and European integration, are also diminishing social cohesion and increasing social and spatial differences between ethnic and socio-economic groups in Central and Eastern European cities.

Social consequences

Since 1990, the socio-spatial differentiation in Central and Eastern European post-socialist cities has been reinforced by industrial restructuring, decentralisation of economic activities, stagnation or bankruptcy of enterprises, privatisation, rising unemployment levels, growing income polarisation, so forth. According to evidence from many cities in Central and Eastern Europe, the process of selective socio-spatial differentiation and segregation has emphasised particular city locations with specific housing, demographic and social structures, and functional land use patterns. This transformation process is linked with the growing dependence of cities on international resources as their local economic and social potentials.

Therefore, the main social consequences of urban sprawl in post-socialist cities are related to: deterioration of the inner city, social and spatial differentiation, unequal distribution of burden among social groups and increased crime rates in suburban areas.

Due to urban sprawl development the inner-city areas are in decline. The large number of vacant dwellings in the inner city of Leipzig is a consequence of the oversupply of housing in suburban areas, the high cost of dwellings in Ljubljana occurred due to deferred provision of affordable housing and speculative urban land banks. As a result, depopulation and aging of the older inner-city areas is visible in both Leipzig and Ljubljana. Decline of retailing in the city centre occurred due to the development of new large shopping centres at the city periphery. Renewal and up-grading of the older housing stock and retail sector has been evident in recent years in many post-socialist cities, with the support of renewal subsidies and 'equity' loans (e.g. combined EU funds, national subsidies, local municipality grants, bank loans, individual investors, etc. through different forms of public–private partnerships).

Spatial segregation is still not a serious problem, but it has been increasing in all post-socialist cities since 1995. The inner-city area is fairly mixed in Warsaw and Leipzig due to low rents in rather large public housing stock. In Ljubljana, despite high ownership of housing, the inner city has preserved its residential function mainly due to lower costs of maintenance in comparison with high property prices for sale and rent, and the firm connection of older residents to their own property. There are very few 'gated communities' in Central European cities as yet, but differentiation is evident between traditional and new types of housing in both inner-city and suburban areas. Life style conflicts are evident between newcomers ('suburbanites') and traditional ('rural') residents.

There are also problems related to unequal distribution and accessibility of jobs, schools, shopping and leisure facilities, so forth, in suburban areas, with increased distances and time consumption that is a burden for young, elderly and women. As a consequence, local authorities in suburban areas will provide more services but, inevitably, they will be forced to increase local taxes for higher maintenance costs.

Policy responses

Physical planning was introduced (or reconstituted after World War II) in the former socialist countries as a tool for urban development in the early 1960s. The physical plans from that time laid down the macro-spatial structure of urban areas, and their general land use patterns, especially focusing on the allocation of land for housing, industrial construction and transport networks. In most of the Central and Eastern European countries, town plans had to be embedded within overall national economic plans, translating the requirements of economic planning into land use proposals, along with centrally prescribed planning and construction standards or norms.

The amount of services at the city levels was also planned according to nationally set standards. The protection of agricultural land and the preference for high-density high-rise housing estates at the inner-city periphery led to the creation of compact urban structures and limited urban sprawl. Another characteristic of the urban fabric, that can be identified as a result of socialist urban planning, is a very low economic utilisation of land in city centres, due to the insignificance of differential land rents and the absence of a 'gravity model' of land values [e.g. lack of definable Central business district (CBD)]. However, the inadvertent benefits resulting from these processes are the well preserved historic cores of most of the Central European cities (e.g. due to a lack of redevelopment driven by increased land values, as was seen in many West European urban areas after the World War II), and also the significant underdeveloped land from derelict nineteenth century industry (e.g. factories, warehouses, gasworks, etc.) that can be released for other uses.

The neo-liberal thinking of the early 1990s was characterised by the low political priority given by central governments to physical planning, regional development and housing policy (Sýkora, 1998; Pichler-Milanović, 1994). The absence of comprehensive national spatial development strategies and coherent regional policies, together with the local and regional government reforms and disputes regarding the basis of new planning legislation, have been significantly evident in some Central and Eastern European countries (e.g. Czech Republic, Hungary, Slovenia). Consequently, land use planning at the municipal level has been characterised by the prevalence of *ad hoc* political decisions rather than long-term strategic vision, weak development control and *laissez-faire* approach to city development.

In terms of spatial planning, this resulted in a kind of 'planning vacuum' in the first half of the 1990s (Nuissl & Rink, 2005) which was aggravated by the fact that:

> 'urban planning has been neglected in the 1990s because of the priorities of macro-economic reforms and the connotation of such planning with the former socialist regime'   (Pichler-Milanovič 2001).

In this situation, it was often easy to get building permits that did not comply with the respective local development plans. Thus, 'market forces, not planning prevailed until the end of 1990s, when the need for planning regulation was recognised to control and direct the spatial development' (Pichler-Milanovič, 2001). This problem was further aggravated by the unresolved property rights (e.g. privatisation and restitution of land and buildings tenure). This lack of planning and regulation results in an outward movement to the city's adjacent municipalities and settlements and drives up the sprawl development.

Since 1995, urban policies have revolved around the search for comparative advantages in order to establish a (revitalised) role within the network of European cities, to establish modern transport networks, to encourage the shift from antiquated industry to service based economies, and to resolve the problems of efficient guidance and regulation of private initiative in the dynamic process of city transformation (Dimitrovska Andrews, 2005; Sýkora, 1998, 1999). In the first half of the 1990s, the common characteristics of development practices in post-socialist cities in relation to urban sprawl can be summarised as follows:

- a liberal approach by central government, as well as local politicians, when assessing urban development proposals, especially in the field of regulation of development, urban planning and housing policy;
- reduced state involvement in as many matters as possible;
- short term, highly individualised, *ad hoc* decisions by local politicians and administrators taking precedence over the preparation of long term plans, strategy or visions of city development;
- the ideological rejection of forward planning as being counter to free market activities, along with the unwillingness of urban planners to identify or adapt to new circumstances, has fostered unregulated, politicised urban development practice;
- weak development control, of special concern regarding regulation of (re)development in the historic cores;

- suburban projects uncoordinated with development in the city; very little or no coordination between the city government and local government of surrounding municipalities in the urban region.

In many Central and Eastern European countries, as a response to pressures of globalisation and competition, a shift can be seen in the planning process, moving from the more traditional 'master plan' model, to strategic planning methods with greater flexibility and adaptability. From the beginning of the 1990s, even the new generation of urban development plans have been prepared in the old fashioned way of physical planning lacking up-to-date implementation mechanisms. There has been very limited use of economic tools to encourage urban development, and consequently, a lack of economic incentives (e.g. the establishment of urban development corporations). However, recent development in urban planning and management of Central and Eastern European cities show positive changes towards comprehensive strategic approaches with enhancement of the image of those cities both as a whole, and the identity of their characteristic areas. *Strategic Plans and/or Development Strategy Concepts* have been introduced in many cities (including the case study cities of Warsaw, Ljubljana and Leipzig) for achieving better effectiveness of the planning process and, subsequently, better quality of physical development. Transparency of urban planning and development, public involvement in the decision making process, integration of physical planning and real estate regulation and urban renewal projects have also been introduced in the process of transformation of post-socialist cities.

Central and Eastern European cities are now competing for international investments and development, which have become a matter of national prestige. This requires commitment from the city planning authorities to pursue market-oriented strategies for economic growth, but at the same time to preserve social cohesion, cultural heritage, and improve quality of life. These new developments are also a way of promoting city competitiveness and international image, and are in line with the new planning paradigm of sustainable development. Instead of controlling and distributing growth, new urban policies intend to promote cities, by reducing the cost or risk of doing business in the area and by improving the social and economic environment. Other changes include:

- transparency of planning and management of the city, for better involvement of the general public in the decision making process;
- greater integration of physical planning and real estate regulation in order to shape the built environment more efficiently;
- simplification of the procedures for planning permission and better responsiveness to developers' needs;

- urban renewal oriented towards reintroduction of vital and liveable public open spaces.

Conclusions: what is needed for 'sustainable' sprawl in post-socialist cities?

In Western European cities, urban sprawl evolved after World War II, before the background of an unforeseen accumulation of welfare and wealth. Living in green areas has become the vision of an affordable lifestyle to the growing middle classes. The governments of these countries encouraged urban sprawl through investment subsidies in the construction of privately owned homes in the surroundings of the large cities. Suburbanisation was seen throughout most of the twentieth century as a positive development, a necessary countermovement to the overcrowding of the nineteenth century metropolis. Virtually the whole planning profession was dedicated to this process, so too were virtually all governments (Fishman, 2005, p. 66).

In general, one can say that the Central and Eastern European countries and the respective cities experienced a process of more or less heavy suburbanisation and urban sprawl in the 1990s. Despite this urban sprawl, the post-socialist cities are still more compact than cities in Western Europe and confirm the vision of the 'European' city. Urban sprawl was stimulated during the transformation period from the supply side through investments in trade, infrastructure and business in the suburban areas, especially in Leipzig, while demand for privately owned detached houses in suburban and rural settlements characterised the suburbanisation process in Ljubljana.

Fifteen years after the fall of the 'iron curtain', the Central and Eastern European countries are still facing huge challenges in economic, social and environmental development, most evident in the rapid transition of urban structure – especially in the capital and larger cities. The function and image of historic cores, inner-city areas, and the outer city (e.g. urban–rural fringe) are changing rapidly. The dangers of damage to historical cultural heritage, uncontrolled urban sprawl, congestion and social segregation are imminent. Therefore, new types and instruments of urban management and planning are needed to meet these challenges. European cities vis-à-vis North American cities are more concerned about the loss of specific culture and urbanity, probably reflecting the fact that cities have always been important symbols and focal points of European societies.

There is no comparable development in social welfare and affluence in Central and Eastern Europe as yet, and living in owner-occupied housing in urban areas is not affordable for most of the people. Thus far there is no comparable social potential for urban sprawl beyond a certain degree. Meanwhile, other social processes are at work in these countries, especially demographic change. More than 200 large cities in post-socialist countries experienced serious population losses (see Oswalt *et al.*, 2006). Their number is continually increasing, even though urban growth will continue to dominate in decades to come in Europe. Yet, of 55 of the 211 regions of the EU, 15 already saw a fall in population during the second half of the 1990s. This is also the case in most of the regions of the new member states (35 out of the 55 regions) in Central and Eastern Europe, because of a natural decrease and net emigration (EC, 2005).

As a consequence of these forces during the last decade, Central and Eastern European post-socialist cities are somehow becoming more alike, struggling to dismantle the negative effects of socialist development and enhance their international status. The cumulative effects of the transformation process on inter- and intra-urban development is essentially a process of international competitiveness, enhanced cooperation and networking, city revitalisation and *reconnaissance* of Central and Eastern European cities, emphasising their cultural heritage, local identity, and a development path towards sustainability. The future of these cities depends now, not only on their (pre)socialist legacies, or the success in adoption of more market oriented principles, establishment of efficient public regulation/control and effectiveness of city governance, but also on their (re)integration into different European and global networks and their implementation of sustainable development goals (EC, 1997).

The observations of current urban planning practices in EU member states have revealed that the ideas of the 'urban plan' as a fixed blueprint for the future has been superseded by reality. Master plans are losing their role, changing from 'compulsory' guidelines to 'strategic' management plans. Managing change and adapting urban fabric in a responsive manner to rapidly shifting economic goals will be essential for the successful non-destructive revitalisation of post-socialist cities, including the continuing process of urban sprawl. Urban management, development and planning have become more varied and complex processes, involving a wide range of actors, who must learn to assimilate change into the very processes of managing that change (Faludi, 2002). In this respect, there is a need for the following:

- additional non-statutory planning documentation, such as visions of strategic alternatives, scenarios, design briefs and guides to help both architects, developers and local planning control officers to reach better and more appropriate design standards in development proposals, preserving local identity and context;

- negotiations with local planning officers regarding any planning proposal, to take account of economic viability both of the scheme, and in relation to satisfying relevant local needs (planning gain);
- involvement of the public in the early stages of preparing statutory development plans.

The need for institutional reforms and the lack of strategic planning are regarded as the major obstacles to urban development. In addition, the lack of coordination between local (regional) and central authorities and, in turn, urban services, has major implications for economic competitiveness and the international image of these cities. However, there is evidence of increasing concern that these problems can only be resolved by an integrated approach between different actors, at both the local (regional) and central (national/state) level. It is also increasingly recognised that a fully integrated economy can only be achieved with the support of a high quality of (coordinated) infrastructure; this requires improvement of both the intra- and inter-urban transport systems and improved environmental quality. City governance is becoming more pro-active in encouraging economic investment and particular public–private partnerships, with cooperation between local (and regional/state) politicians and the business community, essential for promoting the city internationally.

Urban sprawl has been a matter of policy and planning ever since it was acknowledged as a particular pattern of spatial development. The need to control sprawl and develop more compact cities is generally accepted across Europe. As early as 1990, the European Commission's Green Paper on the Urban Environment called for the avoidance of urban sprawl. In 1999, the European Spatial Development Perspective (ESDP) recommended that EU member states and regional authorities should pursue the concept of the 'compact city' in order to have better control over further expansion of the cities. Therefore, the most important aims with respect to management of urban sprawl in post-socialist cities are the following: increasing social and functional mix of areas, smart densification of built-up land use patterns, effective public transport, and the stabilisation of investments in the urban periphery. It is important to underline, as it was found in other city case studies in the URBS PANDENS project, that a well implemented and functioning planning system can be a good institution to work against urban sprawl developments (see also Chapter 8). In combination with effective subsidies and institutional interventions to encourage the regeneration of older urban areas (as seen in Britain), attempts to lower urban sprawl can be very effective. In Britain, where the urban sprawl commenced in the nineteenth century, the rate at which urban sprawl is occurring nowadays is lower than at almost any time over the last century.

There is much evidence that the cities in the Central and Eastern European countries are embarking on a process of des-urbanisation due to demographic change. However, this does not exclude growth in individual cities and urban regions – mainly the capital cities – but these are exceptional cases (such as Warsaw). Likewise, the process of re-urbanisation, which according to the cyclical model of van den Berg *et al.* (1982), follows suburbanisation, is unlikely to become dominant in the Central and Eastern European urban areas. Although there are currently signs of re-urbanisation in some cities such as Leipzig (see Buzar *et al.*, 2007), in the face of low birth rates, out-migration and population decline, it is unlikely that these will become a major continuing trend in the future.

Notes

1   Around 50% of Slovenia's population live in rural settlements, however, less than 5% of the active population is employed in agricultural activities, showing a high share of 'deagrarised' population. This term is used to describe a population living in officially classified rural settlements, but working in secondary and tertiary activities in urban settlements.
2   In Slovenia and Poland more than 80% of land was in private ownership even during the socialist period.
3   Self-built construction of private single-family houses (for personal use) was intensified in Slovenia from the 1960s onwards using the 'informal' or 'semi-formal' (private) land market as a result of housing shortages in urban areas.

References

Andrusz, G., Harloe, M. and Szelenyi, I. (eds) (1996) *Cities After Socialism: Urban and Regional Change and Conflict in Post-Socialist Societies*, Blackwell, Oxford.

Buzar, S., Ogden, P. E., Hall, R., Haase, A., Kabisch, S. & Steinführer, A. (2007) Splintering urban populations: emergent landscapes of reurbanisation in four European cities. *Urban Studies* **44**, 4.

CEC (Commission of the European Communities) (1990) *Green Paper on the Urban Environment*, Office for the Official Publications of the European Communities, Luxembourg.

CEC (Commission of the European Communities) (1999) *European Spatial Development Perspectives: Towards balanced and sustainable development of the territory of the EU*, Office for the Official Publications of the European Communities, Luxembourg.

CEC (Commission of the European Communities) (2005) *Green Paper Confronting demographic change: a new solidarity between the generations.*

Couch, C., Karecha, J., Nuissl, H. & Rink, D. (2005) Decline and Sprawl: An evolving type of urban development – observed in Liverpool and Leipzig. *European Planning Studies* **13**(1): 117–36.

Donner, C. (2006) *Housing Policies in Central and Eastern Europe.* Vienna, Austria.

Dimitrovska Andrews, K. (2005) Mastering the post-socialist city: impact on planning the built environment. In: F. E. I. Hamilton, K. D. Andrews & N. Pichler-Milanovič (eds), *Transformation of Cities in Central and Eastern Europe: Towards Globalization*, pp. 153–88, United Nations University Press, Tokyo-New York-Paris.

EC (European Commission) (1997) *Agenda 2000: For a Stronger and Wider Union.* European Commission, Brussels.

Enyedi, György (1992) Urbanization in East Central Europe: social processes and societal responses in the state socialist systems *Urban Studies* **29**(6): 869–80.

Enyedi, G. (ed.) (1998) *Social Change and Urban Restructuring in Central Europe.* Akadémiai Kiadó, Budapest.

Faludi, A. (ed.) (2002) *European Spatial Planning.* Lincoln Institute of Land Policy. Cambridge Mass.

Fishman, R. (2005) Suburbanization: USA, In: P. Oswalt (ed.), *Shrinking Cities. Vol. 1. International Research.* Ostfildern-Ruit, Hatje Cantz Verlag, pp. 66–73.

French, R. A. & Hamilton, I. F. E. (eds) (1979) *The Socialist City: Spatial Structure and Urban Policy.* John Wiley, New York.

Gutry-Korycka, M. (ed.) (2005) *Urban Sprawl: Warsaw Agglomeration.* Warsaw University Press, Warsaw.

Hegedüs, J., Mayo, S. E. & Tosics, I. (1996) Transition of the housing sector in the east central european countries. *Review of Urban and Regional Development Studies* **8**,: 101–36.

Hamilton, F. E. I., Dimitrovska Andrews K. & Pichler-Milanovič, N. (eds) (2005) *Transformation of Cities in Central and Eastern Europe: Towards Globalization.* UNU Press, Tokyo–New York–Paris.

Hamilton, F. E. I. (2005) The external forces: towards globalization and european integration. In: F. E. I. Hamilton, K. D. Andrews & N. Pichler-Milanovič, *Transformation of Cities in Central and Eastern Europe: Towards Globalization*, pp. 79–115. United Nations University Press, Tokyo-New York-Paris.

Keivani, R., Parsa, A. & Mc Greal, S. (2001) Globalisation, institutional structures and real estate markets in central european cities, *Urban Studies* **38**(13): 2457–476.

Kennedy, M. & Smith, D. A. (1989) East-central european urbanization: a political economy of the world-system perspective, *International Journal of Urban and Regional Research* **13**(4): 597–624.

Kivell, P. (1993) *Land and the City: Patterns and Processes of Urban Change.* Routledge. London.

Marcuse, P. & van Kempen, R. (ed.) (2000) *Globalizing Cities: A New Spatial Order.* Blackwell, Oxford.

Musil, J. (1993) Changing urban systems in post-communist societies in central europe: analysis and predictions. *Urban Studies* **30**(6): 899–906.

Nuissl, H. & Rink, D. (2005) The 'production' of urban sprawl in eastern Germany as a phenomenon of post-socialist transformation, Cities **22**(2): 123–34.

Oswalt, P., Rieniets, T. & Beyer, E. (eds) (2006) *Atlas of Shrinking Cities*. Ostfildern-Ruit, Hatje Cantz Verlag.

Pichler-Milanovič, N. (1994) The role of housing policy in the transformation process of central-east european cities. *Urban Studies* **31**(7): 1097–1115.

Pichler-Milanovič, N. (2001) Urban housing markets in central and eastern europe: convergence, divergence or policy collapse. *European Journal of Housing Policy* **1**(2): 145–87.

Pichler-Milanovič, N. (2005) Ljubljana: from "beloved" city of the nation to central european "capital". In: F. Hamilton, K. Dimitrovska Andrews & N. Pichler-Milanovič, *Transformation of Cities in Central and Eastern Europe: Towards Globalization*, pp. 318–63. United Nations University (UNU) Press, Tokyo-New York-Paris.

Sýkora, L. (1998) Commercial property development: Budapest, Prague and Warsaw. In: G. Enyedi (ed.) (1998) *Social Change and Urban Restructuring in Central Europe*, pp. 109–36, Akadémiai Kiadó, Budapest.

Sýkora, L. (1999) Changes in the internal spatial structure of post-communist Prague, GeoJournal, **49**: 79–89.

Struyk, R. (ed.) (1996) *Economic Restructuring of the Former Soviet Bloc*. The Urban Institute Press, Washington.

Tsenkova, S. (2005) *Trends and Progress in Housing Reforms in South Eastern Europe*. Council of Europe Development Bank, Paris.

United Nations Economic Commission for Europe (UNECE) (1997) *Human Settlement Trends in Central and Eastern Europe*.

United Nations Centre for Human Settlements (UNCHS – Habitat) (2001) *The State of the World's Cities*. UNCHS, Nairobi.

van den Berg, L., Drewett, R., Klaasen, L. H., Rossi, A. & Vijverberg, C. H. T. (1982) *Urban Europe. A Study of Growth and Decline*. Pergamon Press, Oxford.

Vision Planet (2000) Strategies for Integrated Spatial Development of the Central European Danubian and Adriatic Area (CADSES), Guidelines and Policy Proposals.

Węcławowicz, G. (2005) The warsaw metropolitan area on the eve of poland's integration into the EU. In: F. Hamilton, K. Dimitrovska Andrews, & N. Pichler-Milanovič, *Transformation of Cities in Central and Eastern Europe: Towards Globalization*, pp. 223–47, United Nations University Press, Tokyo, New-York, Paris.

5

Decline and Sprawl: Urban Sprawl is not Confined to Expanding City Regions

Henning Nuissl, Dieter Rink, Chris Couch and Jay Karecha

Sprawl in the context of urban decline

Theoretical debate on urban sprawl has, for the most part, been focused on 'successful' cities or urban agglomerations. This can be seen as a general reflection of urban research tending to deal with problems of growth, and assuming that growing cities and regions provide a clue as to the (assumedly) universal patterns of spatial development. Accordingly, the conditions, causes and patterns of urban sprawl, as well as its effects, impacts and meaning to society, have often been discussed by referring either to 'global cities' (Sassen, 1991), such as New York, London, Tokyo and, particularly, Los Angeles, or other towns and cities with astounding growth rates, such as thriving urban centres in predominantly rural regions (e.g. Heim, 2001); or the mega-cities of the developing world (e.g. Xu & Yeh, 2003); or in relation to the emergence of 'edge cities' (Garreau, 1991).

Urban research has, of course, also been concerned with less successful cases of urban development. In particular, attention has been given to problems of urban decline and restructuring in old industrialised cities, or agglomerations of the 'rust belt type' where various forms of shrinking set rather peculiar conditions for urban development. This discourse too has its 'heroes' – for instance, the metropolitan areas of northern England (e.g. Mumford & Power, 2002), the German Ruhr area (e.g. Friedrichs, 1997), the conurbations of Detroit (e.g. Maynard, 2003) and Pittsburgh in the US (e.g. Beauregard, 2002). The focus of this discourse, however, has by and large been quite different from the discussion related to growing cities. Attention has mainly been given to specific problems of urban or regional policy making and planning in declining contexts, such as how to deal with derelict buildings or land, how to resurrect the urban economy or how to create new images for the cities concerned. The issue of urban sprawl in declining contexts, on the other hand, has remained marginal. However, assuming that urban trajectories are path-dependent and rely strongly on existing circumstances (Atkinson & Oleson, 1996, p. 213) it seems uncertain to what extent our knowledge on urban sprawl in growing regions provides a clue for the understanding of urban sprawl in a situation of decline – that is, whether urban sprawl in urban regions that are shrinking could be interpreted only as a variation of what is happening in growing regions.

In urban regions that are thriving, there is obviously a strong link between the general urban development in terms of societal change and economic growth on the one hand, and the physical extension of the urban area on the other hand. The relationship between the urban core and the urban surroundings can be defined as one of overspill. In contrast, in stagnating or declining urban regions the situation is often different. There, the relationship between city and suburbia is often characterised by competition (for inhabitants and investors) as urban sprawl appears to be part of a zero-sum-game, in which new areas are developed at the expense of existing urban quarters. In connection with this, urban sprawl in declining urban regions seems to have a particular impact on urban form, as it usually leads to abandoned houses and derelict land in the inner city areas. For these reasons, urban development policies in such areas have to be geared to the context of decline and pursue realistic goals – which is not an easy task given that most strategies and instruments of urban policy and planning once were mainly designed to organise growth.

In this chapter, the problem of whether urban sprawl may have distinct features in a context of decline is addressed by means of two examples – Liverpool in England and Leipzig in Germany. Both cities reached their historic peak in the 1930s with a population between 700 000 and 800 000 and since then both have experienced considerable urban sprawl in a situation of urban decline. Concerning their history and spatial structure, Liverpool and Leipzig have enough in common to provide a comparable basis for empirical study. On the other hand, both cities are different enough, particularly in terms of urban policy making and planning, to enable an informative comparison. Thus, the two cities together represent a broader spectrum of traditionally industrial European cities of around half a million inhabitants, and their experiences should therefore be instructive for other agglomerations in Europe that face the problems of decline and sprawl at the same time.

The chapter is structured into five parts: the second looks at trends in Britain and Germany; the third part considers the two case study cities while the fourth part makes some comparisons, with particular reference to three questions we deem particularly relevant in terms of urban sprawl in a declining context:

- Why does urban sprawl also arise in combination with urban decline?
- Do the inner city and suburbia converge in a situation in which urban sprawl and urban decline occur at the same time?
- How can urban policy making and planning make use of the situation of urban decline?

The fifth part provides some concluding remarks that pull together our results along the lines of these three essential questions.

Trends in urban sprawl in Britain and Germany

Britain

The control of urban sprawl has been one of the great concerns of the British planning system throughout the twentieth century (Ward, 2004, esp. pp. 52–55 and 226–230). Over the last two decades there has been growing government concern, first with urban regeneration (cf. Roberts & Sykes, 1999) and later with the idea of more compact and sustainable cities (cf. Ward, 2004; Williams *et al.*, 2000). A measure of the success of both of these policies is the proportion of new development that is occurring on previously developed land, rather than converting previously undeveloped land (e.g. agricultural land) to urban use. Although this measure is not necessarily an indicator of urban sprawl (as distinct from urban growth), since in declining city regions we can conceive of urban sprawl (defined in terms of declining dencity) without an extension of urban area, it is difficult to envisage many circumstances where urban sprawl would occur without some development occurring outside the existing urban area. For simplicity only, data relating to residential development is presented below in Figure 5.1. It shows the percentage of residential development built on previously developed land at three spatial scales: England; the North West region and Merseyside (the Liverpool conurbation).

Whereas in England in the mid-1980s the average of residential development occurring on previously developed land was around 38%, by 2001 this proportion had risen to around 55%. This improvement reflects the implementation of urban regeneration and peripheral restraint policies, as local

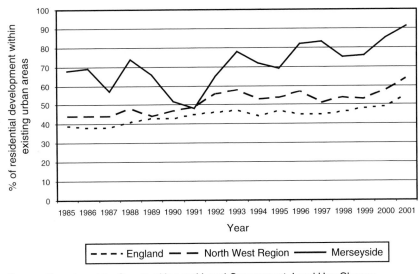

Source: Department for Communities and Local Government, Land Use Change Statistics, Tables D1 & D2, 1985-01.

Figure 5.1   The percentage of residential development built on previously developed land.

planning authorities strive to meet the government's target of 60% of all residential development on previously developed land (Department of the Environment, Transport and the Regions, 1998).

But the picture varies considerably between regions. Across much of the North West region, many towns and cities have experienced the kind of industrial restructuring that has left them in decline, with a legacy of vacant and derelict land. At the same time, the demand for new housing has been less strong than is the case in many parts of the south of England. This has facilitated local planning authorities in the North West in controlling urban sprawl, to the extent that by 2001 more than 60% of all new residential dwellings were built on previously developed land. Merseyside illustrates one of the most extreme cases of a declining agglomeration. Here, the avail-ability of large amounts of vacant and derelict land has coincided with weak housing demand and strong 'green belt' policies, to enable, by 2001, more than 90% of new residential development to be accommodated on previously developed land.

Germany

Since the 1970s, urban and regional planners in Germany have discussed strategies to contain urban sprawl. Until recently, however, this has not had any significant political effect. Rather the federal government has – in contrast to the British government – traditionally neglected its responsibility for the problem of sustainable land use. Yet it is the federal housing and tax policies that have provided strong incentives for urban sprawl, the most famous of which is a subsidy for the acquisition of property by private households (*'Eigenheimzulage'*). Today, the federal government spends around 10 billion Euros a year for this subsidy, thereby supporting the erection of around 30 000 private houses, the vast majority of which are built on greenfield land. More recently, in Eastern Germany, federal housing and tax policies have proven their 'effectiveness' in triggering a building boom, frequently incompatible with the idea of sustainable land use and of limited relevance to a region with a shrinking economy and decreasing population.

Currently, around 105 hectares (which is equivalent to more than 100 football fields) of undeveloped land are being transformed into urban land in Germany every day, approximately half of which will be sealed. It is notable that around one third of this land conversion is taking place in Eastern Germany (excluding Berlin), which is only slightly more than Eastern Germany's share of the country's territory, but which is high given that Eastern Germany accounts for only around 15% of the national population and only around 11% of the gross national product. Figure 5.2 gives an account of land use change in Germany since 1980.[1]

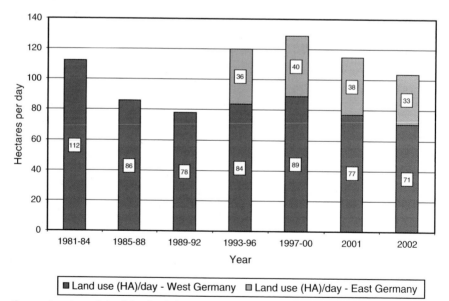

Source: Land use data of the Statistical Office of the Federal Republic of Germany; own calculation.

Figure 5.2 Conversion of open land into urban land in Germany (hectares per day).

Figure 5.2 shows a reversion of a long standing negative trend, in that the rate of land conversion has recently begun to decrease. However, it is not clear whether this reversion will be sustainable or whether it is just an effect of a weak economy. But against the background of severe fiscal problems and in light of the sustainability debate, the government recently abolished the *Eigenheimzulage* so that, despite the strong opposition against this decision, at least some permanent reduction is very likely. Moreover, the 2002 German National Strategy Plan for Sustainable Development fixes the political goal to reduce the rate of sealing to 30 hectares per day by 2020 (Perspectives for Germany: Our Strategy for Sustainable Development, 2002, p. 71), thus calling for a much stronger reduction in land conversion than has been achieved so far.

The two cases

Liverpool

During the first half of the twentieth century, Liverpool was the second most important port in the country serving a large hinterland across the north of England. It was also a major conurbation and industrial centre in its own right. Since the late 1960s, the city has suffered a very substantial loss of jobs and population. Whilst it remains a major port, competition and structural economic changes have reduced its importance in the national economy, thus causing massive problems, urban restructuring and social deprivation. Between 1951 and 2001 the population of Liverpool fell from 790 838 to 439 476 – a decline of over 44% (Couch, 2004, pp. 14–24). Whereas, in recent years, there has been a modest return to employment growth, there is some evidence that this is linked to sprawl, as employment growth rates in the urban core (at 2.1% per annum for the City of Liverpool) have not kept pace with those for the conurbation as a whole (at 2.7% per annum for the Merseyside County area) (Liverpool City Council, 2003, p. 16).

During the 1960s and early 1970s the City Council was engaged in a massive slum clearance programme. This was complemented by the building of overspill council estates, new towns, expanded towns and speculatively built private housing in the suburbs and beyond. By the mid-1970s, in response to concerns about rising costs, falling population and the impact of clearance upon inner-city communities and economies, the programme was being brought to an end. Overspill and the building of new towns were also being cut back. By the 1980s, the clearance of the older private housing stock came to a virtual halt. The approval of the Merseyside Structure Plan and Merseyside Green Belt Local Plan in the early 1980s, led to a strengthening of policies for urban regeneration and stronger restrictions than hitherto upon building outside of the existing urban area. A growing amount of additional housing was being provided within the city through both new build and conversion schemes, although much of this new urban housing took the form of two or three storey dwellings built at suburban densities, even on sites abutting the city centre (Couch & Wynne, 1986). Concurrently, however, there was a continuing out-migration of population. The effects of this were exacerbated by falling average household size, which was greater in the inner city than in the suburbs, as the inner city tended to attract more students and smaller, younger households. In consequence, population densities declined further and faster in the inner areas than in the suburbs.

The effects of these trends can be seen in Figure 5.3. At the scale of the conurbation, a comparison of population trends in Liverpool with those of the whole Merseyside county area provides an indication of the extent to which the city continued to sprawl into the surrounding areas. It will be seen that the rate of sprawl slowed over time, particularly after the move away from slum clearance and overspill housebuilding in the 1980s.

Looking in more detail at the City of Liverpool itself, it is clear that a significant process of urban sprawl has taken place. This is shown in Figure 5.4, which compares the density gradient of Liverpool in 1971 with that for 2001. The graph, showing the actual changes in Liverpool, can be compared with the theoretical model shown in Figure 1.1 in Chapter 1. It will be seen that

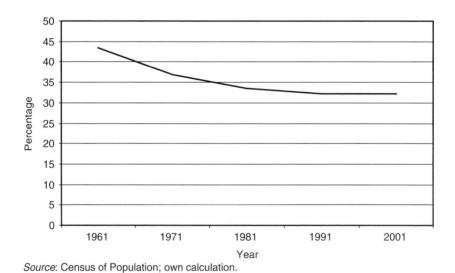

Source: Census of Population; own calculation.

Figure 5.3   The proportion of Merseyside population living in Liverpool.

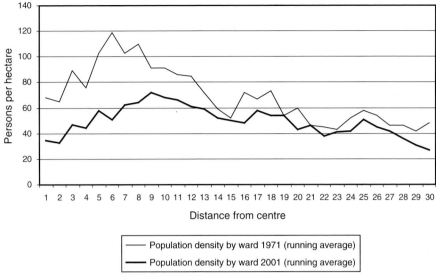

Source: Census of Population; own calculation.

Figure 5.4   Population density in Liverpool.

the shallower gradient in 2001 provides clear evidence of urban sprawl, at least in terms of population density.

The changes in the economy and urban structure, as well as the concurrent population decline, have had a dramatic impact upon the local housing market. Between 1961 and 2001 the ratio of dwellings to households (dph) improved from 0.96 dph to 1.10 dph (i.e. the city moved from a housing shortage to a housing surplus). This surplus is significant because it has reduced demand for the least popular housing. During the 1980s obsolete and peripheral social housing became difficult to let and 'improvement' policies were put in place that invariably led to reductions in housing and population densities in these areas (Liverpool City Council, 1993). In more recent years the phenomenon of low demand has spread to obsolete private housing, especially in the inner ring of nineteenth-century housing that surrounds the city centre (Nevin, 2001). Again, the policy response has resulted in a thinning-out of the housing stock and consequent reductions in housing density. Over the past two decades speculative private housebuilding has dominated British housing production. Whilst the private sector has been willing to invest in the construction of housing in the inner city, albeit usually supported by some form of subsidy, this was, until recently, generally in the form of low-density standardised house types that have been tried and tested in the suburban housing market (Adams & Watkins, 2002, pp. 144–49). Bespoke

Figure 5.5   New housing in Liverpool city centre.

design, higher densities and experimental dwelling forms have rarely been considered financially viable.

Only in the last few years have developers also begun to consider investing in housing in the city centre (see Figure 5.5). There is little tradition of city centre living in British cities, and certainly not in Liverpool. For this movement to occur there needed to be a coincidence of changes in demand and supply. On the demand side, the changing structure of households has been critical. The rise in the numbers of small childless adult households has provided a demand for accommodation that does not need the dimensions of family housing, nor to be near to schools and does not need gardens or green areas for children's play. On the other hand, many of these households do seek out secure dwellings conveniently situated for places of work and urban amenities such as can be found in city centres. On the supply side, important changes have been brought about by the release of commercial and retail floorspace in the city centre. This has been caused by: a) technological changes and increases in productivity that have reduced the employees and space required to maintain the same level of production in city centre commerce and retailing; and, b) urban sprawl, as some retail sectors and some types of office employment have moved away from the city centre in search of cheaper, larger sites, more accessible by car, in suburban and peripheral locations. In consequence there has emerged a large amount of vacant floorspace in search of new alternative uses. Residential development provides such a use (Couch, 1999; Madden *et al.*, 2001).

From the retail sector, and more recently from parts of the leisure sector, in Liverpool as in other cities, demand has come for out-of-centre locations for large free-standing stores and retail parks. However, the combination of a strong planning system and the availability of pockets of vacant or derelict land, within the traditional industrial zones and even in suburban locations, has led to these demands being incorporated at various locations within the existing urban structure. Thus, retailing has sprawled out from the city centre and district centres but, by and large, this sprawl has been contained within the existing urban boundary and has not led to any significant extensions of the urban area (Hillier Parker and Cardiff University, 2004).

Leipzig

The architecture and urban structure of Leipzig reflects and expresses the late nineteenth century and early twentieth century time period, when the city experienced rapid economic development and growth (Hocquél, 1994). By the 1930s, Leipzig had become the fourth largest city in Germany in terms of population. The city was based on thriving commerce and was an outstanding cultural centre. The seizure of power by the Fascists, however, coincided with the first signs of a reverse in the city's fortunes' as Leipzig ceased to grow. World War II then brought about a deep cut in the city's thriving development. By the early 1960s, Leipzig, the German Democratic Republic's (GDR's) biggest city outside of Berlin (the divided capital) became its only major urban centre that was shrinking in terms of population (cf. Schmidt, 1991). This decline was a result of the GDR's politics of urban and economic planning and development, which largely disadvantaged the old industrialised cities and regions in favour of investments in a number of dedicated 'build-up cities' (*Aufbaustädte*) and a few new industrial centres, often situated in formerly rural areas. This neglect of the old industrialised cities and regions at the national level was compounded by socialist urban policy within the region, which laid its emphasis on the building of new housing estates, rather than the preservation and refurbishment of the old housing stock which was regarded as being both symbolically and function-ally typical of the capitalist society (Hoscislawski, 1991). Consequently, the (prefabricated) large housing estates, which are known throughout the for-merly socialist part of Europe, were built on the city's fringes – mainly from the 1970s onwards – petrifying the dividing line between the densely pop-ulated city and its surrounding area, and leading to a redistribution of the city's population from the centre to the periphery (Tesch, 2003).

As around half of Leipzig's housing stock was built before 1918, the city was badly affected by the decay of its traditional residential areas. These areas became unpleasant places to live in and provided poor housing conditions. For instance, in the 1980s only 70% of dwellings in Leipzig were equipped with a bathroom and only about one third had central heating. Almost half of the approximately 100 000 pre-World-War-I-dwellings showed some severe damage, and more than 20 000 of them, being virtually uninhabitable, were vacant. In places, the rate of vacant housing had risen to one third by the end of the 1980s (cf. Kabisch *et al.*, 1997). By the end of the 1970s, several restructuring programmes had been set up in order to maintain the inner city as a living environment. These were aimed mainly at the substitution of old housing, but also involved some investments into the existing hous-ing stock. These programmes, however, suffered from the very beginning from a lack of financial resources and were consequently piece-meal in their nature (Tesch, 2003). Thus, the decay in inner urban housing not only pro-ceeded at a far quicker pace than the construction of new dwellings, but also resulted in making the inner city a place where most people did not want to live.

When the Berlin Wall fell, most experts expected that societal, economic and also spatial developments in East Germany would follow the West German model – with urban sprawl being the dominant pattern of urban develop-ment. Indeed, sprawling urban development began almost immediately with shopping malls appearing in the suburban realm, quickly followed by new industrial and housing estates. The housing estates were made up predomi-nantly of multi-storey apartment blocks (cf. Herfert & Röhl, 2001). Compared with the decaying inner city, this new suburban housing was very attractive to much of the city's population. The legal institutionalisation of restitution (i.e. the principle whereby expropriated owners were to be given back their former property rather than compensated financially) added to the attractive-ness of these new developments. Restitution meant that the reconstruction of old buildings in the city could progress only at a slow pace, and this implied that rents for the (relatively few) refurbished flats in the city were fairly high (cf. Döhler & Rink, 1996). The suburban growth was facilitated by the 'vacuum' in power from the public authorities over the steering of spatial developments (Häußermann, 1997, p. 97). The representatives and employees of the public administrations were often inexperienced with regard to bargaining with private investors, and were also very focused on growth themselves. The result was that private investors had ample scope to get their own way (cf. Coles, 1997).

The activities in Eastern Germany's emerging markets in the real estate and housing sector took place within a context of profound economic restructuring (cf. Kolinsky, 1995). Leipzig suffered severely from this change, losing over 90% of its industrial jobs, which numbered more than 100 000 in 1989. This loss could not be compensated for by the growth of the service sector (Bathelt, 2002; Bathelt & Boggs, 2003). Closely connected with this loss of industrial jobs, was the loss of around 10% of the city's inhabitants within the space of less than ten years, who left in order to search for a job (mostly in the economically more prosperous western part of Germany). A further 10%, however, left in order to move to a new suburban location. (It should be noted that several territorial reform acts enabled the city of Leipzig to 're-capture' a large proportion of the suburbanites, as well as enterprises and retail facilities, by almost doubling the city's area between 1990 and 2000.) Figure 5.6 shows how population figures have developed in the Leipzig region between 1990 and 2001 – differentiating between the core city with its 1990 boundaries; a first suburban ring, containing those municipalities that have been incorporated into Leipzig since then; and a second suburban ring with the (remaining) municipalities that are in close vicinity to Leipzig. It documents the growth of suburbia, alongside a concurrent decline in the region's overall population.

If we focus on the city of Leipzig in its current boundaries (areas a and b in Figure 5.6), it becomes clear that the main issue of urban development is not sprawl, but shrinking. Figure 5.7 repeats Figure 5.4 for Liverpool (but only for the time period of 1991 to 2001).[2]

The graph shows that population losses have been most severe in the most densely populated areas (that is in the nineteenth-century quarters of the inner city and in the large housing estates built in the 1970s and 1980s on the urban fringe). Yet there are some inner-city quarters (including the city centre) where there is no decrease in population, indicating the successful refurbishment of apartments (or construction of apartments) in certain urban quarters (Lütke-Daldrup & Döhler-Behzadi, 2004). It is also clear that the

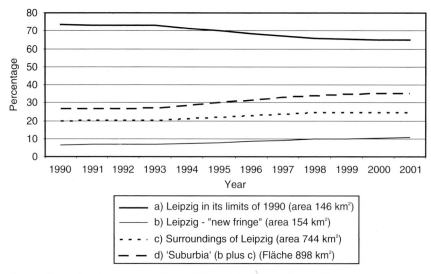

Source: Population data of the Statistical Office of the Federal State of Saxony; own calculation.

Figure 5.6   Distribution of population in the Leipzig region since 1990.

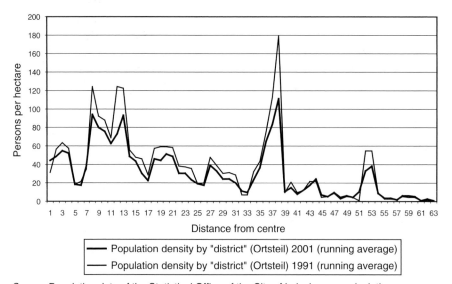

Source: Population data of the Statistical Office of the City of Leipzig; own calculation.

Figure 5.7   Population density gradients for Leipzig: 1991 and 2001.

population density in the more peripheral parts of Leipzig has been constant or has even experienced slight increases in some cases. One exception to this is the large housing estates on the periphery (represented by the two peaks on the righthand-side of the figure). We can see then that, in accordance with the definition for urban sprawl given in this book, Leipzig is sprawling. The most striking feature of urban development in Leipzig is, however, the sudden drops in density in particular areas of the city. These drops account for there being around 50 000 empty dwellings in Leipzig, representing 16% of the city's housing stock (in 2000 the respective figures were more than 60 000 and 20%!) (City of Leipzig, 2004). Although some 20 000 of these dwellings are not yet habitable, the vast majority of them are still being offered on the housing market for rent. Whilst the problem of vacancy occurs across the whole urban region, its distribution is concentrated in particular places. There are large urban areas where the physical urban fabric is eroding and where social problems are concentrated. This is particularly true for the former working class areas and the large pre-fabricated housing estates.

Recently, residential suburbanisation in Leipzig has fallen to very low levels and there are very few peripheral development projects planned or under construction in either the retail or the residential sector. The reasons for this are many. The increase in the power of planning is probably only of lesser significance. The major reason for the decline in peripheral development relates to the ending of the (temporary) fiscal instruments and support programmes that were put in place after unification in order to intensify the influx of capital into the East German real estate market. These measures had proved extremely effective in encouraging development (and in producing urban sprawl). At the same time, the gradual resolution of restitution claims in the city allowed for the renewal of entire inner-city districts, and this resulted in a growing supply of attractive and reasonably priced inner urban housing. Investments into inner urban retail and leisure facilities contributed further to the resurgence of Leipzig's inner city. The persisting economic weakness in Eastern Germany also had an effect. Hence, there are falls in population in several suburban locations and also the problem of vacancy now affects the less favoured parts of the suburban zone too. In these places it has become increasingly difficult to rent out flats or office space and some office parks built only a few years ago are consequently about to be pulled down. (Even in a situation of economic growth, this trend is unlikely to be changed easily. In fact it is possible that this trend could become even stronger as only the more attractive parts of suburbia would be likely to benefit from the new prosperity.) In summary then, we can observe that Eastern Germany is experiencing a deepening of spatial disparities not only between, but also within, regions (cf. Herfert, 2002).

Today, Leipzig, like Liverpool, is experiencing significant urban sprawl only in the commercial and industrial sector. This is due to the fact that both regional and local politics, and also public opinion, are oriented towards the enabling (not the avoidance) of economic growth. As a result, local authorities compete for investors, meaning that investors have a strong bargaining position when it comes to making decisions over these new developments. The most obvious sign of this situation is the huge plant the car-manufacturer BMW has recently established beyond the urban fringe, on a site north of Leipzig which was designated for agricultural use by regional planning. (Note that almost 30 years ago the attraction of a big Ford car manufacturing plant was a key element of Liverpool's strategy to cope with structural change).

Comparisons between Liverpool and Leipzig

The comparison of trends characterising the combination of urban sprawl with urban decline in Liverpool and Leipzig are summarised in Figure 5.8.

Social, economic and institutional conditions

Whereas Liverpool has suffered the fortunes and misfortunes of capitalist development throughout its life, Leipzig was, for around 40 years, protected from market forces and competition and experienced the sudden shock of exposure to western economic competition only after 1989. Accordingly, Liverpool has undergone a gradual (although fairly rapid) decline during the latter half of the twentieth century. The industrial and urban structure of Leipzig, in contrast, was maintained in a more or less stable form throughout the post-war period until the early 1990s when the economy imploded. While Liverpool has suffered a greater loss of population than Leipzig, it is the suddenness of change in particular that evoked a critical situation for the latter. Despite the fall in population, the effect on the demand for housing has, in both cities, been mitigated by a parallel fall in average household size. Changes in household structure have stimulated housing demand for non-traditional dwelling types and locations which means a considerable potential for the regeneration (i.e. renaissance) of inner urban areas.

Although there is usually only limited pressure from industrial or commercial investors in a situation of decline, we find evidence in both urban regions that such a situation makes it particularly difficult to restrict industrial or commercial investments on peripheral (greenfield) sites. The lack of economic growth and the need to create additional jobs obviously enhance the political pressure to allow almost every investor what they demand, that is, to offer weak resistance (and sometimes active support) to the sprawling of employment zones such as research and development facilities, but also big industrial fabrication plants, beyond the existing urban boundary. Thus, in declining regions, the economic development aims invariably take precedence over the aims of sustainable development, and the planning system often plays an active role in stimulating employment sprawl.

Institutional conditions

In Leipzig, the German unification brought to an end the command economy within which a strong planning regime dictated patterns of urban development. The immediate post-reunification period was characterised by a weak planning system and uncoordinated property investment supported by strong financial incentives. The redevelopment of inner-city areas was also hampered by restitution claims. It is only in the more recent period that the traditional strengths of the (West) German planning system have brought development back under stronger controls. In contrast, the Liverpool conurbation has benefited from a strong planning system with (inter alia) two clear and long-standing objectives: the protection of the countryside from urban sprawl and, since the late 1970s, the regeneration of older urban areas. This latter objective has been heavily supported by strong financial incentives and by single-purpose government regeneration agencies. On this basis, a routine of brownfield redevelopment evolved in the UK for which there is no equivalent in Germany (yet).

Patterns of spatial development

In Liverpool, the central business district has shrunk in size due to competition from other centres, technological changes and a sprawling of economic activity seeking new locations beyond the urban core. A coincidence of rising housing demand from small childless households and the emergence of surplus commercial and industrial floorspace within and adjoining the city centre has led to a new form of urban development: city centre housing. Industrial decline has also meant that pressure for large free-standing stores and retail parks has, by and large, been accommodated on 'windfall' former industrial sites spread across the existing urban area. However, such facilities have sometimes also been developed beyond the existing urban fringes; and the same holds for new industrial plants. In addition, a small, but declining, amount of new lower density housing has been built on greenfield land.

While Leipzig was declining in the 1990s, in the surroundings urban sprawl was taking place in all sectors (housing, commerce and retail, industry and infrastructure), bringing about new suburban landmarks such as shopping malls, big industrial estates and huge 'residence parks'. At the same time,

	Leipzig (and region) 1990–2002	Liverpool (Merseyside) 1971–2002
Social and Economic conditions	Poor inner-city housing quality has recently turned into an oversupply of good inner-city housing.	
= *Similarities*	Weak economy encourages the prioritisation of economic development over environmental protection, including allowing industrial/commercial development on greenfield land.	Weak economy has, since the mid-1970s, encouraged the prioritisation of economic development over environmental protection, including allowing industrial/commercial development on greenfield land.
	Decrease/stagnation in population but a stable number of households and a moderately increasing consumption of living space per cap. lead to a stable (or even slightly increasing) demand for housing.	Decline in population and households has reduced the demand for housing.
	Changing household structure (smaller households) is providing a source of demand for housing – including non-traditional dwelling types (e.g. loft apartments) – in the inner/central city.	Changing household structure is providing a source of demand for non-traditional dwelling types (e.g. loft apartments) in the inner/central city.
Institutional conditions	Pressure for urban sprawl in the post-re-unification period accelerated by:	
= *Differences*	– Strong (fiscal) incentives to invest in new buildings; – Restitution claims (making inner city site re-use almost impossible when erection of buildings was subsidised most – until 1996); – Weak planning controls (together with subsidising of building industry, regardless of locations, making greenfield development attractive to investors); This situation has completely changed today.	Strong planning controls, especially over housing development.
	No comprehensive political and planning strategy for brownfield development.	Comprehensive political and planning strategy for brownfield development.

Patterns of spatial development	Urban regeneration gains momentum after mid-1990s	Urban regeneration gains momentum after late 1970s.
	Urban sprawl of housing was heavy in 1990s but has currently faded away due to both an extreme relaxation of the housing market and a change in institutional conditions (see above).	Urban sprawl of housing is substantially brought under control after mid-1980s.
	Oversupply of housing leads to rejection of worst quality housing (older i.e. not refurbished tenements and – a little later – 'slab' housing/large housing estates.	Oversupply of housing has led to a rejection of the worst housing – from mid-1970s to early 1990s this was confined to social housing, since mid 1990s older private housing (especially inner city terraced housing) has been affected, too.
Major issues of urban policy and planning	Attempts to replace (high density) tenements by lower density housing 'of a more suburban kind' in the most precarious parts of the inner city; it is unclear though whether these ideas could be realised.	Redevelopment and regeneration has been associated with a decline in housing densities; first through slum clearance in the 1950s–70s; then through private and social housebuilding on former industrial sites since 1980s.
	Owners oppose density reduction as they are unwilling to remove their – vacant – buildings which diminishes the value of their property.	Little evidence of opposition as owners accept lower density housing as the 'next best use' (higher density re-use is not an alternative).
	Building single or double family houses would change the character of inner districts in Leipzig.	The change from terraced to semi-detached houses is not so great; only 'design professionals' object.

Figure 5.8 Conditions of urban development and the effects on urban sprawl in Liverpool and Leipzig. Reproduced from *Urban Sprawl: European Patterns and Policy* with kind permission from Taylor & Francis journals.

considerable investments into the preservation and development of the existing urban structure were undertaken; the city centre was almost entirely
reconstructed and the adjacent areas – with refurbished late nineteenth/early
twentieth century upper middle class tenement blocks – have become fairly
attractive residential areas. These investments into both the inner city and
suburbia led to an oversupply of floorspace for living as well as commerce,
which exceeds demand. Consequently, in Leipzig, vacancy is the most obvious effect of urban sprawl taking place in a context of decline and has become
a serious problem of urban development. Although the problem of vacancy
affects the whole urban region it is by no means distributed equally. Rather,
we have large urban areas where the physical urban fabric is eroding and, in
the long run, liable to total dissolution. This is particularly true for former
working class areas, on the one hand, and the large pre-fabricated housing
estates on the other.

In our two case study cities the effect of decline and sprawl has been the emergence of a new, more complex pattern of urban structure. The general features
of this urban structure are fairly similar in both cases – notwithstanding
the (historic) differences in the physical form taken by each element within
this structure. For example, in Liverpool, the nineteenth-century working
class housing takes the form of terraced housing, whereas in Leipzig it is
in tenements; in Liverpool, peripheral social housing tends to be low density housing mixed with a few multi-storey blocks, whereas in Leipzig it is
the three- or four-storey apartment-block that predominates. The key differences between the two cities lie not so much in dissimilarities in the nature
of structural change, but in the rate and timing of change and the extent and
power of public policy intervention.

Figure 5.9 presents in abstract form a model of how the structure of the
two cities under scrutiny has been affected by the combination of decline
and sprawl. Since Liverpool is a typical seaside and harbour city with a semi-
circular spatial structure, for this case one should imagine only the upper half
of the concentric figure. The model should be instructive for other European
cities that face the problems of decline and sprawl at the same time. It suggests that cities which are declining and sprawling at the same time are, to
some degree, likely to experience the following changes in urban structure:

- In the city centre there may be a decline in the proportion of floorspace
  devoted to commerce and retailing and an increase in residential and
  leisure uses.
- Much of the former inner-city industrial land can be given over to residential and other 'consumption' uses (retailing, leisure) – a success in
  brownfield conversion, however, is largely dependent on the power of

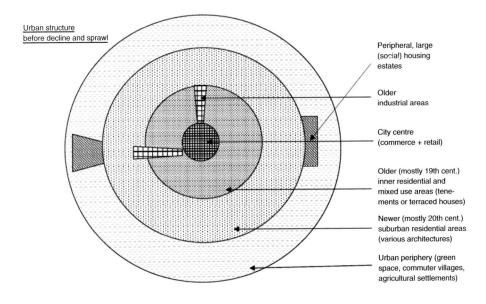

Urban structure
before decline and sprawl

Peripheral, large
(social) housing
estates

Older
industrial areas

City centre
(commerce + retail)

Older (mostly 19th cent.)
inner residential and
mixed use areas (tene-
ments or terraced houses)

Newer (mostly 20th cent.)
suburban residential areas
(various architectures)

Urban periphery (green
space, commuter villages,
agricultural settlements)

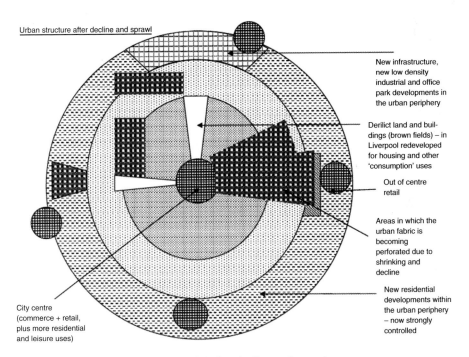

Urban structure after decline and sprawl

New infrastructure,
new low density
industrial and office
park developments in
the urban periphery

Derilict land and buil-
dings (brown fields) – in
Liverpool redeveloped
for housing and other
'consumption' uses

Out of centre
retail

Areas in which the
urban fabric is
becoming
perforated due to
shrinking and
decline

New residential
developments within
the urban periphery
– now strongly
controlled

City centre
(commerce + retail,
plus more residential
and leisure uses)

Figure 5.9   Urban structure before and after decline and sprawl.

planning at the sub-regional level (at present this can be seen in Liverpool but only very rarely in Leipzig).

- Older inner residential/mixed-use areas will continue to deteriorate, become perforated and ripe for renewal, usually at lower densities.
- At the urban periphery the development of new housing can be tightly controlled and limited (if there is a political will to do so), but the development of new industrial, commercial, retail and leisure facilities are more likely to be permitted.

Major issues of urban policy and planning

Urban regeneration has become a major task in both Liverpool and Leipzig and, due to the development of new housing in the course of urban sprawl, takes place under the conditions of relaxed housing markets and rejection of the worst housing. However, whilst in Liverpool much of today's inner-city regeneration is concerned with the redevelopment of social housing from the 1950s and 1960s and earlier rounds of area improvement from the 1970s, urban decline in Leipzig came as more of a shock. Thus, the task of bringing forward the coherent development of whole inner-city quarters is more difficult to pursue in Leipzig and is further complicated by a few more factors. Firstly, the fragmented structure of property and proprietors in most of the old residential areas makes it almost impossible to rebuild entire block-structures. One important reason for the unwillingness of many proprietors to actively contribute to urban redevelopment is the excessive book accounting value of their property – defined in the expectant times of the early 1990s – which exceeds the actual market prices often by four or five times. This means that landowners would incur big losses if they removed (vacant) buildings or sold their property altogether. In addition, there is some opposition by urban planners and stakeholder initiatives against the idea of considerably reducing densities in inner Leipzig. From their point of view, this would deprive the city of its characteristic morphology and its urbanity in general. All in all, it is unlikely that Leipzig will be able to repeat Liverpool's post-war experience of 'gradual downsizing' and there is little chance of an orderly reversion of the city's former expansion by organising a process of inward regression, beginning from the outer fringe. Instead, much of what has recently been built on the periphery will remain whilst, at least in parts of inner Leipzig, we have to expect the dissolution of the compact city.

Conclusions

Taking up the three questions posed above, some broad conclusions can be drawn.

Why does urban sprawl also arise in combination with urban decline?

The suburban zone of declining cities is rather similar to the suburban zones of thriving regions – at places one can observe, however, that developments have not come to an end (unfinished buildings, vacancies, fully developed but mostly empty industrial estates). Not surprisingly, urban sprawl in shrinking cities cannot be traced back to dynamics totally different from urban sprawl in growing cities. The well-known driving forces of sprawl seem to be effective there, too:

- Industrial investors are invariably inclined to develop 'fresh' land if possible (unpolluted and without any restrictions to how and what to build).
- Big, out-of-centre retail and leisure facilities are becoming the focal points of today's shopping and recreation activities.
- Living in a detached suburban house remains a major aim in life for many people.

However, the underlying dynamics of residential sprawl may be specific: the decline of (parts of) the inner city is increasing the wish of inner-city residents to live somewhere else (in particular in suburbia). This problem sometimes occurs in growing cities, too, but is surely aggravated if cities are shrinking. On the other hand, in declining cities, prices and rents are moderate throughout the urban region, and so the refurbished inner urban residential areas provide both an attractive and reasonable living environment. Thus, on balance, there is no increase in 'push-factors'. (The exuberant urban sprawl Leipzig saw in the 1990s was, for the most part, due to the incentives set by the federal policy and was shaped by regulations rather than market forces [Nuissl & Rink, 2005].) Generally, this is true for commercial, retail and leisure facilities, too, but there is also little opposition for the suburban allocation of these facilities in declining regions. On the whole, it seems to be that the dominant problem of these cities is not sprawl but decline.

Do the inner city and suburbia converge in a situation in which urban sprawl and urban decline occur at the same time?

The suburban zone of declining cities is rather similar to the suburban zones in thriving regions – at places one can observe, however, that developments have not come to an end (unfinished buildings, vacancies, fully developed but mostly empty industrial estates). The urban fabric in the inner parts of such cities is perforating with increasing vacancy and a deteriorating urban environment. Suburban and non-urban elements are 'returning' to the cities: in Liverpool in particular single-family suburban houses on private plots; in Leipzig urban micro-parks, mostly covering a few plots, where trees are established so as to contribute to the environmental quality of the respective areas. These 'micro-parks' are seen as an intermediate use until somebody wants to build on these plots. They were also a feature in Liverpool in the 1970s and 1980s. On the whole, 'weakly defined' open spaces within the fabric of human settlements will no longer be typical only of the '*Zwischenstadt*' (urban fringe) (cf. Sieverts, 2003), the anaesthetic assemblage of architectural forms, spaces, functions, and colours which has been emerging on and beyond the outskirts of western cities for about half a century, but may, as brownfields prove permanent, become a characteristic feature also of the inner city.

That the morphology of the inner city develops features which resemble the amorphousness typical of many urban peripheries, does by no means imply that the core city and the suburban municipalities pull together. Instead, their relationship tends to be more competitive than would be normal in a situation of growth. In this vein, the city of Leipzig is arguing against developments in neighbouring municipalities in the existing boards of regional policy, whilst it has recently developed new industrial areas and also some residential neighbourhoods. These activities reflect the core city's fear of population loss, declining tax base and withdrawal of consumer purchasing power. On the other hand, 'Leipzig's land preservation activities are largely focused on the city's floodplain forests which contain only a small share of the region's non-urban land' (Haase & Nuissl, 2007). Thus, the region of Leipzig provides an example of the competition between municipalities tending to become fiercer in a situation of decline. In Liverpool, however, no similar development could be observed, mainly because in the UK local authorities don't rely on their local tax base and have generally less power than in Germany.

How can urban policy making and planning make use of the situation of urban decline?

With regard to urban policy, our first conclusion is that in a situation of urban decline it becomes easier for the planning system to control residential sprawl because of a low demand for housing and, therefore, less vigorous attempts by developers (at least if they operate at the supra-regional level) to seek sites or planning permissions (as compared to a situation in which the rate of profit available would be higher due to a higher demand for floorspace).

On the other hand, it proves to be rather difficult for planning authorities to restrict commercial and, particularly, industrial development on greenfield sites, because there is a strong political pressure on the planning system not to prevent the stimulation of new jobs.

Due to the affluence of available (derelict) urban land in declining cities, the chance for the planning system's aims for a compact mixed-use urban structure to be implemented is particularly high in such cities. Hence, public authorities seek the re-use of urban sites that have had the benefit of many years embedded private capital investment within the site, and public capital investment in the surroundings and general infrastructure of the city. In principle, these factors are also conducive for re-investment in the older urban areas by landowners and proprietors. However, as the comparison between Liverpool and Leipzig shows, without some additional preconditions being fulfilled, private actors will usually refrain from such re-investment. Liverpool provides a good example of what is needed in order to make use of a lack of growth dynamics for the promotion of urban regeneration and redevelopment (cf. Roberts & Sykes, 1999) – and thus the containment of urban sprawl:

- Anchoring the goal of economic use of land (i.e. brownfield redevelopment) in national policy so that regional land use planning can effectively obstruct greenfield developments.
- Establishing an effective monitoring system which gives an account of how much development is taking place on brownfields/greenfields.
- Development agencies on the regional and local level which effectively promote and organise brownfield redevelopments.
- Steering investment programmes towards inner-city brownfields by making the reuse of already developed land a prerequisite for subsidies.

Generally, declining cities like Liverpool and Leipzig should not anticipate a return to their former importance and place in the urban hierarchy, as little demographic growth is to be expected in Europe in the foreseeable future. The past has shown that efforts to attract (and subsidise) industrial investors and to develop big infrastructural facilities with public money, which have been undertaken in both cities, could not stop – let alone reverse – the decline. Besides, since most of these investments have been located on the urban periphery they often have changed the functional structure of the urban space to the further detriment of the inner city. Hence, urban policy making and planning will have to concentrate on the organisation of shrinking and redevelopment. In Liverpool this lesson has definitely been learned during the last decades, and in Leipzig also we see signs of urban governance based on realism after a decade of 'Boomtown-hopes' (Heinker, 2004).

Successful urban policy in a situation of decline requires more than most current activities of urban redevelopment can achieve. First of all it needs to allow for the interdependence of developments in the inner city and sub-urbia. It should help to overcome competition between municipalities (for a diminishing number of investments) in favour of a regional approach to the organisation of spatial development. Another major challenge still to be tack-led will be the downsizing of infrastructures, which will prove inevitable yet also even more difficult to manage than the adaptation of the housing stock to the changing needs of a declining, but increasingly demanding, population which is at the heart of urban redevelopment programmes. It is impossi-ble to simply reduce and trim down such infrastructures, be they technical facilities or social services, in the same way as buildings are eradicated – for instance the council housing of the 1960s and 1970s in Liverpool and pieces of 'slab housing estates' of the GDR era in Leipzig. New concepts and strategies are to be deployed, the development of which has only just begun.

Notes

1   In Germany, unfortunately, no data is available on the percentage of urban devel-opment built on previously developed land. In any case, this share is much lower than in Britain, since no national (federal) strategies for the reuse of brownland have been in place up to now.
2   Unfortunately, no comparable data is available for the time before 1990.

References

Adams, D. & Watkins, C. (2002) *Greenfields, Brownfields and Housing Development.* Blackwell, Oxford.
Atkinson, G. & Oleson, T. (1996) Urban sprawl as a path dependent process. *Journal of Economic Issues* **30**(2): 609–15.
Bathelt, H. (2002) The re-emergence of a media industry cluster in Leipzig. *European Planning Studies* **10**(5): 583–611.
Bathelt, H. & Boggs, J. S. (2003) Towards a re-conceptualization of regional develop-ment paths: is Leipzig's creative industries cluster a continuation of or a rupture with the past? *Economic Geography* **79**(3): 265–93.
Beauregard, R. A. (2002) *Voices of Decline: The Postwar Fate of U.S. Cities.* Routledge, London, New York.
Hillier Parker, C. B. & Cardiff University (2004) *Policy Evaluation of the Effectiveness of PPG6*: Office of the Deputy Prime Minister, London.
Chin, N. (2002) *Unearthing the Roots of Urban Sprawl: A Critical Analysis of Form, Function and Methodology.* Casa Working Paper 47, London: Centre For Advanced Spatial Analysis (Casa), University College London.

City of Leipzig (2004) *Monitoringbericht 2004: Kleinräumiges Monitoring des Stadtumbaus in Leipzig.* Leipzig: Stadt Leipzig, Stadtplanungsamt.

Coles, T. (1997) Trading places. The evolution of the retail sector in the new german länder since unification. *Applied Geography* **17**(4): 315–33.

Couch, C. & Wynne, S. (1986) *Housing Trends in Liverpool.* Liverpool Council For Voluntary Service, Liverpool.

Couch, C. (1999) Housing development in the city centre. *Planning Practice & Research* **14**(1): 69–86.

Couch, C. (2004) *City of Change and Challenge: Urban Planning and Regeneration in Liverpool.* Ashgate Publishing, Aldershot.

Couch, C., Karecha, J., Nuissl, H. & Rink, D. (2005) European planning studies. *Urban Sprawl: European Patterns and Policy* **13**(1): 17–136.

Department of the Environment, Transport and the Regions (1998) *Planning For The Communities Of The Future.*: The Stationary Office, London.

Döhler, M. & Rink, D. (1996) Stadtentwicklung in Leipzig. Zwischen Verfall und Deindustrialisierung, Sanierung und Tertiären Großprojekten, In H. Häußermann & R. Neef (eds), *Stadtentwicklung in Ostdeutschland. Soziale und räumliche Tendenzen*, pp. 263–86. Westdeutscher Verlag, Leverkusen-Opladen.

Ewing, R. (1994) Characteristics, causes, and effects of sprawl: a literature review. *Environmental and Urban Issues* **21**(2): 1–15.

Friedrichs, J. (ed.) (1997) *Die Städte in den 90er Jahren: Demographische, ökonomische und soziale Entwicklungen.* Westdeutscher Verlag Leverkusen-Opladen.

Garreau, J. (1991) *Edge City: Life on the New Frontier.* Doubleday, New York.

Haase, D. & Nuissl, H. (2007) Does urban sprawl drive changes in the water balance and policy? The case of Leipzig (Germany) 1870–2003. *Landscape and Urban Planning*, **80**(1–2): 1–13.

Häußermann, H. (ed.) (1997) *Ökonomie und Politik in alten Industrieregionen Europas: Probleme der Stadt- und Regionalentwicklung In Deutschland, Frankreich, Großbritannien Und Italien.* Birkhäuser, Basel.

Heim, C. E. (2001) Leapfrogging, urban sprawl, and growth management: Phoenix, 1950–2000. *American Journal of Economics and Sociology* **60**(1): 245–83.

Heinker, H. (2004) *Boomtown Leipzig.* Faber und Faber, Leipzig.

Herfert, G. & Röhl, D. (2001) Leipzig – Region zwischen Boom und Leerstand, In K. Brake, J. Dangschat & G. Herfert (eds), *Suburbanisierung in Deutschland: Aktuelle Tendenzen*, pp. 151–62. Leske + Budrich, Leverkusen-Opladen.

Herfert, G. (2002) *Disurbanisierung und Reurbanisierung – Polarisierte Raumentwicklung in der ostdeutschen Schrumpfungslandschaft.* Manuscript, Leipzig: IFL – Institut für Länderkunde (Forthcoming).

Hocquél, W. (1994) Leipzig, Ein großstädtisches Denkmalensemble des Historismus: Zustand, Möglichkeiten, Aufgaben, In P. Peters (ed.), *Leipzig: Zwischen Planung und Investoren*, pp. 28–34. Müller, Köln.

Hoscislawski, T. (1991) *Bauen Zwischen Macht und Ohnmacht. Architektur und Städtebau in der DDR.* Verlag für Bauwesen, Berlin.

Johnson, M. P. (2001) Environmental impacts of urban sprawl: a survey of the literature and proposed research agenda. *Environment and Planning A* **33**(4): 717–35.

Kabisch, S., Kindler, A. & Rink, D. (1997) *Sozial-Atlas der Stadt Leipzig.* Manuscript, Leipzig: UFZ – Umweltforschungszentrum Leipzig-Halle.

Kolinsky, E. (ed.) (1995) *Between Hope and Fear: Everyday Life in Post-Unification East Germany – A Case Study of Leipzig.* Keele University Press, Keele.

Lütke-Daldrup, E., Döhler-Behzadi, M. (eds) (2004) *Plusminus Leipzig. Transforming the City.* Mueller + Busmann, Wuppertal.

Liverpool City Council (1993) *Key Statistics, Liverpool Wards 1971/81/91.* Liverpool City Council, Liverpool.

Liverpool City Council (2003) *Liverpool Economic Bulletin.* Liverpool City Council, Regeneration Policy Division, Liverpool.

Maynard, M. (2003) *The End of Detroit: How the Big Three Lost their Grip on the American Car Market.* Currency/Doubleday, New York.

Mumford, K. & Power, A. (2002) *Boom or Abandonment. Resolving Housing Conflicts in Cities.* The Chartered Institute Of Housing, Coventry.

Madden, M., Popplewell, V. & Wray, I. (2001) *City Centre Living as the Springboard for Regeneration: Some Lessons from Liverpool.* Working Paper 59, University of Liverpool, Department of Civic Design, Liverpool.

Nevin, B. (2001) *Liverpool's Housing Market Research Programme, 1999/2001: A Review of the Main Findings and Policy Recommendations.* Liverpool City Council, Regeneration Policy Division, Liverpool.

Office of the Deputy Prime Minister (ODPM) (Annual) *Land Use Change Statistics, Tables D1 and D2.* The Stationary Office, London.

Nuissl, H. & Rink, D. (2005) The 'Production' of Urban Sprawl in Eastern Germany as a Phenomenon of Post-Socialist Transformation. *Cities* **22**(2): 123–134.

Peiser, R. (2001) Decomposing Urban Sprawl. *Town Planning Review.* **72**(3): 275–298.

Perspectives For Germany: Our Strategy for Sustainable Development (2002). Press- and Information Office of the Federal Government of Germany, Berlin.

Roberts, P. & Sykes, H. (eds) (1999) *Urban Regeneration: A Handbook.* London, Sage.

Sassen, S. (1991) *The Global City: New York, London, Tokyo.* Princeton University Press, Princeton.

Schmidt, H. (1991) *Die metropolitane Region Leipzig – Erbe der sozialistischen Planwirtschaft und Zukunftschancen.* ISR-Forschungsberichte 4, Österreichische Akademie der Wissenschaften, Institut für Stadt- und Regionalforschung, Vienna.

Sieverts, T. (2003) *Cities without Cities: An Interpretation of the Zwischenstadt.* Spon Press, London.

Tesch, J. (2003) *Bauen in Leipzig 1945–1990.* Rosa-Luxemburg-Stiftung Sachsen, Leipzig.

Ward, S. V. (2004) *Planning and Urban Change.* 2nd Edn. Sage, London.

Williams, K., Burton, E. & Jenks, M. (eds) (2000) *Achieving Sustainable Urban Form.* E & FN Spon, London.

Xu, J. & Yeh, A. G. O. (2003) Guangzhou. *Cities* **20**(5): 361–74.

6

No Place Like Second Home: Weekends, Holidays, Retirement and Urban Sprawl

Karl-Olov Arnstberg and Inger Bergstrom

The largest industry in the world

Summer is the time when we consume specific values, from barbecues and scuba diving to a beautifying sun tan. Summer is the time for travels, for vacation, for leisurely lifestyles. In a way, summer is also the time for *sprawl*. Not only urban sprawl, but sprawl in the widest sense of the word. People go for vacation to different parts of the world and all over Europe people have summerhouses – *second homes* – where they invest a lot of money and work. The countryside has in many places become the playground of society at large (Bunce, 1994, p. 111). From a small upper class phenomenon, tourism has become a massive industry. We do not only have the usual sun-and-beach-tourism, cultural tourism and alpine tourism. We also have eco-tourism and a fast growing market of international residential tourism, a phenomenon rare in the past. (Leontidou & Marmaras, 2001, p. 257). There is even a kind of anti-tourism, where the worst places on earth attract visitors. Oblast Kaliningrad becomes a realistic alternative to the Taj Mahal.

One of the forms of second home that has been heavily realised in recent years, is big complexes of houses in the form of separate villas in large estates, developed by private building societies. We find them in the Mediterranean area – in Greece, France and Spain. They are especially common on islands such as Corsica and Mallorca (Marmaras, 1996, p. 3).

What speeded up the process of second homes in other countries was, of course, the law from 1993, which permitted EU citizens to buy property anywhere within the region. As a result the border line between international residential tourism and international migration is not always clear. Leontidou and Marmaras discern four types of movers (2001, p. 259):

- families splitting their time between a job in the city and leisure in the countryside abroad (often involves mixed marriages);
- entrepreneurs who combine leisure with income earning in the countryside;
- artists, intellectuals and people who seek alternative lifestyles;
- retirement migrants moving to the Mediterranean coasts and islands.

Summertime is the time for 'the other and lazy life', the life people would like to live forever, if they only had enough money; at least they often say so. In reality it is doubtful if people are happier during their summer vacation than when at work. In fact, statistics in Sweden tell the opposite; many divorces are decided during vacations. But if asked, summer and vacation time is almost always seen as the best.

To many Europeans the summerhouse is of a much higher symbolic value than the permanent home. The summerhouse is the happy place where they spend the high value time of vacation, while the home is a necessary requirement, tied to work, the daily rat race and sheer survival. Families feeling alienated in urban mass housing need to recover during summer. Tenants, not entitled to do much in their high-rise flats on the urban periphery, can compensate for this in rented cottages, caravans or, when they can afford it, in their summerhouses. To urban people the summerhouse is a question of power and love, nothing less. Subsequently we treat summerhouses owned and used by urban citizens as attached to the city.

Of course, second homes are also relevant for people living in the countryside, but if rural people do not see any economic advantage to a different life during summer, there is really no point in having a summerhouse. Vacation, yes of course; maybe a visit to a city for a couple of days or just being lazy on one of Europe's many beaches. But a summerhouse at home, who needs it?

There is also a sprawling market for people with no interest in summerhouses. Vacation and travelling are, for many among us, almost synonomous. From a European perspective, tourism has been promoted, since it is understood as a part of the integration of Europe. No wonder summer is big business in Europe, as in many other parts of the industrialised world. Taken together leisure, recreation and tourism creates the largest industry in the world.

A short history of the summerhouse

Wealthy Mesopotamians and Egyptians probably had summerhouses. We know at least that they had the same feeling of being urban and a nostalgic interest in agrarian rusticity (Bunce, 1994, p. 5). In the Roman Empire the very rich usually had a second home, a *villa suburbana*, where they could experience *amoenitas*, the pleasures of a country retreat. Preferably it was a huge seaside villa surrounded by a garden with fish ponds and a swimming pool, but it could also be a quite modest country house, a *villa rustica* (Balsdon, 1969). There the Romans could walk in the woods, hunt and behave as gentleman farmers (White, 1977).

This idea of being a 'gentleman farmer' links the country house of Roman civilisation to the Italian renaissance country houses (Bunce, 1994, p. 78). These, in their turn, had a strong influence on the English country estates from the sixteenth century and onwards (Newton, 1971). An expanding and affluent upper middle class were motivated both by the idea of a country retreat and by the possibility of property investment. The English *country gentleman* was born and, in Victorian England, he was a quite visible character, with his country house as a status symbol. Urban people moved, if they could afford it, away from the unhealthy and, during summer, hot and stinking towns and cities, to the countryside and the seaside.

From 1887 there was even a *Country Life* magazine published, marking the importance of the country house and leisurely life style to the upper middle class. By the end of the century, however, the decline started. The houses were too big and the fortunes not as bottomless,as previously. Many second homes were turned into hotels, vacation homes, so forth.

The Roman ideal also inspired country houses in other parts of Europe, but they did not become a mass movement until after World War II (Bunce, 1994, p. 87). It was not only a question of money. The *weekend* and the *holiday* first had to be shaped.

The summers of my childhood

When we search the web for the very specific phrase 'The summers of my childhood' we get 89 600 answers. Many of them take the summerhouse for granted. They tell us about an existence where time is *forever*, and as memories they are as sweet and breathless as the first kiss. No responsibilities, nor any hints of this *forever* being a limited number of years between a guarded early childhood and the problematic storms of adolescence. Yes, among all summers, those of childhood are without competition. Like the poet John Tobias writes:

> 'During that summer
> When unicorns were still possible;
> When the purpose of knees
> Was to be skinned;'

Summerhouses are of major interest to urbanites and 'summering' at the cottage has become a symbol for a happy family life – which in some places has deeply problematic effects.

Take the Mediterranean coast as a frightening example. Retirement tourism is especially common in Spain, and Spain has around 22 million home-owners. Close to four million of them are foreigners and this figure is growing. Around 1 25 000 foreigners buy each year a second home or a house for permanent living in Spain. British buyers are driving the Spanish, as well as the European, market. In Spain they are no less than 36% of foreign property owners, while the Germans come in second place at 23%. Although the prices are quite high, they jumped 17% the first three months of 2004. More distant areas are also affected. In southeast Spain, inland towns such as *Murcia* and *Almeria* have become popular. A flat there is a good prospect in comparison with the more expensive *Costa del Sol* or *Costa Brava*. One indication that is as good as any of what's happening is that people are acquiring more four-wheel drive cars than ever. In 2003 the sales went up by 40% in the area. (The Webpaper *Expatica*, June 2004).

People deploy their growing wealth for both investment returns and leisure. Property analysts believe the overseas markets for second homes could even overtake the domestic markets as people see better property investment opportunities abroad and low-cost airlines shrink travel times. The most popular destination is Spain, followed by France.

Portugals 'Associação Nacional de Empreiteiros de Obras Públicas' (ANEOP) reported in 2004 that one in four Portuguese had a second home. This means that the country has around one million second homes, which is the highest number in Europe and double the figure for France. Most of these second homes are of recent construction, signifying that despite being a low wage economy, Portugal is 'real estate-rich'.

In Greece there has been stronger resistance against promoting the country to second-homers. The reason is partly that there are not any budget flights to Greece yet. Also, the bureaucracy makes it harder for foreigners to buy property. Nevertheless, Corfu is one of the most attractive addresses in the world for blue bloods with old money. Property prices there are as high as in the French Riviera. Corfu's most impressive villas face the clear blue Ionian Sea and distant Albanian mountains. They are equipped with swimming pools, tennis courts, personal chefs and boats in private marinas. But of course we also find this upper class tourism elsewhere.

The villas lining the coasts of Nice bear witness to the roots of international residential tourism in the early twentieth century and even before, when English elites used to live seasonally in the French countryside. The French, for their part, used to reside in their colonies in North Africa. In early twentieth century Tunisia, the picturesque Andalusian-style village of Sidi Bou Said owed its fame to three young painters who stayed there after 1914: Paul Klee, August Mache and Louis Millet. However, it is difficult to speak of international residential tourism in this case, as well as other cases of diaspora communities in colonies; the French communities in Algeria, Italian ones in Libya, Egypt, Erytrea, the Greek communicates in Egypt are not properly 'touristic' (Leontidou & Marmaras, 2001, p. 259)

In the north of Europe, many beaches are also heavily exploited. Take the Danish coast, where nearly all of the second homes as well as holiday and leisure facilities are situated. Since most of the settled population also live quite close by, the coast is threatened by different kinds of land use demands, as well as by pollution from agriculture. Summer cottages and different built-up areas – harbours and technical installations – occupy one third of the total coast. The rest is rather a rural area, of which some parts still are exposed to sedimentation and active erosion.

Two homes

The two ideal housing situations in Europe are: either inner-city living with easy access to service, schools and cultural activities; or living in the much less dense countryside with open space, a piece of land of ones own and a life style attached to the nature. Usually urban dwellers would love to have both kinds of housing. The 'favourite solution' is to have a large enough apartment in a city, designed for 'winter and work' and a complementary detached house for summer and leisure somewhere else, preferably close to water. Summerhouses are for swimming and seaside life, of course, but also for skiing and different winter sports, as well as just recreational and slow-paced country life – people cultivating flowers and talking walks in the nature around them. The summerhouse can also be used as a weekend house and, if it is suitable, even during the cold season. In rich western countries it is an almost 'normal' situation to have a summerhouse and a car for journeys there.

The Sweden of today is a highly urbanised country but, only fifty years ago, a majority of Swedes still lived in the countryside. This means that many middle-aged and elderly people were either born, or have their origins, in the countryside. Because of this, they also often have a cottage, a country house or sometimes a small farm, where they go in the summertime and, if it is not too far away, also at weekends.

In Sweden there are four kinds of summerhouses with different historical backgrounds. Today they are merging into 'just summerhouses', a minority among them very luxurious and a majority more adapted to normal incomes. The situation is about the same in the other, also sparsely populated, Nordic countries.

First we have summerhouses attached to pasture in the woods and mountains in the north of Sweden. In pre-industrial times a certain culture developed, with the farmers' daughters and sons living under simple conditions close to their livestock, making cheese, butter and other dairy products, for consumption in the winter. *Chalets* are, of course, also known from the Alpine countries, such as Austria and Switzerland, where this culture has played a major role in the shaping of national identities and stereotypes. In regions of Europe where stock-farming was more important than agriculture, the peasants moved out to their chalets, in order to live with their cattle. Today these houses are very often turned into summerhouses.

The second kind of summerhouse is the cottage, originally built and used by craftsmen, farmers and farmhands. This category also includes houses designed for other kinds of production. In Sweden, fishing hamlets especially, but also former ironworks and other industrial communities, are quite popular for summer vacations.

Ideally they should be at a distance that is possible to commute to over weekends, which means that they should be no more than, say, 100 km away. At least if we have a look at the market, we can see that prices within this distance from the larger cities are quite high. The difference between this category and the chalets is, of course, that these houses were never meant for summer use only.

Thirdly, we have wealthy citizens who, in the latter part of the nineteenth century, built large seaside summerhouses, especially on the Baltic Sea Archipelago and on the West coast. The Swedish have a special name for them, hard to translate since it doesn't sound as good in English: wholesale dealers' houses ('*grosshandlarvillor*'). In contrast with the first two categories, these houses are meant for leisurely summer use only. Since heating costs could be counted out, they are quite spacious, with high ceilings and large windows, preferably with a seaside view.

The fourth type is the modest cabin, usually built by and for workers after the World War II. As a single object, it could be situated almost anywhere away from cities and towns, but is very often located on a small green plot – with hundreds of other cabins and weekend cottages as neighbours. It is a step up from the very popular allotment-garden areas, where people often have cottages too, but which are usually too small to live in.

Making and maintaining roots

To give another European example, French urbanites – throughout all social groups – strive for two homes. Like in other European countries, in France the home in the city is the regular dwelling and the home in the countryside is for holidays. But in contrast to the usual European situation, it is only recently that the French countryside has lost some of its productive dimension and these parts have turned into the recreational landscape they already have become in, for example, Sweden. The social anthropologist Sophie Chevalier has written about the French two-home project as a materialisation of family identity (Chevalier, 1999). Having a summerhouse and being there is a kind of exodus. It can be understood as an escape to the reminiscences of a traditional world with manmade artefacts. Although 'mild', it is nevertheless a protest against the industrial society with its mass produced material products.

In terms of family history, the link to life in the countryside is strong. The house in the country symbolises 'the family'. This means that selling the 'family residence' is considered deeply problematic, even if the link really isn't there. Summerhouses are not for consumption, they are taken out of the market exchange. Newly bought houses also usually become tied to the family, which means that they can be bought but never, or only under very special circumstances, sold again. The furniture also becomes immovable:

'As the contents and decor of the family residence are also inalienable, no family member moves furniture items from the family residence to his or her apartment. This is not only for practical reasons, because these old pieces of furniture are often too big for a flat, but also for symbolic reasons, because these pieces belong to the family residence. There is a strong link

> between the decor and the house itself, between the architecture and the
> style of the furniture'   (Chevallier, 1999, p. 93).

The country house is meant to be the meeting point for the members of the lineage. Therefore, unlike a mass produced flat in the urban landscape, the summerhouse should be personalised and integrated in the family. The ambition, of course, is to maintain roots, and if there aren't any, shape them. Keeping the summerhouse as it 'always has been' is a way to add to the value of one's past. People keep or buy houses in the country in order to anchor their lineage (Chevalier, 1999, p. 83). The place doesn't then have to be spectacular. Summerhouses are neither meant for consumption nor for creating an impression. So it was, anyway. Lately one can notice that people talk about places like possessions, they boast about the address of the summerhouse that also shows the actual value of the house and thereby the prosperity of the owner.

Recreation, retirement ...and investment

If one doesn't have any roots to a specific place in the countryside and if one is rationally minded, why not investigate widely? What's wrong with finding this holiday paradise in some other part of the world? If farm-land in Holland is not three but thirty times as expensive as in Poland, why not buy a summerhouse in Poland instead, and get much more value for the money? In a world where *placelessness* is a realistic option, one could as well have a summerhouse in a place where a foreign language is spoken. There could even be an exotic edge to it. In Denmark and Sweden, this is a reality. In the wooden areas of southern and western Sweden there are villages populated only in summer and where the majority speak German. The local estate agents advertise their properties in both Swedish and German.

In Denmark, before it became a member of EU, the ambition was to stop seaside houses from being bought by Germans for only a third of the prize of the German equivalent. The Danes were, however, not very successful, as the principal is that citizens of EU should be equal in all matters. Because of this, neither have new member states such as the Czech Republic and Poland been able to obtain lasting exemptions.

In Sweden, Germans in general are welcome to buy summerhouses. Tensions between them and locals are not considered a problem big enough to reach the media, although now and then there is some friction.

In other parts of Europe the tensions seem to be more substantial. Two British planning researchers, Nick Gallent and Mark Tewdwr-Jones, spent three years studying the growth of second homes in Europe, more specifically in north Wales and the Highlands of Scotland, together with Galicia in Spain, west Sweden and Savo in Finland. Some of the regions studied actually welcomed second homes, as they were seen as an economic benefit, helping the local economy. But their research also showed that in some places there were indeed considerable tensions between incomers and local inhabitants. Their solution to this was to suggest more houses being built in rural areas.

The ambition to stop summerhouses can also be domestic. Especially in Scotland and Wales, the mainstream housing stock was used up in providing second homes. And, because these properties were lying empty for the most part of the year, the settled population, who couldn't afford to pay the prices, simply had to move away. In some parts of north-west Wales as much as one quarter of the homes in certain villages are second homes, which has lead to a desperate shortage of low cost housing for local people. The same is true for certain parts of Skye, where second homes have contributed to depopulation.

In Exmoor National park in south-western England, British authorities in September 2001 proposed that no more outsiders should be allowed to buy second homes, a radical solution indeed. The proposed rules would also keep extensions to houses small, to keep the prices from going up. Otherwise locals were priced out of the market. The new rule against outsiders was explained as a tool against gentrification. The majority of recent sales were from buyers outside the south-west and resulted in some villages not being occupied for more than a few weeks a year.

Retreat to a loved place

Many urban Swedes dream of moving to a summerhouse, simply because this means moving to a happier place. The opportunity comes when commuting time is shortened, when they work part time or when they don't have to go to work each day. But this is not only an opportunity; it is also an economically important situation. Sometimes, due to a lowering in incomes, people are forced to move to their summerhouses. When the city grows, the market price and the following taxation make the summerhouse too expensive to keep as a complement to the permanent home. In the Urbs Pandens Project, Austria, Slovenia and Sweden are countries that remarked that converting summerhouses into permanent dwellings is one of the patterns spreading the city. Factors of relevance for this version of sprawl are:

- If the public communications are improved, or if the road is upgraded, there is the possibility of commuting. Young families move out from the city.
- Retired people often move there when they have made the house fit for living in during the wintertime. The number of retired people will increase when the 'baby-boomers' of the 1940s retire.
- A growing number of people have a flexible working schedule, they work part time or at home. These people can accept a long commuting time, as they don't go every day.

People moving to the countryside can be categorised into three groups; those *moving home*, those *moving back* and those *moving out*. People *moving home* go back to the place where they grew up but left for studies or work. They move to the homes of their childhood or close to the old home. Many of them made up their mind about moving back home very long ago. Those *moving back* do not go to their original home, but to a similar place, seeking the same kind of life style. The individuals and families *moving out* often carry a romantic and idyllic view of the countryside, they imagine a peaceful, quiet and natural life. They often believe that stressful urban life is bad for children. Often, they move out when awaiting their second child.

Common to all three groups is the fact that the individuals have chosen to change their lifestyle in order for the opportunity to live a healthier life. Their claimed motives for moving from the city are:

- more influence over their life (i.e. their time, although the result often turns out to be the opposite, if commuting to the city);
- to leave the stress of the city; and
- to come close to nature.

People who move to the countryside often regard home and family as the main priotities in life. Many of them have a combination of two occupations or more, to make their living. One could say that they rather work for living than live for work.

Those *moving out* bring the urban life style to the countryside, and even if tensions between them and the locals are rare, the two groups have not much in common; they live parallel lives. Those *moving home* fit almost naturally into local everyday life and those *moving back* are also quite familiar with the rural culture. The latter may be urbanites, but having spent their summers in the countryside they are used to the way of life and can interact socially with the locals (Feldmann, 2002).

Inhabitants of Värmdö, outside Stockholm, were asked in a survey, what was the most important question for them, relating to their second home. They all answered: communications. This is also the greatest planning issue of the comprehensive plan of the Värmdö municipality. In that respect planners and inhabitants make the same priorities.

In the Stockholm region today, about one thousand summerhouses are converted each year for permanent living. From the planners point of view this is a problematic process since with this move follows difficulties with traffic, water supply, sewer systems, so forth. Further, the municipality is obliged to serve all registered people with schools and other social facilities, as well as with public transport.

Värmdö, a sprawled community in the Stockholm region

We would like to end this chapter with some comments on Värmdö, a municipality in Stockholm chosen as a local study, since a discussion on second homes and sprawl cannot be had without a discussion on, and clarification of, scale. On the largest level, the city level, we define the municipality of *Värmdö* as the most sprawled municipality in both Sweden and Stockholm. This, however, does not imply that every part of Värmdö is sprawled in a physical meaning. For example, Gustavsberg, the old industrial community in Värmdö, does not sprawl, although it most certainly is affected by the sprawl of the municipality in different ways. It is also too strained to see parts of the sparsely populated Baltic Sea Archipelago as sprawled, despite they are both influenced by sprawl in the municipality as a whole and also expose some of the criterias of sprawl (Figure 6.1).

Second homes are of major importance for this community on the outer fringe of Stockholm, but what we also find are summerhouses transformed into homes for permanent living. In Värmdö there is both sprawl attached to permanent living and a seasonally increased sprawl during the warm season. Altogether 10000 persons, two thirds of the gainfully employed in Värmdö, commute to other parts of Stockholm. In summertime the commuting increases, as there are around 15000 summerhouses in Värmdö. This means that the population during summer is doubled, from 32500 to around 60000 inhabitants. A majority of the people living there, when not on holiday, also commute to other parts of the Stockholm region. In 30 years there will be no summerhouses anymore in the central parts of Värmdö, only houses for permanent living.

Figure 6.1 Family homes in Värmdö.

Figure 6.2 New housing in Värmdö, 2002.

Värmdö is seen as a suburb to Stockholm where housing is considerably cheap, and still of high quality (Figure 6.2). If one has a small firm and needs extra space to stock merchandise or park heavy transport and work equipment – like big trucks, dumpers and excavators – just to give a few examples, Värmdö is a rational choice. If one takes the trouble of commuting by car and being stuck for a couple of hours in the daily traffic jam, one gets first class housing quality to budget price. This is also relevant for people in owner's apartments. A few have been built in the last two decades and, after some shaky years around 1990, the prices are steadily going up. Actually this is understandable as, if you avoid rush hours, it takes only 20 minutes by bus to reach central Stockholm.

Värmdö scores high when it comes to environmental qualities. As a seaside municipality, Värmdö contains a large part of the highly appreciated archipelago of Stockholm. There is also a varied landscape with real woods and lakes, this kind of 'wilderness' around the corner, which is typical for Scandinavian and Finnish cities, but more seldom found in other parts of the densely populated Europe. Värmdö is thus a rational choice for inner-city Stockholmers with small children as well as for retired people, who are more fond of woods and water than streets and restaurants. To young people, dedicated to urban lifestyles, Värmdö is, however, has little to offer and if you are young, happen to live there and do not have a drivers license and a car, you also have difficulties getting home late in the evening. There are buses, of course, but the timetable is loose.

For ecological reasons, most of the Värmdö archipelago is protected in various ways. Seashores, shallow waterland, wetlands, deciduous forests, older coniferous forests and natural pastures – such as dry, calcareous meadows and shore meadows – are considered as being of indispensable value. Large unexploited areas are protected because they serve as wildlife habitats and ecosystems – important places for reproduction of otherwise threatened species such as birds of prey, seabirds and seals. In Värmdö today, there are no first class shopping facilities or markets. Due to this, a majority of the inhabitants shop on their way home, when commuting.

Tourism and recreational activities are, in many ways, of growing economical importance to the municipality. Many people visit and stay as guests in the municipality for a variety of reasons. Summer guests and day visitors require activities, communications, food and lodging. The first and economically most important groups are, of course, the summer guests, who give the necessary customer potential to groceries, service businesses, restaurants and lodgings. Another large group is people arriving to, and cruising in, the archipelago in their own boats. Bullandö is one of the largest small boat harbours in the Stockholm region. On the mainland there are golf courses and some cultural facilities like art exhibitions and museums. Gustavsberg is still considered to be something of a Swedish centre for artistic china and ceramics.

Värmdö municipality is visited by a lot of tourists, both from other parts of Sweden and from abroad. There are boat clubs and golf courses, and no less than three harbours with regular ferries to different parts of the archipelago. This archipelago with literally thousands of islands is seen not only as a national, but even a worldwide, attraction. No wonder these scattered islands are the prime pride of the Värmdö municipality. Here are rich possibilities for sailing and other forms of boating, as well as experiencing the coast, the Baltic Sea and the archipelago in many different ways.

When it comes to the permanent living population of the archipelago, the process is reversed to the one transforming summerhouses into permanent dwellings. In the archipelago permanent fisherman's cottages and small farms are sold as summerhouses to wealthy Stockholmers. One of the things speeding up this process is the, in Sweden much discussed – and also heavily criticised by right wing politicians – real estate taxation. The prices on summer places in the archipelago are very high, and since taxation follows the market, old lakeside settlements often become too expensive to keep for the owners, who have often been born there and whose families have been living there for ages. A very attractive small farm could well have a tax imposed based on a value estimation of 650 000 Euro. This means a yearly real estate taxation of 1.5%. To this, a capital tax of 1% can be added. Altogether this means 16 250 Euro in taxes every year. To manage such a heavy taxation takes more than average earnings.

These are state taxes and cannot be changed or handled by the local authorities. Their interest is, also with a taxation perspective, to have the maximum number of domiciled inhabitants in the municipality. In the archipelago this is of extra importance, since the municipality cannot otherwise offer the necessary service to the lucrative tourist trade.

Värmdö is one of the smaller of the 26 municipalities in the Stockholm region when it comes to the number of people living there. It has a fairly young population compared to the rest of the region. The average age for both men and women is 36 and the big age groups are 0–10, 28–45 and 50–58. Statistically the youngest group is also the largest group moving in, which clearly indicates Värmdö's popularity among families with children.

Around 55% of the population lives in their own permanent houses, 20% in summerhouses and 25% in apartment blocks. The latter are mainly to be found in the central parts of Gustavsberg, were the density is highest. The average household density is circa 2.7 person/dwelling, more than the average for the Stockholm region – which is 2.1. Around 16 000 people live alone or as single parents. Their children are included in this number. There are 11 500 married couples, 3000 are divorced and 1000 are widows and widowers. There are 3700 with a foreign background – most are from Finland and tied to the china factory as workers or former workers there. Around 1900 have foreign citizenship.

Traditionally the villages situated in Värmdö got their food and merchandise for trade from fishing and the hunting of seals and seabirds. Farming and stock farming was necessary but still of minor importance. Piloting has also become an important sideline occupation in this part of the archipelago, known for being very difficult to navigate in, since all boats heading for Stockholm have to pass Värmdö.

In around 1820 a china factory started up in Gustavsberg. It was to become very well known in Sweden and at the turn of the twentieth century it was one of the biggest factories in Sweden with around 1000 workers. This was unfortunately closed down in 1994, but another factory remains, which employs between 350 and 400 workers. Gustavsberg, then, is the second biggest employer in the municipality. The biggest by far is the municipality itself.

During the latter part of the nineteenth century steamship traffic made two things possible. First, and most importantly, the Stockholm bourgeoisie started to build their summerhouses in this region. Spacious and richly decorated summerhouses were raised along the steamship lines, and villages such as Stavsnäs and Sandhamn turned into summer playgrounds for artists, authors (e.g., August Strindberg) and affluent Stockholmers, which is, by the way, still true – especially for Sandhamn, where it is almost ridiculously expensive to acquire a summer house today. The Royal Sailing Society of Sweden is situated there. There are also expensive restaurants and tourist traps to be found, and Sandhamn is the only island in Värmdö municipality to which working people today commute from the mainland.

If summer guests are the first of the characteristics of Värmdö since the nineteenth century, strawberries are the second. The steamboats made it possible to transport fresh strawberries to the markets in Stockholm and strawberries from Möja, another island in the archipelago, became so famous that strawberries cultivated in other islands were also called Möja-strawberries. Even today these strawberries are known for being very delicious, but the competition from imported strawberries is too fierce and not many derive their livelihood from cultivating strawberries anymore.

Unfortunately the withdrawal from city life and positive outlook on a green lifestyle is not the same as an ecologically attractive lifestyle. The reason for this is sprawl, which is experienced by the Värmdö municipality as a major planning problem. Individual solutions for water supply and drainage in a former summer-household area, result in sanitary inconveniences and people getting salted instead of fresh water in their taps. Still, there is no easy answer for the municipality on how to enlarge the public water supply and the sewage treatment works. Their capacity is already fully developed, in contrast with the situation in the Stockholm region as a whole, where the technical supply systems have been extended and modernised over a long period.

The municipality realises that the growing population must be accompanied by major infrastructural investments. One of the problems, the insufficient sewage treatment works, must result in either a major extension or a connection with the works in Lidingö, another – and more wealthy – of the Stockholm municipalities.

When it comes to roads, requirements do not only concern roads for cars, but also for pedestrians and bicycles. The planners believe that many local journeys which now are done by car, for example to park-and-ride facilities and bathing-beaches, could as well be done by bicycle, if safe cycle ways were available. Schools and day care centres are also required, and it all ends up on the agenda of the municipality. Taken together, the extension of the infrastructure into a sprawled and sparsely populated landscape is a costly undertaking.

For a municipality in the late modern Swedish welfare society it is not possible to treat these questions in a slapdash way, to handle the problems as they arrive. The taxes in Sweden are among the very highest in the world and the citizens usually believe they are entitled to demand a well functioning and smooth running public service. The infrastructure is expected to just be there, reliable and working.

The two prime actors causing sprawl are *the family* and *the developer*. Families are attracted by life in a sprawled urban landscape for three major reasons. First is the wish for family life (the nuclear family as a cosmos of its own). Second is 'placelessness' (people liberated from the social obligations and economical necessities of a certain working-place). Last, but not least, comes consumer behaviour (competence in making rational choices when it comes to housing-careers, shopping, means of transport and other merchandise that in cooperation makes sprawl). In more detail, 'customers on the housing market of Värmdö' comprise:

- Stockholm families with a wish to acquire a 'greener' life and live in a detached or semidetached house of their own – either a summerhouse or a house for permanent living. These families are recruited from the whole Stockholm region, including both Värmdö and downtown Stockholm. One or both spouses usually work elsewhere and commute by car. The main reason for this choice of housing is the children. The inner-city

life, so favoured among young and childless people, is usually considered
unhealthy due to air pollution. Also, the children's possibility to move
freely is limited, because the traffic. It is possible in the Stockholm area
to make a switch from an inner-city apartment, to a detached and spacious house in Värmdö, or some other place in the periphery, and get a
raise in housing standard without this being especially costly. A three-
bedroom-owner's-apartment in inner Stockholm costs about as much as a
considerably bigger one-family-house in the suburbs. When moving out,
these families have three basic choices. First, and probably most commonly, they buy a suitable house that is for sale, due to different reasons
(divorce being a quite common one, because this life is not meant for the
single, not even for single-parent households). The second alternative is
to buy a new house, situated in a housing estate, with more or less identi-
cal homes, built by a developer. The third alternative is to buy a site and
commission an architect to build an individually designed house.

- Stockholm families and retired senior citizens, who do not have to commute, and because of this decide to move away from the stress and other
disadvantages attached to city life, and permanently settle in their summerhouse. This is not as expensive as buying a detached house. For
the municipality, this summerhouse sprawl 'infrastructurally seen' is
problematic, since these houses often have their own ecologically cum-
bersome solutions, with own springs (with salted groundwater as a result),
high energy consumption and individual sewage disposal systems, with
eutrophication as a consequence.

The Stockholm region has multiplied its built environment after World War
II. This development is mainly conditioned by the topography. Stockholm is
situated in a landscape with plenty of water, which has affected the physical
enlargement as well as the regional planning. There is continuous discussion
on land exploitation and how it should be conducted. Often, economically
as well as socially attractive projects have been dismissed due to ecological
reasons. In Sweden, ecology is usually equivalent to the saving or enlargement of green areas and unspoiled watersides. Concerning Stockholm this
often is a difficult project, in relation to the objective of compactness.

Sprawl is also a reality in Stockholm, but it is not possible to treat sprawl in
terms of insufficient planning and lack of legislation, resulting in an uncontrolled urban increase. Rather it is the other way around. After World War II
a widespread growth occurred in the Stockholm area, but this is the outcome
of controlled planning. Governmental norms and recommendations, as well
as governmentally directed loans to the public housing sector have, together
with the planning monopoly and development and building legislation, held
Stockholm's urban growth in a tight grip.

The thinning out of the physical urban milieu, with plenty of space, air and green areas, as well as a thoroughly accomplished function and traffic separation, has for long been the objective in urban planning not only in Stockholm, but in Sweden as a whole. During the last decade this goal has, however, been reversed. Today the responsible politicians in Stockholm have the well integrated, physically concentrated European town as their prime goal. In overall and regional planning for Stockholm this objective is clearly marked. A recently published program says: 'The town environment should have the traditional European qualities: compactness, a wealth of variety, public spaces and green structure'.

So we end on a demand for a denser and greener urban life. The inner city of Stockholm is, compared to other European cities, quite green, but hardly the answer. Värmdö is certainly very green, but not dense enough. The answer to this quest seems to be the same as before: city life combined with a nice second home – for those who can afford it.

References

Balsdon, D. (1969) *Life and Leisure in Ancient Rome.* The Bodley Head, London.

Bunce, M. (1994) *The Countryside Ideal. Anglo-American Images of Landscape.* Routledge, London.

Chevalier, S. (1999) The french two-home project. Materialization of family identity. In C. Irene, (ed.), *At Home: An Anthropology of Domestic Space.* Syracuse University Press, New York.

Feldmann, B. (2002) *Inflyttare till Stockholms skärgård. Livsstil, livsform och skärgårdsfrågor,* Unpublished research report, The Ethnological Department, Stockholm University.

Gallent, N. & Tewdwr-Jones, M. (2000) *Rural Second Homes in Europe: Examining Housing Supply and Planning Control.* Ashgate, Aldershot.

Leontidou, L. & Marmaras, E. (2001) From tourists to migrants. Residential tourism and "littoralization". In: Y. Apostolopoulos, P. Loukissas & L. Leontidou (eds), *Mediterranean Tourism: Facets of Socioeconomic Development and Cultural Change.* Routledge, London.

Marmaras, E. (1996) *Migration and Tourism Development in Marginal Mediterranean areas: Foreign Second Home Owners in Spain and Greece,* Research Report, Department of Geography, King's College, London.

Newton, N. (1971) *Design on the Land: The Development of Landscape Architecture.* Belknap Press, Cambridge, Mass.

The Webpaper *Expatica,* June 2004. http://www.expatica.com/actual/article.asp?channel_id=1&story_id=30986

Thompson, F. M. L. (ed.) (1982) *The Rise of Suburbia.* introduction, Leicester University Press, Leicester.

White, K. (1977) *Country Life in Classical Times.* Paul Elek, London.

Part III

Models, Urban Policy and Sustainability

7

Modelling Urban Sprawl: Actors and Mathematics

Matthias Lüdeke, Diana Reckien and
Gerhard Petschel-Held

In this chapter we discuss urban sprawl as a process that results from the decisions of multiple actors. Amongst the many possibilities for decisions taken by these actors we concentrate on locational decisions (see, e.g., Colombino & Locatelli, 2001) which – as an aggregated effect – change the conditions of the location for subsequent actors' locational decisions: actors who move – according to their preferences – to low density zones, contribute to densification and thereby change the conditions for further 'low density seekers'. This is only one simple illustration of a multitude of such feedback mechanisms which occur in economic, social and environmental dimensions. In explaining cases where a complicated net of such feedbacks leads to urban sprawl, a system dynamics approach seems appropriate (Meen & Meen, 2003; Deal & Schunk, 2004). This opens the door to the application of formal methods of deduction (formal logics, mathematics) widening the scope for establishing hypotheses with a larger number of explicit relations than can be evaluated by 'unsupported' reasoning alone. However, it should be stressed that the deductive step which can be improved by the application of these formal methods is only one in the complex process of scientific understanding, while the inductive, or dialectic, process of hypothesis formulation from empirical material (Shank, 2001) is largely untouched.

In the next sections of this chapter we will discuss the step from many individual actors to 'actor classes'; the relations between structural variables; and an actor-based understanding of the sprawl process. These ideas are then applied to a number of case study areas. There is then a section devoted to the mathematical formalisation of these relationships: known as Qualitative Dynamic Modelling. The next section shows some simulation results and discusses how they can be used for validation of the hypotheses on actor-class preferences and feedbacks. Finally there is a discussion about the ways in which qualitative dynamic modelling can be used in the policy making process.

Actors, actor classes and sprawl

The archetypes of sprawl explained in the preceding chapters address the spatial scale of the whole agglomeration or – at least – the whole sprawling area, thereby following rather a macro-perspective (in contrast to the micro-perspective of single individuals). These macro-processes can be understood as the aggregation of the consequences of a multitude of single decisions, made by different individuals (see, e.g., Filion *et al.*, 1999). In the context of sprawl, two types of actors have to be distinguished: actors who take decisions related to their *moves in space* (locational decisions of residents, retailers, industry) and non-moving actors (political authorities, developers, etc.) who influence sprawl by directly setting conditions for the decisions of the moving actors.

For various reasons a system analytical treatment seems to be more promising for the moving than for the non-moving actors. Firstly, the space-function feedback is much more direct for the moving actors and their decisions directly affect the physical phenomenon of sprawl. Secondly, a system analytical approach demands a clear setting of the systems boundary. To endogenise, for example, mechanisms which generate specific spatial policy decisions (i.e. decisions of a non-moving actor) would interfere strongly with our aims, namely to assess or develop promising policy options to regulate sprawl. This touches on the reflexivity problem of social sciences, which cannot be solved in general, but where at least a clear statement can be made about the actual hypothesis – who is the observer and what is observed. So we follow a system characterisation that allows us to reasonably ask questions such as: what is the influence of the establishment of a Green Belt on further settlement development? that is, decisions of non-moving actors are treated as boundary conditions for the systems dynamics and have to be set as scenarios.

The next question is about the right level of aggregation of the moving actors. Is it adequate to speak about 'young families with middle income' in an aggregated manner, or is it necessary to address each single household as one actor in its relation to all others? The latter is realised in 'multi agent-based modelling' (Epstein, 1999; Hare & Deadman, 2004) which is mainly aimed at explaining emerging macro-properties from micro-interactions. The former finds its application in mainstream economic theory, which is based on one representative household.

In the case of the urban sprawl analysis, the question of the appropriate aggregation can be investigated empirically. An aggregation of households into an actor class is appropriate when they are homogenous with respect to the properties relevant for the relations in the sprawl context, in particular their preference structure and their specific influences on the regions they move to (White, 1981; Thill, 1993).

For the case study area of Wirral/Liverpool a sample of the population was surveyed by a postal questionnaire. Responses were fed into a cluster algorithm to test if homogenous actor classes could be formed (Couch & Karecha, 2006). The survey sought the preferences for specific residential locations. Fourteen characteristics of locations were pre-given and the respondents ranked the importance of each in influencing choice of location. The ranking ranged from irrelevant – slight importance – fairly important – very important – crucial. Furthermore, 24 potential characteristics of the respondents were also sought, including family status, profession, age of the heads of households, their commuting time and the number of cars available in the household. From this empirical material three very persistent clusters of high preference homogeneity emerged (independent from the applied clustering algorithm):

- *Retired people* and those over 60 years old. They were mostly adult couples (60%) and elderly persons living alone (26%) with one car (64%). They preferred being in a low-crime and quiet neighbourhood near the countryside or coast, with good road connections, good bus and railway links, and in proximity to food shopping.
- *Professional and managerial households with child/children* which mostly comprised adult couples with child or children (88%) in professional or managerial positions (78%). The head of household was mostly of middle age (91% between 35–59 years old) and in possession of two or more cars (100%). Most were looking for a low-crime and quiet neighbourhood with good schools. The proximity of countryside and coast was also of interest for the actor class.
- *Professional and managerial households without child/children* represents adult couples (93%) in professional or managerial positions (100%). These were mostly young people (64% younger than 34 years of age) or of middle age (29% between 35–59 years old). This actor class sought, as did all other actor classes, low-crime and quiet neighbourhoods; but with this group the availability of affordable housing was an additional preference.

Table 7.1 Actor classes as defined independently by the different case study groups

Case Study	Actor I	Actor II	Actor III	Actor IV	Actor V	Actor VI
Leipzig	Middle income households	High income households	Industry/ businesses	Large retail/leisure centres		
Värmdö (Stockholm)	Upper class older couples without children	Upper class families not feeling connected to Värmdö	Family enterprises feeling connected to Värmdö	Old residents	Summerhouse converter (for permanent living)	Summerhouse owner (use it temporarily)
Vienna	Young DINKs	Young families	Single parents	Middle-aged DINKs*	Retired people	
Nadarzyn (Warsaw)	Middle income green-seeker	High income green-seeker	Nadarzyn-Fans	Dwelling-standard-fans		
Wirral (Liverpool)	Retired people	Professional and managerial households with children	Other households	Professional and managerial households without children without children	Lower-middle class households	

* DINKs – Double income no kids; green-seeker – households seeking a home with good access to the countryside.

Furthermore but with less strength, the algorithm also revealed:

- *Lower-middle class households* with and without children, mainly between 35 and 59 years old (61%) but also some of younger age (24%) and distributed among many occupations. This group sought a low-crime and quiet neighbourhood with affordable housing near to friends and family.
- *'Other' households (single adult and adult couples)* are mainly unemployed persons, with 95% under 60 years. They consist of single adults living alone in most of the cases (70%) and some adult couple households (15%). Here also living in a low-crime and quiet neighbourhood ranks highest importance, but the provision with good bus and railway links, the proximity of friends and family and affordable housing were all of significance.

This case shows on an empirical basis that the aggregation of households into sufficiently homogenous actor classes is possible. In Table 7.1 we summarise the relevant moving actors as identified in our research for the respective case study areas. In the different regions different characterisations of the actor classes were necessary. In Figure 7.1 we show the position of the residential actor classes in a scheme of economic status, age and family status

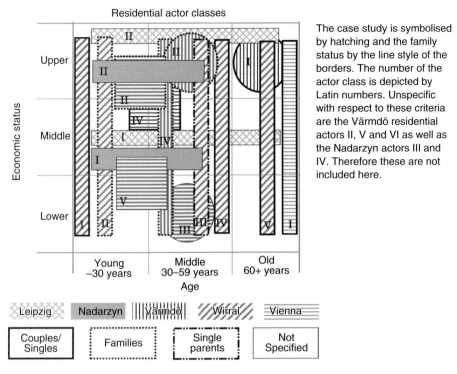

Residential actor classes

The case study is symbolised by hatching and the family status by the line style of the borders. The number of the actor class is depicted by Latin numbers. Unspecific with respect to these criteria are the Värmdö residential actors II, V and VI as well as the Nadarzyn actors III and IV. Therefore these are not included here.

Figure 7.1 Position of the residential actor classes in an economic status/age scheme.

which clearly shows the heterogeneity of the actor class sets of the different cases. For example, the Vienna actor classes are age oriented while the Leipzig and Nadarzyn (Warsaw) classes are separated by economic status. This may reflect the differences between countries in transition and Austria as a saturated capitalistic system where places are already more class-homogenous. Wirral and Värmdö each show a different and complex mixed structure reflecting specific relevant mechanisms of sprawl.

The actor versus the structural perspective on sprawl

The question now arises how the more structural properties of the urban system relate to the actor perspective. To do this, a moving-actor class oriented process model has to be defined in some more detail.

Classes of actors (different kinds of residents, retailers, etc.) are characterised by homogeneous ways in assessing the attractivity of different urban zones with respect to their decision to move there. The attractivity of an urban zone will be used here in an extended sense, closer to the migration decision: it comprises the usual locational properties and the affordability to move for the actor class being considered. In this notation a zone which, for example, does not offer affordable housing, is not attractive for a specific actor class, regardless of other advantages. The attractivity assessment for an actor class depends on three aspects:

a. the fixed characteristics of the respective zone;
b. the presence of other actor classes (competition, synergies, homogeneity, customers, etc.); and
c. externally influenced properties (incentives, taxes, infrastructure ...).

Actor classes migrate along attractivity gradients (move from a zone of lower to a zone of higher attractivity). Thereby they reduce their population in the zone they leave (zone of origin) and increase their number in the zone they move to. This migration may change the attractivities of both zones for all actor classes with respect to mechanism (b) and cause further changes in migration fluxes. This means that the mechanisms cited in (b) can be endogenised into the formal model while (a) and (c) will be considered exogenous.

The qualitative attractivity migration model: QUAM

The following section discusses some important macro-variables as commonly used in structural explanations of sprawl (as, for example, applied in other chapters within this book) and shows how they are related to the actor class oriented structure (called QUalitative Attractivity Migration model: QUAM). It is clear that the macro-variables (indicated by italics in the following paragraph) may either be exogenous to the QUAM-model and cause:

1. a **C**hange in **A**ttractivity of a zone for a specific actor class (type **CA**);
2. a **C**hange of the **N**umber of actors in a specific class (type **CN**);

or address aspects which are endogenous to the model, that is,

3. the **D**ynamics of the spatial **D**istribution of actor classes (type **DD**).

The macro-variables concern:

- The topic *demographic and household change* is mostly interpreted in terms of increasing one-person households, changes in the population pyramid or changing family status, which can be mapped on a change in total size of actor classes like 'young single', 'old single' or 'young family' (type CN).

- The *migration, segregation and filtering* aspects are much more diversely interpreted, but aspects like immigration (either foreign or rural) and emigration can also be mapped onto the change of the total size of respective actor classes (type CN) while aspects like social homogeneity, east–west divide, gentrification of inner-city areas, concentration of foreigners in old densely built-up outer areas, migration from inner-city areas to rural areas and filtering processes are represented by the dynamics of the spatial distribution of actor classes (type DD).

- With respect to the *sectoral composition and transformation of the economy* the processes of industrialisation/de-industrialisation and tertiarisation are of importance. From the residents point of view this modifies the attractivity of different zones for specific employees depending on commuting distance, and may influence the attractivity of expensive housing zones for different actor classes, depending on income (type CA). The trend to smaller firms with more flexible location decisions has to be mapped on the change of the respective actor class (type CN). Labour market structure changes do not add new paths of mapping, the same is true for foreign investments and shifts of location of economic activity: they change the attractivity of a zone for residential actor classes (type CA).

- *The lack of space in inner city* maps on increasing or decreasing supply with adequate dwellings which can be represented as increasing or decreasing attractivity for residential actor classes in the model (type CA).

- *Changes in income, the distribution of incomes and spending patterns* in the sense of income growth, polarisation of income distribution, household expenditure, so forth. can be mapped onto changes in the size of actor classes of different income levels (types CN, DD) or a change in the attractivity of, for example, a housing area for a fixed actor class with changing income (type CA).

- *Changes in land prices and/or housing costs* due to supply changes can be reproduced by a shift of the attractivity functions of the different actor classes (type CA).

- *Infrastructure investments – transport and other* increases the attractivity of remote places for most of the actor classes (type CA). Transport itself depends on the spatial distribution of specific actor classes (residents, industry).

- With regard to *public regulation, taxes and subsidies* the competition between municipalities and spatially specific, as well as demand side, taxes/subsidies are of importance. These can be mapped on changes of attractivities with respect to a region and/or an actor class (type CA).

- *Public regulation, land use planning, housing policy* includes aspects such as tenant-protection, housing privatisation and problems of restitution (type CA).
- The aspects subsumable under the *quality of the inner city* are of type DD: reputation, supply with adequate housing, infrastructure (cultural, schools, traffic, water supply, etc.).

This list shows that almost all structural and macro-properties usually used in sprawl explanations can be represented by an actor class oriented approach.

Identifying the feedbacks

The example of the Leipzig periphery is used to illustrate the second step in defining an actor based process model: the identification of actor specific preferences and feedback from the actor class population on the characteristics of the location (see also Lüdeke *et al.*, 2004). This is a crucial element in sprawl related dynamics.

For the urban fringe of Leipzig, four relevant actor classes have been identified (see Table 7.1). For them, seven potentially relevant dimensions of attractivity to the choice of location have been identified. According to empirical studies and literature review (Lüdeke *et al.*, 2004) the seven dimensions concern:

- dwelling standards (heating, bathroom, windows, etc.);
- dwelling prices (rents or purchase prices);
- the physical environment (density of settlement, proximity to natural landscape, etc.);
- infrastructure (roads, train and bus lines);
- the neighbourhood (social environment and image);
- the accessibility of major centres (e.g. a shopping mall); and
- the catchment area (number of customers able to visit a shopping mall).

The last dimension is only relevant for actor class 4 (large retail/leisure centres) while the standard of flats only applies for actor class 1 – the middle income households (according to empirical studies). Prices, physical environment, neighbourhood and infrastructure are relevant for both residential actor classes 1 and 2 – middle and high income households. Infrastructure also matters for the economic actor classes 3 and 4 (industries/ businesses and large retail/leisure centres), as does the availability to large plots. These issues are summarised in Table 7.2.

Table 7.2 Dimensions of attractivity of the Leipzig periphery identified to be relevant for the actor classes

Attractivity-relevant aspects	for actor
standard of flats (heating, bathroom, etc.)	P_1
prices (rents, prices of houses)	$P_{1,2}$
physical environment (density of settlement, proximity to natural landscape)	$P_{1,2}$
infrastructure (roads, train lines)	$P_{1,2,3,4}$
neighbourhood (social environment)	$P_{1,2}$
availability of large plots (e.g., for a shopping mall)	$P_{3,4}$
catchment area (number of customers able to visit a shopping mall)	P_4

P_1 – Middle income households; P_2 – High income households; P_3 – Industry/business; P_4 – Large retail/leisure centres.

Starting with actor class 1, the middle income households, the assessment of the Leipzig case study group revealed that the attractivity dimension dwelling standard of flats is not significantly influenced by further in-movement of any actor class. The supply of high quality dwellings/flats is, and probably will also be for the nearer future, sufficient due to attractive depreciation possibilities for investors throughout the 1990s. The second important dimension is price. Here, experts do not expect an increase from scarcity of building land, but an increase of prices due to an improvement in the image of the zone when the population of the high income households grows. Therefore, increasing high income households has a negative influence on this attractivity dimension for the middle income households.

The attractivity due to the physical environment is not influenced by in-movement because of the still low settlement density and the generally low aesthetic quality of the Leipzig periphery compared with the inner-city. Traffic infrastructure is abundant and congestion is not yet a serious problem. In a wider sense of *infrastructure*, the development of shopping malls in the periphery is welcomed by the middle income households. With respect to the *social environment*, a slightly positive influence of in-movement of high income households on the attractivity can be observed. So an increase in high income households has two competing effects on the attractivity of a region for the middle income households (increased prices due to an improved image and better social environment). The net effect will be negative, as for the middle income households the *price* effect is more important than the *image* effect.

Regarding the attractivity of the zone for the high income households, we find a somewhat reversed situation: here the *social environment/image* plays a much more important role than the price. Therefore, the positive effect of increasing high income households yielding more social homogeneity more than compensates for the negative impact on prices. In the case of *infrastructure* and *physical environment*, these aspects will be left unchanged under population change for the same reasons as mentioned above. The difference is that the development of new retail/leisure centres will not increase the attractivity of the zone for high income households, because these centres are much less attractive to them as compared with middle income households.

The attractivity of a peripheral region for industry/business appears to be determined by availability of large plots and *infrastructure*. Due to the strong competition between communes for jobs and profitable businesses, the first dimension is not a limiting factor, as land is likely to be made available in response to the wishes of potential investors. With respect to *infrastructure* there is a synergistic effect between the different industries/businesses resulting in a positive influence of industries/businesses on their specific attractivity.

For large retail/leisure centres the *catchment population* is a crucial aspect – but closer inspection shows that in the era of high car ownership this is the total population in the whole agglomeration and thereby does not contribute to the retail/leisure centres' decision to move to the periphery or not. Instead, availability of land is important. This dimension of attractivity is not significantly influenced by a hypothesised increasing demand, as communes will offer adequate spaces to attract investors. But it appears that the provision of *infrastructure* is influenced positively by the presence of industry parks: synergetic effects appear.

In Table 7.3 all attractivity dimensions and their dependence on changes in the actor populations are summarised. A_1 represents the attractivity of the region for P_1 – the middle income class; A_2 stands for the attractivity for P_2 – the high income class, A_3 indicates the attractivity for P_3 – industry/businesses, and A_4 shows the attractivity of the region for P_4 – the retail/leisure centres.

As shown in section 'The actor versus the structural perspective on sprawl', attractivity is influenced by:

a. the fixed characteristics of the respective region;
b. the presence of other actor classes (competition, synergies, homogeneity, customers, etc.); and
c. externally influenced properties (incentives, taxes, infrastructure ...).

Table 7.3   Attractivity dimensions and their influences

a) Attractivity dimensions of the Leipzig periphery for the four actor classes (ordered according to importance for each actor) and how they are influenced by actor population changes. For details see text.

A_1	P_1	P_2	P_3	P_4	Remarks
standard of flats	o	o	o	o	oversupply
Price	o	–	o	o	oversupply, image
phys. environ.	o	o	o	o	still low density
infrastructure	o	o	o	+	oversupply
neighbourhood	o	+	o	o	image
AGGR. EFFECT	**o**	**–**	**o**	**+**	
A_2	P_1	P_2	P_3	P_4	
neighbourhood	o	+	o	o	image
phys. environ.	o	o	o	o	still low density
Infrastructure	o	o	o	o	oversupply
Price	o	–	o	o	competition
AGGR. EFFECT	**o**	**+**	**o**	**o**	
A_3	P_1	P_2	P_3	P_4	
accessibility of large areas	o	o	o	o	competition of communes
Infrastructure	o	o	+	o	Synergies
AGGR. EFFECT	**o**	**o**	**+**	**o**	
A_4	P_1	P_2	P_3	P_4	
catchment area	o	o	o	o	not sprawl-relevant
accessibility of large areas	o	o	o	o	competition of communes
Infrastructure	o	o	+	o	benefits from P_3
AGGR.EFFECT	**o**	**o**	**+**	**o**	

b) Resulting aggregated attractiveness matrix (Attractively is a mathematical, commonly used term in English)

$$\text{sign}\left(\frac{\partial A_j}{\partial P_i}\right)$$

Population→ ↓Attractivity	P_1	P_2	P_3	P_4
A_1	o	–	o	+
A_2	o	+	o	o
A_3	o	o	+	o
A_4	o	o	+	o

Columns: influence of on the attractivity A_j of this region for each actor class j.

"o" means no relevant influence; "+" a positive; and "–" a negative influence.

P_1 – Middle income households; P_2 – High income households; P_3 – Industry/business; and P_4 – Large retail/leisure centres.

Reading example (row 1 of the attractivity matrix): for actor class 1 an increase of the population P_2 would decrease the attractivity while an increase in P_4 would increase the attractivity of the region. Changes in the population of P_1 or P_3 would not affect the attractivity of the region to P_1.

Table 7.4   Attractivity matrix for Leipzig including the additional external effect on the attractivity for the residential actor classes, represented by the "t-column"

Pop.;Time→ ↓Attractivity	sign $(\partial A_j / \partial P_i)$				
	P_1	P_2	P_3	P_4	t
A_1	o	−	o	+	−
A_2	o	+	o	o	−
A_3	o	o	+	o	o
A_4	o	o	+	o	o

As time t – in contrast to the P_i - increases always, the fifth column acts as a continuously negative influence on A_1 and A_2.

P_1 – Middle income households; P_2 – High income households; P_3 – Industry/business; and P_4 – Large retail/leisure centres.

So far we have discussed mechanism (b) (Brainard, *et al.*, 2002) in this section. But if we want to describe the Leipzig case after reunification external influences (c) have to be taken into account, which is in the case of Leipzig the continuous increase (from 1990 to 2000) in the supply of attractive dwellings in the inner city mainly due to clarification of ownership relations and the shift in subsidies from support for new dwellings to the restoration of old buildings. These external influences tend to reduce the difference in attractivity between inner city and periphery for the residential actor classes and thereby the net attractivity of suburbia. This reflects back onto the attractivity matrix. The modified matrix is displayed in Table 7.4: in addition to the four columns P_1–P_4 which characterise the influence of population changes on the attractivity for the different actor classes, a fifth column is added to describe the external influence. Additionally, to the population effects, the factor t influences the attractivity of the periphery for the residential actor classes P_1 and P_2 negatively over time. This factor competes with the population related influences and may or may not be overcompensated by other matrix elements in Table 7.4.

We illustrated the system analytic characterisation of a sprawl region using the Leipzig case. As mentioned in the introduction of this chapter, this allows for the application of formal, mathematical methods to perform further deductive steps, including model validation and policy analysis. In both cases the aim is to deduce the dynamic behaviour (i.e. the time course) of the actor populations – in system analytic terms the 'trajectories' of the system – from the stated interrelations as summarised in Table 7.4. This mathematical method is relatively new and has some interesting properties bridging the gap between quantitative and qualitative methods.

Operationalising the qualitative attractivity migration model

The mathematical theory which allows us to evaluate system descriptions as in Table 7.4 is called 'Qualitative Differential Equations' or QDEs (Kuipers, 1994). The method is based on system theoretical process thinking, that is, the state of a system is related to its rate of change. In the realm of usual quantitative modelling this is formalised by differential (since Leibnitz and Newton) or difference equations where explicit numerical relations between the variables and their rates of change are needed. In contrast, QDEs try to deduce the time development of the variables from a much weaker, namely a 'qualitative' understanding of the interactions of the system elements. This has some advantages. In particular, it is very appropriate for the evaluation of social systems' behaviour where indicators are difficult to specify and especially to quantify.

This qualitative understanding can be characterised by the following hierarchy of determination:

1. Which elements are directly related (e.g., A and B are directly related, A-B)?
2. What is the direction of the influences (e.g., B influences A: A <- B)?
3. Is it a strengthening or alleviative influence (e.g., B alleviates A)?
4. Is it an influence on the variable or its rate of change (e.g., B alleviates the rate of change of A)?

Levels 3 and 4 imply that it is possible to describe the elements of the system by ordinal scale variables, that is, a 'greater/less than' relation can be defined. At level 4 of determination, QDEs can be applied and generate the time course of the variables by their trends and trend changes. As QDEs are a generalised system analytic method, the boundaries of the system, its elements, their qualitative relations and exogenous drivers have to be identified. In all cases where this can be done at least in parts, the method is applicable. To apply QDEs, the construction of an influence diagram is necessary in order to depict the system's elements and their qualitative relations. To obtain this, techniques of qualitative data collection (interviews, oral history, focus groups, delphi groups) and data analysis (hermeneutics, discourse analysis, grounded theory) can be applied – for the potential role of these techniques in the different stages of model development and interpretation of model results, see Luna-Reyes and Anderson (2003).

The method was originally applied by Kuipers and his group to qualitative physics and human physiology. In the realm of sustainability science it was applied to smallholder agriculture in developing countries (Petschel-Held & Lüdeke, 2001; Sietz *et al.*, 2006), fisheries management (Eisenack *et al.*, 2005) and industrial agriculture (Lüdeke & Reusswig, 1999). Here the aim was to calculate possible future developments from qualitative systems understanding, to choose from these sets of possible futures the desirable ones, to identify critical branching points and to assess policy options to influence the development positively. The scale of application is characterised by an intermediate functional resolution, resulting in a number of interacting elements not larger than about 40. This means, for example, that the algorithm in its present form is not applicable to typical Multi Agent Based modelling (MAB) which deals with hundreds of agents.

The outputs of the method are time developments in terms of trend combinations of the variables and possible future changes of these combinations. Depending on the input, branching and/or cyclic time developments may result, that is, different possible futures. The strength of QDEs is that powerful mathematical system theoretical methods become available, even if only qualitative knowledge of the interactions of the system's elements is available, for example, in the form of an influence diagram. One disadvantage is that in some cases the result, that is, the qualitative trajectories, may be very ambiguous in the sense that very many branching points occur. The extreme case would be that the filtering ability of the qualitative model is so weak that almost every future development is possible. But this simply means that the input – our knowledge of the system – is insufficient to make any forecasts. This method can be directly used to evaluate models like the one shown in Table 7.4. For a more mathematical formulation see Appendix 1.

Validation and future scenarios

To illustrate the validation process of a QUAM model we return to the Leipzig example. Here it was possible to obtain a qualitative description of the suburbanisation development since 1989 with respect to the population trends (a so called 'qualitative trajectory') in the periphery of the city for the four identified actor classes.

The graphical representation of the results (as in Figure 7.2) is as follows: a rectangle depicts a dynamic state of the zone. This state is characterised by the actual trend of the population of each actor class, depicted by an upward or downward arrow. A rhombus symbolises an undefined trend. The rectangle is partitioned by columns, depicting the actor classes from the left

a) observed change of
trend combinations:

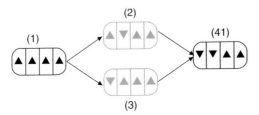

b) possible trajectories realising
the observed trend change:

a) Trend combinations for the Leipzig
periphery as observed during the 1990s
(left hand side state) and 2006 (right hand
side state).
b) As it is improbable that the trends of P_1
and P_2 changed their sign exactly at the
same time two different qualitative
trajectories reproduce the observation.

In columns:
P_1 – Middle income households,
P_2 – High income households,
P_3 – Industry/business and
P_4 – Large retail/ leisure centres.

Figure 7.2   Trend combinations for Leipzig.

to the right $(P_1, P_2, \dots P_i)$. The dynamic state of a zone is changing, if at least one defined trend of one P_i changes its sign. Then a new rectangle is drawn as the successor to the former development stage. Possible successors of a dynamic state are indicated by long arrows between the qualitative states. A typical property of QDE-solutions is that there may be more than one successor for a given dynamic state.

The observation reveals an increase in all actor class populations during the 1990s while at present the trend of the residential actor classes P_1 and P_2 becomes negative (see Figure 7.2a). The exact sequence of the trend reversals of P_1 and P_2 is not known, but two different qualitative trajectories are in accordance with the observations (see Figure 7.2b).

The model is validated if the above observed trajectory can be reproduced. Evaluation of the model from Table 7.2 with the algorithm described in the preceding section yields the graph as shown in Figure 7.3. It includes a branch consistent with the observed state sequence (1)->(3)->(4). This proves that it is possible to reconstruct the observation.

The verified model can now be used to discuss possible future developments (scenarios). Assuming that the exogenous influence which increases the attractivity of the inner city persists, the graph from Figure 7.3 stays valid. Starting with the present situation of an emerging decrease in residential populations (P_1, P_2) and a continued increase of the commercial actors

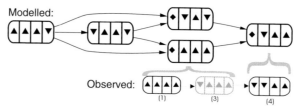

Modelled:

Observed:

(1)   (3)   (4)

Graphs resulting from the attractivity matrix of Table 7.2. The columns in the 'state rectangles' represent P_1 to P_4. Furthermore it is shown that a branch of this graph reproduces the observed qualitative trajectory.

Figure 7.3   Modelled and observed trends in Leipzig.

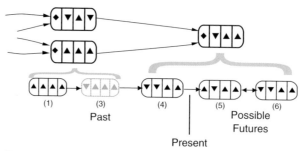

(1)   (3)   (4)   (5)   (6)

Past   Possible
                         Futures

Present

Possible futures of the Leipzig periphery as calculated by the model: firstly the P_2-trend will change [state (5)] and later on possibly oscillate [(5)–(6)].

Figure 7.4   Possible futures for Leipzig.

(P_3, P_4), the model predicts the possibility of a future trend reversal for P_1: the middle income households may start again to generate net-migration into the periphery, even under increasing attractivity of the inner city. Looking further into the future, a kind of 'oscillation' between states with increasing and decreasing P_1 is possible (see Figure 7.4). If the external influence considered in the model were to stop, a straightforward analysis with the QDE algorithm reveals that the oscillation would stop and the middle income families would constantly contribute to sprawl.

Using a QUAM model for policy analysis

There are two different ways illustrated here of how the QUAM models can support policy advice:

1. moving from general targets to the identification of specific policy mechanisms which have to be influenced in order to control urban sprawl;

2. the evaluation of alternative suggested strategies and policy instruments to control urban sprawl.

As an example of the first, we use the results of a stakeholder workshop held in Leipzig (Petschel-Held *et al.*, 2004), where a consensus on a list of targets for the control of urban sprawl was achieved amongst the participating stakeholders and scientists. As an example of the second use, we have employed the results of a questionnaire on strategies to combat urban sprawl and its consequences in the different case study areas.

From general targets to specific policy mechanisms: a model analysis

During the Leipzig workshop, the project partners and stakeholders from seven European cities elaborated on general targets for urban development related to urban sprawl. Major goals for the political and planning system were formulated. These can be summarised as:

- an increase in the functional and social mix of urban areas;
- densification of the urban regions while avoiding over-densification;
- a limit on urban sprawl.

Each of the goals will now be discussed within the modelling framework for one or more of the project case studies.

Increasing the functional and social mix of urban areas, examined in case studies of Vienna and Nadarzyn/Warsaw

The goal is to enable or to increase the functional and social mix of urban areas. This is represented by a persistent trend combination where all actor classes show the same trend direction: either all actor populations increase or decrease. In contrast, mixed trend directions would yield (at least in the long run) a decrease in functional and/or social mix.

Although the initial situation of the descriptive model runs performed so far was frequently characterised by an increase in all actor class populations (due to the choice of hotspots of sprawl), this combination was never persistent. In particular, the final trend combinations were never homogenous.

Vienna (Peripheral zone A3a, south-western municipalities of Mistelbach district and adjacent municipalities of Gänserndorf-district). From a previous study about the 'dreams of habitation' in the Vienna agglomeration (Tappeiner *et al.*, 2001) and further statistical material, five clusters were chosen to represent the actor classes involved in sprawl in Vienna:

- P_1 – Young DINKs: describes young couples in the age of 15–29 years, both persons are working, have no children and are financially well off.
- P_2 – Young families: with only one person working, the financial budget of the household is fully committed.
- P_3 – Single parents in the age of 30–45 years.
- P_4 – Middle aged DINKs: defines couples between 30–59 years of age, the financial background is robust.
- P_5 – Retired people, the budget of the household becomes smaller.

Starting from the existing model developed for Vienna, the attractivity matrix for the five actor classes is shown in Figure 7.5.

The projected final state of the zone is not very favourable from the viewpoint of social and functional mixture. The middle-aged DINKs and retired people are steadily increasing while the other actor classes constantly move out. Here the hypothesis is that the social mix would increase if all actor classes would move into or out of the zone (so inducing either an increasing or decreasing total population). To ensure that one of these trend combinations is persistent, one needs to go back to the attractivity matrix. Here we see that the attractivity for P_1, P_2 and P_3 decreases when more people of P_4 move in. This is due to the stimulation of rising dwelling prices by this actor class (middle aged DINKs). For a higher social mix in the region the negative influence of the middle aged DINKs on the attractivity of the young DINKs, the young families and the single parents needs to become negligible. The '−' have to change to 'o'.

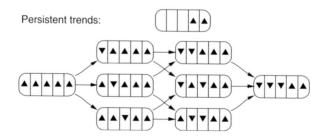

Figure 7.5   Sequence of trend combinations for the Vienna zone A3a.

Table 7.5 Attractivity matrix for Vienna's suburban zone A3a

Population→ ↓Attractivity	P_1	P_2	P_3	P_4	P_5
A_1	o	o	o	–	o
A_2	o	o	o	–	o
A_3	o	o	–	–	o
A_4	o	o	o	o	o
A_5	o	o	o	o	o

P_1 – Young DINKs; P_2 – Young families; P_3 – Single parents; P_4 – Middle aged DINKs; P_5 – Retired people.

If this change in the matrix can be induced, the social mix of the region will increase because all actor classes will persistently rise or fall in numbers once such a migration pattern has been activated.

This result from mathematics can be summarised as follows: eliminate the negative influence of rising P_4 on the attractivity of the considered region for P_1, P_2 and P_3. According to the model assumptions, this influence is generated by market mechanisms.

The choice of policy instruments to achieve this outcome is for local planners to determine in relation to local circumstances. However, likely alternative policies include the direct provision of affordable housing, subsidies for non-profit housing and rent controls.

Nadarzyn/Warsaw. Here, a survey of inhabitants revealed the following actor classes involved in the urban sprawl process:

- P_1 – Middle Income Greenseeker;
- P_2 – High Income Greenseeker;
- P_3 – Nadarzyn-Fans;
- P_4 – People interested in dwelling standard.

As in the former examples, a good social mix is thought to be represented by a homogeneous trend combination for all actor classes. The output from the modelling of the dynamics in Nadarzyn is shown in Figure 7.6.

Table 7.6 shows that the financially well-off actor groups – represented by P_2 (High Income Greenseeker) and P_3 (Nadarzyn-Fans) – move there because of the positive reputation of Nadarzyn. If they move to the zone they influence the housing market in that the prices for the available premises rise faster

Persistent trend:

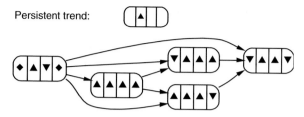

Figure 7.6   Trend combination sequence for the Nadarzyn zone.

Table 7.6   Attractivity matrix for the case study of Nadarzyn

Population→ ↓Attractivity	P_1	P_2	P_3	P_4
A_1	o	–	–	o
A_2	o	o	o	o
A_3	o	+	+	o
A_4	o	–	–	o

P_1 – Middle Income Greenseeker; P_2 – High Income Greenseeker; P_3 – Nadarzyn-Fans; P_4 – People interested in dwelling standard.

than they would have with the only influence of shrinking availability. In the matrix for Nadarzyn this is reflected by the negative influence of increasing P_2 and P_3 on the attractivity of the region for P_1 and P_4. By eliminating these negative influences, a persistent homogenous trend combination, and thereby a development consistent with social mixing, would be possible.

An instrument to avoid the impact of the higher income actor classes on prices in Nadarzyn can help to achieve/preserve social mixing. Which precise policy instruments would be successful (e.g., rent limits, supply of affordable housing, subsidies for non-profit housing, etc.) will depend on the specific situation and would have to be decided by local experts.

Densification of suburban areas, examined in the case study of Leipzig

Here we ask the question: how to generate a more dense development in the Leipzig periphery? As, at the moment, 're-urbanisation' is the predominant trend, this question is aimed at establishing a future where the development of the inner city to a reasonable density (avoiding over-densification) will be

Table 7.7 Attractivity matrix for the case study of Leipzig

Population→ ↓Attractivity	P_1	P_2	P_3	P_4
A_1	o	–	o	+
A_2	o	+	o	o
A_3	o	o	+	o
A_4	o	o	+	o

P_1 – Middle income households; P_2 – High income households; P_3 – Industry/business; P_4 – Large retail/leisure centres.

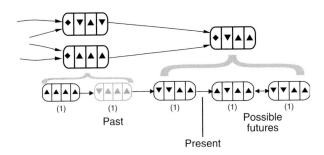

Figure 7.7 Trend combination for the Leipzig periphery.

completed, and further growth in the periphery could occur as Leipzig tries to establish itself as a 'growth pole' in Eastern Germany.

Under current conditions (see Table 7.7), the following scenario for the further development of the Leipzig periphery was deduced (see Figure 7.7):

We anticipate a further increase of the population of actor classes P_1 (middle income households), P_3 (industry) and P_4 (shopping malls/leisure parks). Inspection of the attractivity matrix, that is, the underlying assumptions, suggests that spatial competition between the actors is very low – due to the large abundance of vacant land. One can expect that development under these conditions will be at relatively low densities because there are only weak restrictions on the availability of land. Aiming for a dense development in the periphery would mean that the supply of building land has to be limited. Such a limitation would change the conditions for the Leipzig periphery: now competition between the different actors will occur and generate new interactions. Consequently, the attractivity matrix is changed according to Table 7.8.

Table 7.8 Attractivity matrix for the case study of Leipzig under land restrictions

Population→ ↓Attractivity	P_1	P_2	P_3	P_4
A_1	–	–	o	+
A_2	–	–	–	–
A_3	o	o	–	–
A_4	o	o	–	–

P_1 – Middle income households; P_2 – High income households; P_3 – Industry/business; P_4 – Large retail/leisure centres.

Table 7.9 Modified attractivity matrix for the case study of Leipzig under land restrictions

Population→ ↓Attractivity	P_1	P_2	P_3	P_4
A_1	–	–	o	+
A_2	–	–	–	–
A_3	o	o	+	o
A_4	o	o	+	o

P_1 – Middle income households; P_2 – High income households; P_3 – Industry/business; P_4 – Large retail/leisure centres.

If a simulation is performed on the basis of this modified matrix, we get a new dynamic end-state. It is now characterised by the situation that the populations of all actor classes except those for industry/businesses decrease, which means one gets *less development* instead of more and *denser development*. This is not what was intended. So the question arises: are there measures to enable further development under politically restricted land resources?

To get an idea how these measures have to modify the interrelations between the actor classes (i.e. the attractivity matrix) to be successful, all theoretically possible changes were analysed with respect to their impacts on the expected development. The most promising modification is depicted in Table 7.9, which assumes that the mutual negative interaction between the industry/businesses and the retail/leisure centres (P_3 and P_4) can be avoided. Simulation on the basis of this new matrix generates a dynamic end-state which consists of increasing populations including the high income households.

Table 7.10 Attractivity matrix for the case study of Värmdö

Population→ ↓Attractivity	P_1	P_2	P_3	P_4	P_5	P_6
A_1	o	o	o	o	o	o
A_2	o	o	o	o	o	o
A_3	+	+	−	+	+	+
A_4	−	−	o	o	−	−
A_5	o	o	o	o	o	o
A_6	o	o	o	o	o	o

P_1 – High income older couples; P_2 – High income families; P_3 – Family enterprises; P_4 – Old residents; P_5 – Summerhouse converters; P_6 – Summerhouse owners.

It is now a question of choosing the right policy mechanisms to realise a situation where competition for land between residential and other uses exists, but not between industry and large retail. In case that such a set of measures can be defined by local experts, a dense expansion of the city could be achieved.

'Limiting sprawl', examined at the case study of Värmdö

Accepting that sprawl is sometimes unavoidable but should be kept in reasonable limits, the aim here is to reduce net migration to the periphery, that is, the aim is to stabilise the suburban population.

In the case of Värmdö, we describe the mutual interactions between the six actor classes with the following matrix:

From this we calculate further in-migration of the high income older couples, the high income families, the summerhouse converters (converting from temporarily to permanent use of the summerhouse) and the summerhouse owners (temporarily use), an out-migration of the old residents and an undefined situation for the family enterprises in the future. Looking at the changes in in-migration trends, none of them is decreasing, that is, we cannot expect a stabilisation of the population of Värmdö. How can the situation be modified to generate a stable trend combination with decreasing rates of migration?

A situation where the increasing populations of the high income older couples, the high income families, the summerhouse converters and the

Table 7.11   Modified attractivity matrix for the case study of Värmdö

Population→ ↓Attractivity	P₁	P₂	P₃	P₄	P₅	P₆
A₁	−	o	o	o	o	o
A₂	o	−	o	o	o	o
A₃	+	+	−	+	+	+
A₄	−	−	o	o	−	−
A₅	o	o	o	o	−	o
A₆	o	o	o	o	o	−

P₁ – High income older couples; P₂ – High income families; P₃ – Family Enterprises; P₄ – Old residents; P₅ – Summerhouse converters; P₆ – Summerhouse owners.

summerhouse owners (P₁, P₂, P₅ and P₆) will saturate the zone can be achieved by measures which add negative feedbacks of these actor classes on their respective attractivities (A₁, A₂, A₅ and A₆). This means that an increase of their own population decreases the attractivity of the zone for the respective actor class (see Table 7.11). The effect is that the currently observed trend combination will not change their signs but net migration will become smaller and smaller, resulting in a stabilisation of the total population. Again, it is for local planners to determine the precise policy instruments to be used. One possibility might be to intensify market mechanisms by restricting the supply *specifically* for the respective actor classes (an unspecific restriction of building land would not work because this would add additional minuses to the matrix).

So far we have shown how certain general targets of urban development can be achieved. The results leave open questions of detail but they give hints as to which aspects of the urban system have to be modified.

In the following section we ask the question the other way around and test the consequences that might be expected from specific policy choices.

Discussion of case specific strategy – suggestions from a QUAM perspective

In the following section, the model is used to test the impact of a range of policy instruments in selected cities. In this framework a strategy describes a recommendation that can be implemented through a combination of instruments, while an instrument will be understood as a tool or mechanism to achieve specific goals.

Leipzig

The Leipzig model showed that the present state of emerging residential re-urbanisation was not explained by mutual actor class interactions, but by external influences on the relative attractivity of the inner city and periphery. These external influences are represented by the following suggested strategies (as proposed by the case study experts):

1. improving the quality of inner-city environment;
2. increasing the proportion of owner-occupied dwellings;
3. abolishing incentives for suburban development.

Strategies 1. and 3. are already in use and are – according to the model results – already successful with respect to residential re-urbanisation. With respect to the future situation, the model shows that the population of the middle income households in the periphery will increase again. This unfavourable trend change can occur independently from the continuation of the above measures. It would generate middle class driven sprawl and a kind of gentrification of the inner city. It therefore follows that a further strategy:

4. ensuring reasonable rents and land prices in the inner city

is of great importance for the further development of Leipzig. Therefore, instruments have to be developed to operationalise this strategy. With respect to business and industry the model predicts further sprawl. Here the suggested strategy:

5. cooperation between municipalities (including the City of Leipzig), in order to mitigate (land-consuming) competition (for investments and inhabitants)

becomes important in order to minimise the land consumption of necessarily increasing economic activities in the periphery. The strategy:

6. raising the awareness of politicians for the negative effects of sprawl

touches the preconditions of any measure against sprawl. Here the model does not make specific statements as it concentrates on the 'moving actors', not on the actors which set the framework for urban development. But the model result underpins the importance of this strategy, as an uncontrolled and moving actor driven sprawl would be disadvantageous.

7. Making urban development and land use change less attractive for
   municipalities

touches on the question of whether incentives or disincentives should be
used to influence the decision of a potential mover to the periphery. As a
general conclusion from the QUAM model, the incentive-strategy (making
the inner city more attractive) is preferable, as disincentives (making the
periphery less attractive) could potentially lead to 'evasive actions' of the
movers, which can only be avoided if the disincentives are equal across all
areas – a condition that is difficult to realise. The strategy of:

8. land use regulation

can be discussed from a similar point of view: only if the implemented regulations are ubiquitous can effects, such as a tendency for development to
leapfrog over the green belt, be avoided (Brown *et al.*, 2004).

Nadarzyn/Warsaw

The Nadarzyn model results show a future decline of middle income actors
and a further increase of upper class residents, driven by the interactions
between the actor classes. This will lead to a greater homogeneity among
newcomers and impact on the social cohesion in the sprawl zone. To promote
the integration of newcomers into the existing social structures of the old
residents the strategy:

1. promoting social cohesion

should be taken seriously and implemented by various means. On the other
hand, it needs to be questioned whether such a homogenisation of the social
structure is desirable. If not, specific strategies that support the retention of
the less prosperous inhabitants and avoid gentrification have to be implemented before the out-migration of this actor class starts. The calculated
scenario underpins the importance of:

2. managing the direction of sprawl

as an increasing number of well-off people will build houses and probably try
to get environmentally preferential locations, thereby generating a splinter
development which damages the landscape and generates high infrastructure costs. These costs could, in principle, be borne by the future well-off
inhabitants. Therefore the strategy of:

3. ensuring the infrastructure by private investors

could be successful. But it should be kept in mind that such a policy would reinforce the tendency of social homogenisation towards the high income actor classes.

Wirral/Liverpool

Current strategies for the control of sprawl in Wirral include:

1. increasing employment opportunities in the inner city;
2. improving the environment of urban neighbourhoods;
3. restricting development on peripheral land.

The first two strategies particularly concern the improvement of the inner city of Birkenhead and Liverpool – the latter affects the outer areas. Both factors are related to the model, as they change the attractivity for the different actor classes for the different zones. They will potentially alter the population dynamics in comparison to those calculated without these interventions.

The strategies concerning the outer areas aim to reduce the supply of peripheral land. In the model this is represented by an increasing price for available premises. Certain actor classes are sensitive to price changes and the attractivity of the zone for these actor classes decreases. The questionnaire survey revealed that professional and managerial households with children, lower-middle class households and 'other' households are especially price sensitive, and would therefore tend to move out of the zone. The model shows that it is important whether lower-middle class households or 'other' households move out first. If the lower-middle class households increase first it is likely that Outer Wirral would develop into an attractive zone for other actor classes. But, if 'other' households migrate there first then the opposite trend is more likely. The zone would become less attractive to the retired, the professional households with children and the lower-middle middle class, which successively move to other zones.

If this development can be pursued in combination with the instruments that valorise the existing urban areas, a re-urbanisation process seems possible. Another strategy was to:

4. secure social mixing in residential neighbourhoods.

The model shows that all actor classes move away from 'other' households since they decrease the perception of a low crime and quiet neighbourhood, as postulated (Witt, *et al.*, 1998; Fagan & Freeman, 1999; Carmichael & Ward,

2000; 2001; Raphael & Winter-Ebmer, 2001; Lagrange, 2003). It needs to be underlined that this does not correlate with actual crime rates but is the result of how people perceive the presence of others (Taylor & Jamieson, 1998; Jefferies & Swanson, 2004). Apart from that, all other actor groups show a fairly similar development, in the way that they are willing to move to other areas successively, independently from the other actor groups except 'other' households. Therefore, the issue of social mixing and integration seems a challenging but crucial task for the Wirral area.

Vienna

There are two levels of intervention proposed for the Vienna region. Many problems with Vienna's urban development, for example, urban sprawl, seem to be associated with the fact that there are three different administrative units responsible for Vienna and its surrounding areas. Therefore strategies have been proposed that:

1. raise awareness, improve communication and set joint databases for the cooperation between different levels and divisions of government.

These strategies act on an organisational meta-level which is not explicitly incorporated in the model approach, since here only moving actors (in contrast to administrative actors) have been taken into consideration. Nevertheless one can argue, if the results of the endogenous dynamics under current planning procedures do not lead to a favourable development, planning structures have to altered and adjusted.

The second level of planning recommendation concerns strategies which aim at specific aspects of urban development, and are thereby related to the model assumptions and results.

Here it was suggested that there should be:

2. provision of flexible housing developments dependent on personal biographies, including alternatives to the single-family house.

Simultaneously, the image of housing types other than single-family houses needed to be improved. A further strategy called for:

3. flexible, customer oriented planning of business locations.

Both strategies 2. and 3. concern the future share of actor classes. If one looks at the model results it is possible to predict what kind of housing and businesses might be needed in the future. For example, in the outer city zone K3 (south-western municipalities of Gänserndorf-district) in the final state of the modelling for this zone all actor classes except that of the middle-aged DINKs are increasing. Therefore, all kinds of housing and shopping needs will be demanded, for couples, families and retired people: a broad range of housing forms and local business would be necessary.

In the peripheral zones A3a and A4a (eastern municipalities of Tulln-district) the model suggests that there will be a high demand for the requirements of seniors and middle-aged DINKs. Therefore, there will be a need for housing and shopping facilities for people from medium age (30 years) onwards. There will be less demand for family houses and the needs of younger DINKs. An additional specific strategy asks for:

4. ecological 'consequential charges' after spatial development activities.

Regarding this point, we can assume that such a strategy will affect more intensively the socially middle or lower actor classes than it will touch upper class people. The most financially stressed actor classes are young families and single parents. Both actor classes have increasing populations in the final state for the projection of K3. This means that the implementation of such a strategy of charging for ecological consequences will perhaps hamper the development in region K3, but also result in a driving out middle class people who, at present, contribute to the social mixture in this zone.

Conclusions

It is possible to demonstrate that an approach to urban sprawl which is based on classes of moving actors and the qualitative characterisation of their interactions is able to reproduce observed trajectories of urban development. This means that the actor-oriented approach can yield some important insights into the process of urban sprawl. Sprawl can be understood in part as a socially generated and reproduced process of actors' decisions. The characteristics of actors, their preferences towards certain attractivities and their interactions on these attractivities represent important issues for sprawl. Projections generated with this approach have – due to their qualitative nature – more the character of scenarios (exploring possible futures) than of predictions resulting from quantitative modelling. This fits well with recent understanding of an adequate mapping of the future of human systems (Laumann *et al.*, 2006) and respects the local situations. We regard this feature of qualitative modelling as a strong advantage: local experts and planners are given decisive insights into the process whereas the decision about the implementation of specific appropriate instruments is left open to them. This can ensure a very interdisciplinary approach which could support the decision making processes of politics and planning.

We clearly defined the borders of the system to be modelled by exogenising various macro-influences and considering them as well defined boundary conditions. This does not mean that these are of minor importance; it just means that we do not think that it is possible to explain them sufficiently with a formal mathematical model.

On the other hand, this choice of model boundary reflects one of the main problems of steering urban development: how do endogenous mechanisms (of markets, social relations, etc.) interact with exogenous attempts to intervene? The method of qualitative modelling is very appropriate here, as it preserves the uncertainty of the outcome of opposed effects – so we frequently get less specific results than from quantitative modelling, but the results are more reliable.

In the preceding section we showed the kind of policy assessment which is possible with a qualitative actor based system analytical approach to urban sprawl. One conclusion is that social mixing seems an important issue influencing urban sprawl in the European context (as, e.g., reported in Canada by Filion *et al.*, 1999). Frequently, the price driving impact on the property market by a well-off actor class is an obstacle to social mixing, while other influences – such as age structures – seem less important.

Another very important result is the recognition that the local situation is of high importance with regard to policy success. The implementation of a specific instrument in one case study area did not necessarily have the same impact on spatial development as in another. Frequently, to be successful, measures have to address different actor classes specifically, as shown in Leipzig concerning densification and in Värmdö concerning the limitation of sprawl. In contrast, a uniform implementation of measures will often not be sufficient. (see also Kasper, 2003).

We have to assume that there is some persistence in the quality of actor classes (e.g. in their preferences) and the structure of their interactions. Under these conditions, valid statements on consequences of external interventions are possible. One has to keep in mind that structural persistence is a much weaker assumption than trend persistence which is still assumed in many practical policy assessments.

Appendix

General formulation

Attractivity A of a region i $(i = 1, \ldots, n)$ for an actor class k $(k = 1, \ldots, m)$ depends on the populations P_{ik} of all actor classes in this region: $A_{ik} = A_{ik}(P_{i1}, \ldots, P_{im})$.

Dynamic equations for the attractivity–migration approach for n regions and m actor classes:

$$\sum_i P_{ik} = P_k \qquad 0 \le P_{ik} \le P_k \qquad A_{ik} \ge 0$$

$$\frac{dP_{ik}}{dt} = \sum_{\substack{l=1 \\ l \ne i}}^{n} A_{lk}(P_{l1}, \ldots, P_{lm}) - (n-1) \cdot A_{ik}(P_{i1}, \ldots, P_{im})$$

In its qualitative formulation the right hand sides of the above equations are only defined by the signs of their partial derivatives

$$s_{ikj} = sign\left(\frac{\partial A_{ik}}{\partial P_{ij}}\right)$$

which denote for each region i how its attractivity for actor class k is influenced by the population of actor class j in this region.

Reduced formulation

If one exogenises the attractivity development for all actor classes k $(k = 1, \ldots, m)$ in all regions except the sprawl region, the endogenous dynamics is described by the following m differential equations:

$$P_k \ge 0 \qquad\qquad\qquad\qquad (7.1)$$

$$\frac{dP_k}{dt} = A_k(P_1, \ldots, P_m) \qquad\qquad (7.2)$$

Again, in its qualitative formulation the right hand sides of the above equations are only defined by the signs of their partial derivatives

$$s_{kj} = sign\left(\frac{\partial A_k}{\partial P_j}\right) \qquad (7.3)$$

which denote how the attractivity for actor class k is influenced by the population of actor class j in the sprawl region.

References

Brainard, J. S. & Jones, A. P. *et al.* (2002) Modelling environmental equity: access to air quality in Birmingham, England. *Environment and Planning A* **34**(4, April): 569–758.

Brown, D. G. & Page, S. E. *et al.* (2004) Agent-based and analytical modeling to evaluate the effectiveness of greenbelts. *Environmental Modelling & Software* **19**(12): 1097–109.

Carmichael, F. & Ward, R. (2000) Youth unemployment and crime in the English regions and Wales. *Applied Economics* **32**(1): 559–71.

Carmichael, F. & Ward, R. (2001) Male unemployment and crime in England and Wales. *Economic Letters* **73**(2001): 111–15.

Colombino, U. & Locatelli, M. (2001) *Modelling Household Choices of Dwelling and Local Public Services*, pp. 1–12. Centre for Household, Income, Labour and Demographic Economics, Turin.

Couch, C. & Karecha, J. (2006) Controlling urban sprawl: some experiences from Liverpool, *Cities* **23**(25): 353–63.

Deal, B. & Schunk, D. (2004) Spatial dynamic modeling and urban land use transformation: a simulation approach to assessing the costs of urban sprawl. *Ecological Economics* **51**(2004): 79–95.

Eisenack K., Welsch, H. & Kropp, J. (2005) A qualitative dynamical modelling approach to capital accumulation in unregulated fisheries. *Journal for Economic Dynamics and Control* (DOI:10.1016/j.jedc.2005.08.004).

Epstein, J. M. (1999). Agent-based computational models And generative social science *Complexity* **4**(5): 41–60.

Fagan, J. & Freeman, R. B. (1999) Crime and work. *Crime and Justice* **25**: 225–90.

Filion, P. & Bunting, T. *et al.* (1999) The entrenchment of urban dispersion: residential preferences and location patterns in the dispersed city. *Urban Studies* **36**(8): 1317–47.

Hare, M. & Deadman, P. (2004) Further towards a taxonomy of agent-based simulation models in environmental managment. *Mathematics and Computers in Simulation* **64**(2004): 25–40.

Jefferies, T. & Swanson, N. (2004) Wohnformen der Angst. In P. Oswalt (ed.), *Schrumpfende Städte*, pp. 280–88. Hatje Cantz Verlag, Ostfildern-Ruit.

Kasper, B. (2003) Wohnen wie in den Ferien – *Lebensstile, Mobilität und Wohnen im suburbanen Raum.* Report des Fachgebiets Verkehrswesen und Verkehrsplanung Nr. 7. Universität Dortmund, Dortmund, Germany.

Kuipers, B. (1994) *Qualitative Reasoning: Modelling and Simulation with Incomplete Knowledge.* Cambridge and London, MIT Press.

Lagrange, H. (2003) Crime and socio-economic context. *Revue Francaise de Sociologie* **44**(5): 29–48.

Laumann, G., Fischer-Kowalski, M., Gallopin, G. C., van der Leeuw, S. E., Lüdeke, M. K. B., Veldkamp, A., Anderies, J. M. & Haxeltine, A. (2006). Modelling global change dynamics. Submitted to *Global Environmental Change.*

Lüdeke, M. K. B., Reckien, D. & Petschel-Held, G. (2004) Modellierung von Urban Sprawl am Beispiel von Leipzig. *In: Schrumpfung und Urban Sprawl – Analytische und Planerische Problemstellungen*, pp. 7–18. Hrsg.: Henning Nuissel, Dieter Rink. UFZ-Diskussionspapiere 3/2004, Leipzig.

Lüdeke, M. K. B. & Reusswig, F. (1999) *Das Dust Bowl-Syndrom in Deutschland. Machbarkeitsstudie über die Formulierung systemanalytischer Indikatoren für integrierte Strategien einer nachhaltigen Entwicklung in Deutschland am Beispiel der Probleme der Intensivlandwirtschaft.* PIK/HGF, Report.

Luna-Reyes, L. F. & Anderson, D. L. (2003) Collecting and analyzing qualitative data for system dynamics: methods and models. *System Dynamics Review* **19**(4): 271–96.

Meen, D. & Meen, G. (2003) Social behaviour as a basis for modelling the urban housing market: a review. *Urban Studies* **40**(5–6): 917–35.

Petschel-Held, G. & Lüdeke, M. K. B. (2001) Integration of case studies on global change by means of qualitative differential equations. *Integrated Assessment* **2**(3): 123–38.

Petschel-Held, G., Lüdeke, M. K. B. & Reckien, D. (2004) Reflection of the work within the 2nd stakeholder workshop URBS PANDENS in Leipzig, 4–6 November 2004: *Discussion of the strategies for managing urban sprawl in relation to the QUAM-model.* URBS PANDENS working paper, Potsdam Institute for Climate Impact Research, Potsdam 2004. http://www.pik-potsdam.de/urbs/projekt/st_ws_2.pdf.

Raphael, S. & R. Winter-Ebmer (2001) Identifying the effect of unemployment on crime. *Journal of Law and Economics* **44**(April 2001): 259–83.

Shank, G. (2001) It's logic in practice, my dear Watson: an imaginary memoir from beyond the grave [96 paragraphs]. Forum: *Qualitative Social Research* [On-line Journal] **2**(1). Available at: http://www.qualitative-research.net/fqs-texte/1-01/1-01shank-e.htm [Date of Access: April 20, 2005].

Sietz, D., Untied, B., Walkenhorst, O., Lüdeke, M. K. B., Mertins, G., Petschel-Held, G. & Schellnhuber, H. J. (2006) Smallholder agriculture in Northeast Brazil: Assessing heterogeneous human-environmental dynamics. *Regional Environmental Change* **6**: 132–146.

Snelgrove, A. G. & Michael, J. H. *et al.* (2004) Urban greening and criminal behavior: a geographic information system perspective. *Horttechnology* 2004: 48–51.

Tappeiner, G., Schrattenecker, I., Lechner, R., Walch, K., Stafler, G., Sutter, P., Oswald, P., Koblmüller, M. & Havel, M. (2001) *Wohnträume – Nutzerspezifische*

Qualitätskriterien für den Innovationsorientierten Wohnbau/Hauptbericht. Östereichisches Ökologie-Institut, Wien.

Taylor, I. & Jamieson, R. (1998) Fear of crime and fear of falling: english anxieties approaching the millennium. *European Journal of Sociology* **39**(1): 149–75.

Thill, J.-C. (1993) Mental maps and fuzziness in space preferences, *Professional Geographer* **45**(3): 264–76.

White, S. E. (1981) The influence of urban residential preferences on spatial behaviour. *Geographical Review* **71**(2): 176–87.

Witt, R. & Clarke, A. *et al.* (1998). Crime, earnings inequality and unemployment in England and Wales. *Applied Economics Letters* **5**(1998): 265–67.

8

Lines of Defence: Policies for the Control of Urban Sprawl

Henning Nuissl and Chris Couch

The aims of policy

Urban sprawl has been a matter of policy and planning ever since it was acknowledged as a particular pattern of spatial development. The desire to control the dynamics of urban sprawl was one of the earliest motivations for state intervention in spatial development.

In earlier chapters, great differences were identified in the causes of urban sprawl in different parts of Europe. Nevertheless, there is a remarkable consensus between different European countries and between different levels of government about the overall aims of policy with regard to urban sprawl. It is now almost universally acknowledged that sprawl causes ecological damage, increases the need to travel, makes service provision more expensive and has additional, though often difficult to measure, social and economic impacts (European Environment Agency, 2006). The need to control sprawl and develop more compact cities is widely accepted by governments across Europe.

As early as 1990 the European Commission Green Paper on the Urban Environment called for the avoidance of urban sprawl:

'The separation of land use and the subsequent development of extensive residential suburbs have in turn stimulated commuter traffic, which is at the heart of many of the environmental problems currently facing urban areas .... Strategies which emphasise mixed use and denser development are more likely to result in people living close to work places and the services they require for everyday life'   (CEC, 1990, p. 60).

In 1999, the European Spatial Development Perspective recommended that:

> 'Member States and regional authorities should pursue the concept of the "compact city" (the city of short distances) in order to have better control over further expansion of the cities. This includes, for example, minimisation of expansion within the framework of a careful locational and settlement policy, as in the suburbs and in many coastal regions. It will only be possible to stem the expansion of towns and cities within a regional context. For this purpose co-operation between the city and the surrounding countryside must be intensified and new forms of reconciling interests on a partnership basis must be found'   (CEC, 1999, para 84).

The report 'Towards an Urban Renaissance' (Urban Task Force, 1999), commissioned by the Office of the Deputy Prime Minister, was very influential in Britain and some other countries. The report wrote of 'regaining our urban tradition' and contrasted their perception of the current (UK) situation of dispersed urban areas, dispersed facilities, leapfrogging development and erosion of the countryside, with a vision for the future that would include compact urban areas, clear urban districts, distinct neighbourhoods, a clear urban edge and protection of the countryside (Urban Task Force, 1999, pp. 52–53). Figure 8.1 shows the theoretical model of urban form advocated by the Urban Task Force.

The mechanisms of policy

It is generally acknowledged that policies to control urban sprawl need two elements: the discouragement of sprawl and the encouragement of urban regeneration. Traditionally the discouragement of urban sprawl has relied heavily on the regulation of peripheral development through land use zoning and, in some cases, the virtual prohibition of peripheral development through instruments such as the British 'green belt'. The encouragement of urban regeneration is a newer idea in planning, but since the 1970s a variety of mechanisms have emerged, principally locationally-specific development subsidies or tax-breaks, relaxed planning controls and the creation of special agencies to promote the regeneration process.

Against this background, across Europe a variety of new policy responses to sprawl are now being developed. These include: the introduction of regional planning agencies which can apply a strategic vision and control the competing development demands of local authorities (e.g. Knieling, 2003); urban regeneration schemes aiming to re-establish the attractiveness of the inner urban areas (e.g. Haase *et al.*, 2005); changes in land taxation laws and new

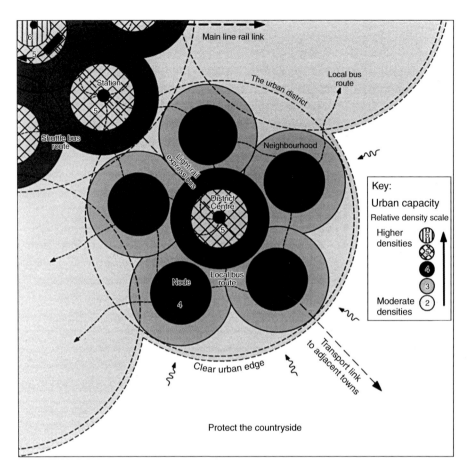

Figure 8.1 A form of urban development that minimises urban sprawl and maximises efficiency in the transport system. *After*: Urban Task Force, 1999.

legislation on public financing that reduce the dependence of municipalities on their local tax base (e.g. Bizer, 1998); road-pricing schemes to make road users aware of the true socio-environmental costs of commuting:

'because of the long term nature of transport planning we will seek political consensus in tackling congestion, including examining the potential of moving away from the current system of motoring taxation towards a national system of road pricing' (Alistair Darling, UK Secretary of State for Transport, 2005).

Given both the range of the debate over potential policy responses to urban sprawl as well as the variety of policy instruments actually put in place across different European countries, it seems appropriate to classify these

Table 8.1   Policy types with regard to the control or amelioration of urban sprawl

Policy type	Examples of policy
Regulation	Spatial (land use) planning
	Restrictions on specific land uses
	Density controls
	Phasing and sequential testing
Economic intervention: direct investment, taxation or subsidy	Provision of infrastructure: transport, utilities and social facilities
	Subsidies (especially towards urban regeneration)
	Development taxes
	Property taxes
	Trading in development permits
Institutional change, management and advocacy	Change of size and function of municipalities
	Special agencies (especially for urban regeneration)
	Advocacy, partnership and policy dialogues
	Information, targets and league tables

various strategies and instruments into groups that reflect the nature of the approach being used. A common approach to policy analysis is to divide public policies into those concerned with regulation, spending, taxation and subsidy, and advocacy. Looking at urban sprawl in the USA, Bengston *et al.* (2004) recently employed a three-part classification of policy types for the control of urban sprawl. Adopting and slightly modifying their approach, we also propose a three-part classification of existing and potential policy responses, although our definition of classes is slightly different, as shown in Table 8.1. Such a classification is, of course, based on ideal-types. In reality policy responses are frequently complex combinations of approaches. The important consideration in policy formulation is that any combination of approaches is integrated, complementary and mutually supportive towards achieving common aims.

Regulation

The main policy field in which we find a regulation approach to the problem of urban sprawl is spatial planning. Throughout Europe, the principal instrument of spatial planning consists of the preparation and legal enforcement of land use and development plans for particular areas. Being mainly introduced as a reaction to the need to organise and steer the rapid outward expansion of urban areas in the course of industrialisation, the very existence of planning laws and the consequent praxis of plan making and plan enforcing can be regarded as the earliest policy response to urban sprawl. This response, however, did not emerge simultaneously across the countries of Europe. Rather, in contrast to the cradle of modern urban planning in Western, Northern and Central Europe where the idea of development plans is well established and accepted, there are countries where the current planning legislation and planning practice is comparatively new and at times still a highly contested area of policy. In Greece, for instance, the largely unorganised development of urban areas was only perceived to be an urgent problem in the 1960s, and modern planning legislation was introduced only in the 1970s (cf. Chapter 4).

Obligatory and legally binding formal spatial planning takes place at different levels of governance. Municipalities typically provide a comprehensive land use plan which covers their entire territory, defining the location and nature of future development. In many countries these local plans are framed by plans prepared at regional levels, that is, by medium tiers of administration. Where such an intermediate level of spatial planning is lacking, there is sometimes a distinctive antagonism between the state on the one hand and the communes on the other. In addition to the comprehensive land use plans, in some countries, such as Germany (*Bebauungsplan*) and the Netherlands (*Bestemmingsplan*), detailed plans, specifying the physical form of future development, are prepared, especially for areas where some new development is to be expected. Other countries, such as the UK, rely mainly on the comprehensive land use plan and supplementary policy to control development, without the preparation of detailed building plans.

For example, as shown in Figure 8.2, in North West England the 'Regional Spatial Strategy' provides a strategic framework for the control of urban sprawl by encouraging the concentration of most development within what is known as the North West Metropolitan Area (essentially the two regional cities of Liverpool and Manchester and the area between). Local Development Frameworks (formerly County Structure Plans and Unitary Development Plans) provide elaboration and must conform to the regional strategy. Hence, the Unitary Development Plan for Wirral, as shown in Figure 8.3, includes both a detailed description and boundaries for the 'green belt' policy, where virtually all development is prohibited, as well as further policies that concentrate development within the built up, or urban, part of the Borough lying within the North West Metropolitan Area.

In principle, the system of formal spatial planning provides a mechanism that is capable of controlling urban sprawl. In particular, this system enables the authorities to implement the various models and ideals of spatial development and organisation of space, such as 'decentralized concentration'[1] or 'urban growth boundaries'[2]. But these are not really new ideas: as long ago as 1944, Abercrombie's Plan for Greater London successfully employed

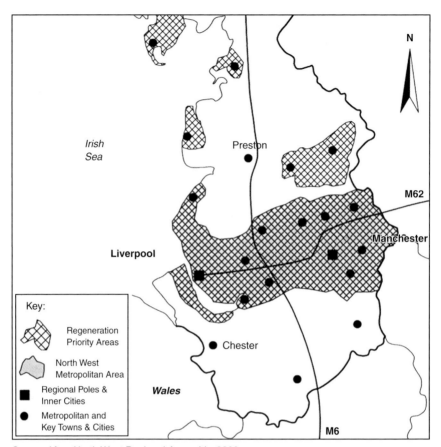

Source: After: North West Regional Assembly, 2003.

Figure 8.2   Regional spatial strategy for North West England (extract).

the idea of a boundary around the metropolis, surrounded by a 'green belt' and combined with the idea of 'decentralised concentration' – a series of 'new towns' were earmarked as decentralised growth centres beyond the green belt.

In some cases, the concern about urban sprawl has even led to the introduction of new elements into the planning legislation that improve the potential to constrain urban sprawl. In Germany, for instance, with the amendment of the federal planning law in 2004, municipalities were entitled to withdraw the right to build if it was not taken up within a specified period of time. This enables local authorities to cut back the amount of land zoned for urbanisation when revising their comprehensive development plans. Likewise, the EU recently called for an obligatory test for ecofriendliness of all spatial plans. However, the existence of powerful planning legislation does not guarantee

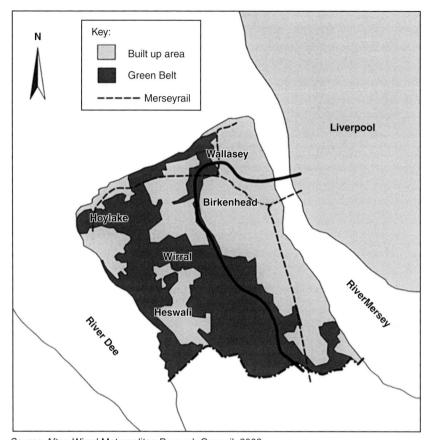

Source: After: Wirral Metropolitan Borough Council, 2003

Figure 8.3   Wirral 'green belt'.

its use. Frequently, the problem is not the availability of legal controls but their *usage* by different public agencies who may not always regard the control of urban sprawl as their top priority. Three types of planning agency are particularly important here.

In general, the core cities can be regarded as 'natural allies' of an anti-sprawl policy. Arguing that they also have to bear the lion's share of the costs of growth, they typically strive to 'keep' as much developmental activity as possible inside their own boundaries by both increasing the density in existing areas (infill development and the re-use of derelict land) as well as releasing new land. The latter is possible where the administrative area of core cities is big enough to comprise a good deal of undeveloped land (which is the case in many European countries but, notably, not in France). The development plan of the city of Vienna of 1994 provides a good example for this strategy by claiming that:

> ' "inner" district expansion will hardly suffice to meet the increased demand for housing, the required renewal of some densely built-up urban zones. Population growth and social change force planners to fall back on land outside the built-up areas to develop new neighbourhoods. However this form of "outer-district" urban expansion must not lead to a further spreading of car traffic and to urban sprawl and landscape spoliation in and around Vienna. (Vienna Urban Development Plan, 1995, p. 15, translated by A. Hamedinger, p. 13).

This typical strategy of core cities may be described as 'yes to urban growth but in an integrated manner'. However, in the pursuit of this strategy short-comings can sometimes be observed. Firstly, whereas the concentration of development on the core city does indeed limit sprawl if measured on the basis of administrative units, it is by no means synonymous with an actual prevention of urban sprawl (be it measured in terms of land use change or a declining density gradient), in that it does not guarantee that less green-field land is developed nor that the land developed is the most appropriate. It is not uncommon for the desire to accommodate growth within their own boundaries to tempt core cities to sacrifice green areas or to dedicate land to urban development that might be rather unsuited for this purpose.[3] Secondly, the densification and extension of the core city may prove detrimental to the environmental quality and the attractiveness of those areas where the development is taking place, by reducing the amount of green space, increasing the distance to the open countryside, or raising the price of housing. In the long run, this can actually increase the demand for residential sprawl. In their evidence to a British Government Committee, the Town and Country Planning Association (TCPA) stated that:

> 'At a time when the capacity of urban areas to accommodate future house-hold growth is much debated, and there is a strong countryside protection lobby, the TCPA believes that it is essential to keep in mind the need to avoid "town cramming". The protection and *creation* of urban green space is essential in this regard'   (Town and Country Planning Association, 1999).

In contrast to the core cities, suburban municipalities in many European countries are prone to promote urban sprawl. They tend to use their competence for spatial planning to attract investors seeking a suburban location, often neglecting the future social and environmental costs of such development. Many suburban municipalities are engaged in a fierce multi-directional competition for investment and inhabitants, both with the core city and with other suburban municipalities. The main reason for the notorious growth orientation of suburban municipalities is the reliance of local authorities on their own tax base to fund their spending (cf. Wassmer, 2002). In many European countries, as in the USA, a high proportion of local government income comes from the taxation of local inhabitants and firms. In countries where the local tax base is of less importance for the provisions of local authorities, such as the UK, suburban municipalities seem less prone to such pressures. Moreover, suburban opposition to further growth was one of the forces leading to the phase of higher density and multi-storey redevelopment in the UK that occurred in the 1950s and 1960s (Ward, 1994, pp. 161–65). The Stockholm suburb of Värmdö (see Chapter 6) provides a paradigmatic example of the growth orientation of suburban communes: Värmdo is permanently short of money and therefore almost desperate for taxpayers, developers and employers. The keyword for its politicians is not sprawl but growth – but the latter, one might add, is in this case, tantamount to the former.

Thus, although the planning law provides the local municipalities with the means to counter urban sprawl, the same is true of the opposite as well: such powers are often used to promote growth rather than contain development. By and large it is only saturated and prosperous municipalities which, often under the influence of protectionist local residents and environmental groups (so called 'Nimbys' – 'not-in-my-back-yard') (cf. Dear, 1992), plan their development around 'no growth' strategies (e.g. Nuissl, 1999). However, in a situation of strong pressure for land development this behaviour of suburban municipalities may even push urban sprawl further out to the countryside.

Since the orientation on growth is widespread among municipalities, the subregional or regional level of spatial planning can play a key role in controlling urban sprawl. Regional planning can impose a set of aims and provide a spatial framework for the operation of planning in lower tiers of government. Commenting on the situation in the USA, Bengston *et al.* suggest that:

> 'with regard to vertical coordination … growth management is most effective within a statewide context, so that each level of government coordinates their plan with other governmental levels. Horizontal coordination is needed to help avoid situations in which growth management policies in one jurisdiction undermine policies or create burdens in neighboring communitie'   (Bengston *et al.*, 2004, p. 289).

The situation is little different in Europe: regional spatial planning can bring both vertical as well as horizontal coordination to municipal spatial planning. However, also on the regional level of spatial planning, there are two potential obstacles to a positive response to urban sprawl. Firstly, the reluctance to implement anti-sprawl policies, which can be seen at the local level, may also occur at the regional level. In some federal states in Germany, for instance, the responsibility for regional planning lies with an association formed by the local authorities in a respective region. In these cases it is very difficult to fix goals for regional planning that require restrictions on the growth potential of particular municipalities. Secondly, regional agencies can have difficulties in developing strong anti-sprawl policies for the same reasons as municipal authorities: they too are in competition for development, not between municipalities but at a different scale – between regions.

So, regional agencies too are faced with conflicting and often mutually exclusive aims: economic development on the one hand and environmental protection on the other. In the Leipzig region, for instance, there are several examples of the Land government promoting 'sprawl', such as the development of a large car manufacturing plant, the building of a tangential motorway, or the extension of an exurban shopping mall (in the neighbouring federal state of Saxony Anhalt) which are all development projects that affect environmentally sensitive areas. Against this background, regional planning is frequently a rather contested field in which the rationality of professional planners has to be enforced against 'competing' rationalities. The German planning system thus illustrates that even if regional planning is vested with legal powers, it is often difficult to achieve its objectives. Indeed, in a study of Israel, Razin (1998) has questioned the likelihood of urban sprawl being successfully controlled by 'macro-scale regional plans' and planning regulations, and argues in favour of changes to both local tax regimes and local government structures as a more effective approach.

Planning systems also sometimes include regulations aimed at the control of specific types of development (rather than their location). These regulations can also have the effect of limiting urban sprawl. The legislation restricting large out-of-town (and entirely car-dependent) retail facilities in Norway, Finland, and now also most German Lander provides a good example for this kind of indirect spatial policy.

The phasing of development can be an important control ensuring the efficient use of existing or planned infrastructure, avoiding unnecessary and wasteful investment in underused facilities and preventing development from 'leap-frogging' beyond the urban boundary. In England, the 'sequential test' required by 'Planning Policy Statement (PPS) 6: Planning for Town Centres', is a good example. It requires local authorities to seek suitable brownfield areas first before preparing greenfield land for new retail or leisure development.

'The sequential approach to site selection should be applied to all development proposals for sites that are not in an existing centre ...In selecting sites, all options in the centre should be thoroughly assessed before less central sites are considered. The sequential approach requires that locations are considered in the following order:

- first, locations in appropriate existing centres where suitable sites or buildings for conversion are, or are likely to become, available within the development plan document period, taking account of an appropriate scale of development in relation to the role and function of the centre; and then
- edge-of-centre locations, with preference given to sites that are or will be well-connected to the centre; and then
- out-of-centre sites, with preference given to sites which are or will be well served by a choice of means of transport and which are close to the centre and have a high likelihood of forming links with the centre' (DCLG, 2005, PPS6, paras 3.14 and 2.44).

More recently the concept has been extended to planning for residential development (Planning Policy Guidance Note 3 [PPG3]). Thus, the Government expects local planning authorities not only to provide sufficient housing land to meet the needs of the community, but also to give priority to re-using previously developed land within urban areas, bringing empty homes back into use and converting existing buildings in preference to the development of greenfield sites. This strategy is particularly relevant with respect to those regions where urban sprawl occurs in combination with decline (see Chapter 5).

Economic intervention: direct investment, taxation or subsidy

There is considerable evidence that investment in public infrastructure (highways, public transport, utilities, etc.) stimulates development and therefore urban sprawl by altering the 'attractiveness-balance' in an urban region. The planning of transport infrastructure is one of the most controversial and contested policy fields when it comes to the discussion of how to change the incentives and disincentives for urban sprawl. For instance, radial rail lines for rapid transit, together with park and ride facilities, support a sprawling behaviour by enhancing the attractiveness of suburban locations as compared to the inner cities because suburban accessibility is being improved and the journey from suburbia to the urban core becomes more convenient. The building of new transit lines is often one of the biggest desires of suburbanites in Europe (such as the inhabitants of Värmdö, highlighted in Chapter 6), whereas, contrary to the USA, fears of a social downgrading of suburban areas connected by transit lines to the inner city (and thus the poorer population) seem to be less pronounced. On the other hand, investments into public transport clearly help shift modal split away from the motor vehicle and improve the inner-city environment by keeping car traffic out of town, and thus set an incentive for inner-city living.

An alternative to enacting restrictive regulations in order to steer urban development is the possibility to influence the behaviour of those actors who potentially bring about urban sprawl in such a way that 'sprawling' behaviour becomes less tempting to them:

> 'Instead of attempting to replace one urban spatial structure with another structure as master planning often does, we should seek to alter incentives and the dynamical path we are on'   (Atkinson & Oleson, 1996, p. 610).

Public policy can influence the behaviour of different actors with regard to urban sprawl in a number of ways. For example, it can use financial incentives and disincentives (positive subsidies or negative taxation) in order to make certain behaviour relatively cheaper or more expensive respectively. Likewise it can increase, or reduce respectively, the attractiveness of a particular location in relation to another location, for instance by regeneration programmes or similar strategies. This concerns both actors whose movement in space is actually tantamount to urban sprawl (households and firms moving to the urban periphery), as well as actors who encourage and promote urban sprawl (real estate companies and developers).

A number of studies have shown financial incentives can play a big part in determining patterns of urban development (Brueckner, 2000; Brueckner & Kim, 2003; Gihring, 1999). This can go as far as in Eastern Germany in the 1990s, when a sizeable wave of urban sprawl was an unintended side effect of development subsidies and tax breaks intended to stimulate the restructuring of the economic situation (cf. Nuissl & Rink, 2005). The growing concern about a sustainable use of natural resources, including land resources (i.e. greenfields) has recently prompted a debate about how incentives for an economical use of land can be encouraged by both changes in tax policies and the introduction of economic elements into the planning systems. In Germany, for instance, various economic instruments are currently being discussed, including a system of tradable permits to legally dedicate land for urban use (Schmalholz, 2004).

Public intervention in the land and housing market by tax policies, subsidies and political programmes often prove more stimulating to urban sprawl than to urban regeneration. Usually aiming at the promotion of economic devel-opment and an increase in housing supply, they rarely make any proposition on where the development should take place. The steering of development to specific urban locations is not usually an objective of urban tax policies. The impact of these policies in fostering urban sprawl is therefore normally assessed as a side effect of social or economic policies. It would be possible, however, to accord inner urban investments considerably higher subsidies than 'exurban' developments.

The same is true for other tax measures that aim at goals that have nothing to do with urban sprawl. The congestion charge is an example where the impact is not yet fully known (Vickerman, 2005). It could be argued that the effect of charging for car access to the city centre will discourage property investment in that location and shift property development pressures to suburban loca-tions beyond the charging zone, thereby exacerbating sprawl. On the other hand, it might equally well be argued that the improved environmental con-ditions in the city centre brought about by less traffic congestion will make the zone more attractive to property investors. At a time when there is much debate about the introduction of much more comprehensive urban road pric-ing in European cities this is an important question. A recent proposal by the British Department for Transport to fund some road pricing demonstration projects and evaluations appears to be concerned only with impacts inter-nal to the transport system, such as the effects on congestion or modal split (DfT, 2006). Road pricing could have a major and, as yet, unknown, impact on land use and urban sprawl. It is very important that these impacts are explored as part of any demonstration project before wide-scale road pricing is introduced across Europe.

Generally, it seems that a policy which really aims at the strengthening of disincentives for urban sprawl has to be much more decisive in support-ing inner-city (in comparison to suburban) developments than is the case today. In particular, this could mean that subsidies and tax-depreciations are allowed only for inner-urban projects. It would also be a disincentive to urban sprawl if investments in traffic infrastructures that facilitate urban-peripheral mobility were cut back. However, neither of these measures is likely to win much political or public support in the near future.

Institutional change, management and advocacy

Beside the 'hard' legal and economic instruments urban policy has at hand, there is a wide array of 'soft', informal instruments that are based on the idea of commitment to a common goal. Generally speaking, the soft instruments attempt to find cooperative solutions to particular problems arising from conflicting demands on land use, whereas the traditional, hard, instruments seek to solve these problems by exertion. Reflecting the experience that the 'blue-print-planning', operating mainly with legal tools, is often unable to achieve its goals due, in part, to its inability to handle the true complexity of the processes that produce urban space (Friedman, 1987; Healey, 1997), these soft instruments are advocated as an alternative means of progressing. In place of, or at least supplementing, legal instruments, can be found such mechanisms as round-table discussions, partnerships and workshops.

Attempts to manage urban development by means of soft instruments tend to involve public actors in the first instance. In particular the competition between territorial entities of one particular level is relevant here – competition between municipalities, regions or even national states respectively. As has been argued above, this competition is a major driver of urban sprawl. Accordingly, administrative fragmentation proves to be an important reason of urban sprawl, as it increases the number of competing 'actors' (cf. Carruthers, 2003). Warsaw may serve as an example here: the Polish capital consists of 11 districts all of which have the legal power of spatial planning; in addition there are around 50 further communes in the metropolitan area designing their own development plans. The competition between these authorities has recently led to a huge oversupply of land ready for development (cf. Nowakowski, 2002).

The size of local government units is also important in other ways – the bigger they are the less they are likely to be reliant on one particular investor or project, and less vulnerable to the influence of individual land owners with regard to planning policies and decisions. Therefore, in the UK, where municipalities have an average size of 127 000 inhabitants (which is far larger than those in any other European country), suburban localities are far less oriented towards a 'pro-growth strategy' than, for instance, in Germany, where the average municipality amounts to a population of just over 7 000. Against this background, various options of administrative reform of local authority have been discussed throughout Europe so as to mitigate municipal competition – for instance the merger, that is, incorporation, of local authorities, or the installation of regional boards, to name but a couple (Council of Europe, 1993).

Clearly, the commitment to a common idea on the future of a particular region can be conducive to a more sustainable, and less sprawling, development strategy of local governments in this region. Such commitment might be strengthened if the municipalities are involved in the process of designing a common plan, beyond the usual consultations – irrespective of whether this is a formal or informal plan. The involvement of local authorities in the process of regional planning, for example, can assist in mediating between the conflicting interests of neighbouring municipalities. It is precisely the promotion of such ideas or plans which is the major matter of concern for most agencies for regional development – be these agencies concerned with spatial planning; promoting economic development; or place-marketing.

It hardly comes as a surprise that soft instruments of spatial development work fairly well in situations that entail a win-win-structure: for instance, if the national government has decided to make a big infrastructure investment in a particular region and municipalities have to discuss and agree about details of the project. On the other hand, if a 'zero-sum-game' is to be played, it is much more difficult to convince the officials in charge to engage in some kind of cooperative action. This becomes manifest, for example, with most attempts to persuade, or push, municipalities to transfer some of their formal competences in spatial planning to the regional level, that is, a new supra-local authority.

In a situation where it is not only municipal borders that have to be bridged, it is particularly difficult to instigate cooperation between communes or to put up a 'regional umbrella' to integrate local planning. However, the coordination of local development strategies and spatial plans is also nec- essary where urban agglomerations stretch across national borders (as is the case, for instance, with the agglomerations of Basel/Mulhouse/Lörrach, Liege/Aachen/Maastricht or Lille/Tournai) or touch several federal states (as is the case with Hamburg, Berlin, Bremen and Frankfurt/Rhein-Main in Germany, or Vienna in Austria). In many of these cases several administra- tive and legal solutions to the problem of coordination have been devised in the past decades. These solutions are sometimes rather sophisticated and have the harmonisation of spatial development as one of their major objectives. As a rule, the cross-border coordination of local development policy requires considerable effort (and time) by public authorities, but its success in managing spatial development and urban sprawl is usually obvious.[4]

Another soft instrument of spatial planning, which is persuasive rather than restrictive, is the provision of information for those actors whose decisions actually determine the pattern of spatial development. This con- cerns both public and private (as well as individual and collective) actors. With regard to the public actors, the monitoring of spatial development and land use change has long been discussed as a means to promote sus- tainable development. The focal point of this discussion is the assumption that an enhanced knowledge on the environmental and social drawbacks of urban sprawl may lead policy makers to the conclusion that they should call for more efficient forms of spatial development. Decision makers should therefore be provided with as much knowledge about the consequences of their actions as possible, so as to enable them to reasonably judge development proposals and to act in a responsible way. (As in the retail sector, where supermarkets now list the salt and fat content of food, not to coerce consumers into particular purchasing patterns but to provide information upon which a more informed choice can be made). Moreover, such knowledge can serve as an additional source of legitimacy for the efforts of those – regional or governmental – authorities who strive for a containment of urban sprawl. Accordingly, various 'planning information instruments' have been developed that aim at continuously providing information on spatial developments for decision makers, and sometimes also the public (cf. Siedentop, 1999). For example, in the UK, the government has established a 'Targets and League Table' culture, at the heart of which is the measurement and publication of a range of local authority performance indicators.

The provision of performance-based league tables has had a significant effect in a number of fields of UK public policy, particularly in the health and education sectors. However, they are also being used in the planning field. One of the UK Government's key indicators for the reduction of urban sprawl is the proportion of new dwellings built on previously developed (i.e. brownfield) land. The target is to achieve 60%. As might be expected, in areas with a substantial legacy of industrial change and dereliction the proportion is high (e.g. averaging 88% in Merseyside between 2001 and 2004) whereas in more rural areas the proportion is typically low (e.g. only 42% in Cumbria). This becomes an interesting policy tool where two apparently similar areas achieve two very different levels of performance. For example, in the 'home counties' west of London, the figure achieved in the former county of Berkshire was 79%, but in adjoining Buckinghamshire the figure was only 38% (Land Use Change Statistics for England, 2004, Table A2). Whilst there may be very good reasons for differences in the level of performance between these two counties, the publication of such an indicator does direct the eye of policy makers to areas of concern. In other words, the use of these performance indicators and league-tables operates as a form of 'mixed-scanning' allowing Government to maintain a relatively low-cost overview on the control of urban sprawl, but also directing higher cost investigations to specific instruments or areas where performance appears to be poor.

Today, we find a continuous monitoring of land use changes, facilitated by the recent progress in the interpretation of satellite data, almost everywhere in Europe. These monitoring efforts, however, are rather different in terms of explanatory character. They provide a description of how the land use or vegetation has changed over time – which is quite useful information that helps to raise the awareness of the problems of sprawl. On the other hand, monitoring systems which provide information on both environmental and social consequences of spatial developments are still comparatively rare. Here, we find a field for future research that should eventually help to design more carefully targeted policy responses to urban sprawl.

Apart from providing decision support to professionals, the publication of data from land use monitoring systems also facilitates public awareness and participation in the planning process. Whilst much of the decision making surrounding urban sprawl can be attributed to the calculation of economic costs and benefits by individual firms and households with little concern for wider socio-environmental matters, it is interesting to speculate on the extent to which behaviour might be changed through 'promoting a non-sprawl culture…through education and dissemination' and by 'advertising and marketing techniques' (Kolyvas, 2003, p. 19), similar to previous campaigns against, for example, smoking in public places, or in support of the notion of 'recycling'.

Conclusions

'Planning culture' and the control of urban sprawl

The brief overview of policy responses to urban sprawl in Europe has shown that there exists a wide range of strategies and instruments that are employed in order to get sprawl under control. It could also illustrate that, seen from a somewhat broader perspective, the strategies and instruments on urban sprawl that are in use in different countries share many basic features – however different they may be in detail, in particular due to the peculiarities of the respective legal system. But the existence of a similar set of policy strategies and instruments in different contexts is by no means tantamount to their practical relevance also being similar in these contexts. Rather, many of these strategies and instruments are often either not implemented at all or do not work well in the particular situation. Furthermore, it is difficult to come to any overall assessment of the utility of these instruments. To use an example from the USA for this problem: when comparing federal states with and without growth management programmes, Nelson (1999) and Kline (2000) arrive at completely contrary conclusions as to the success of these programmes.

On the one hand, the complexity of processes in which these policy instruments are to intervene makes it difficult to assess their effectiveness. On the other hand, however, this difficulty is also due to the latent power of culture since the differences between national planning systems stem from both 'variations in national legal and constitutional structures and administrative and professional cultures' (Healey & Williams, 1993, p. 701). In this vein, Newman and Thornley (1996) distinguish five (ideal types of) administrative cultures in Europe, which they say are the result of different political histories: British, Germanic (Central European), Napoleonic (Western and Southern European), Scandinavian and, as a kind of residual category, Eastern European administrative cultures, with the first being the most liberal one and the latter the most state-oriented one.[5] This is, of course, still a somewhat bold characterisation but it hints at two important aspects: firstly, we have to acknowledge that the 'European way' to cope with urban sprawl in fact seems to be more heterogeneous than the – manageable – differences of policy instruments may indicate. Secondly, we have to take into account not only the legal framework in which policy has to respond to urban sprawl; instead the 'soft' context of informal institutions and cultural habits, which is deeply rooted in a particular region's political history, is also important. The examples of two European capital cities may serve as an illustration for this argument:

> 'The relationship between government and civil society has always been a mixture of benevolence and co-optation leading to a lack of participatory culture in Vienna'   (Novy *et al.*, 2001).

The political culture described in this quote has probably determined the spatial development of Austria's capital city much more than the availability or non-availability of certain policy and planning instruments. The Greek capital then gives an even clearer example of the necessity to pay attention to the issue of planning culture:

> 'Plans are drafted, but shelved. The Structure Plan of Athens has been published in the Government Gazette ..., but it is often violated or ignored by the government itself. Many interventions with a spatial impact remain uncoordinated: legislation on the building code, rent levels, land "legalization", urban expansion and industrial decentralization. Administrative and bureaucratic inertia, multi-authority interference, non-devolution of government, clientelist politics, pressures by landowners and the low ecological consciousness of the population are major barriers. ...This amounts to what is called disjointed incrementalism'   (Leontidou, 1996, p. 265).

The 'disjointed incrementalism', which was described in the debates of planning theory, becomes tangible here as an outcome of the political and administrative culture in which planning is taking place rather than a general attitude of urban policymakers or planners towards their business. Or, to take another example of the importance of the cultural framework, the centralised and top-down nature of power-relations in governance of urban areas in the UK allows central government to set and enforce targets upon lower tier levels of government. In other countries, particularly those with federal structures, such top-down approaches may be unfeasible, unwanted or unenforceable.

The theoretical implications that become visible when the policy responses to urban sprawl are interpreted against the cultural background in which they occur cannot be explored in depth here. However, in order to wind up this brief overview of policy responses to urban sprawl, at least a few hints shall be given as to how the 'different types' of urban sprawl discussed in this book are both an outcome but, vice versa, also a determinant of the planning culture into which they are embedded.

The planning vacuum in the context of post-socialist transformation

A major lesson of post-socialist transformation in Central and Eastern Europe has been that the rapid evolution of formal institutions did not bring about the intended results immediately. Rather the implementation of new laws was obstructed by the inexperience of authorities and, at least to some degree, the lasting influence of informal institutions that had been shaped in former decades. In terms of spatial planning this resulted in a kind of planning vacuum in the first half of the 1990s (e.g. Nuissl, 1999) which was aggravated by the fact that urban planning was neglected in the 1990s because of the priority being placed on macro-economic reforms, economic regeneration and the connotations of such planning with the former socialist regime (see Chapter 5). In this situation it was often easy to get building permits that did not comply with the respective development plans (cf. Gutry-Korycka, 2005). Only at the end of 1990s did the understanding spread again, that spatial development needed regulation and control.

The unenforceability of planning in contexts of unprecedented growth

Particularly in Southern Europe, many major cities, such as Rome, Madrid and Athens, experienced a period of rapid development and growth in the second half of the twentieth century. The urban sprawl that occurred there was hardly steered by policy interventions – not least because much of this development did not even seek planning permission: it was illegal but the legal systems were not enforced. Land was developed despite existing development plans forbidding urban use, and much of what was built, mostly by people who migrated from the rural parts of the respective countries (and in the case of Greece from Asia Minor), was legalised only much later (cf. Kreibich *et al.*, 1993).[6] The planning culture that developed in this situation hardly drew on the policy instruments discussed above, but was characterised by political processes that took place beyond the established realms of public decision making (cf. Chapter 4).

Compliant urban planning in contexts of decline

As has been argued in a previous chapter of this book (see Chapter 5), concerning the chances to control urban sprawl, the situation in declining city regions is rather ambiguous. On the one hand there is less pressure for the development of land than in thriving regions. On the other hand, in a context of decline the political pressure to welcome (almost) every investor and every kind of development, with limited regard for environmental impacts, is particularly high. Against this background, it is less likely that the aspiration to control urban sprawl will be enforced as strongly in a region experiencing decline as in a more prosperous region.

Lessons learned

Looking to the future, it seems that spatial planning systems and the regulation of land use are being strengthened across most of the European Union, and supported by stronger requirements for the environmental impact of development to be considered before development plans are drawn up or before planning permission is given. These changes are likely to slow down the rate of sprawling in most European countries. On the other hand, some regions, such as South-East England, are under extreme growth pressures and it is difficult to see how such pressures can be accommodated entirely within existing urban boundaries without distorting land use patterns within existing settlements and raising densities to the point where such changes become socio-environmentally and politically unacceptable. This raises questions about urban density and form (cf. Williams *et al.*, 2000). What are the maximum acceptable densities and what urban form is acceptable? Here the answers are likely to be culturally and locationally specific. In England and Scandinavia there is a strong tradition of living in houses which imposes powerful limits on the highest acceptable residential densities. Across much of Central and Southern Europe the tenement block is a widely accepted urban form. So here, a higher density and a different form of housing are possible. In the inner cities of Paris, Madrid or Athens even greater densities and mixtures of uses seem to be tolerated.

However, in general, it seems likely that there has to be a trade-off. In regions of population and economic growth there will be some sprawl, but it needs to be controlled, managed and steered to the most acceptable locations. Here, the British notion of sequential testing may provide a model for other countries, providing a mechanism for the orderly phasing and location of urban development. Clearly, if the sequencing of development is to be politically and socially acceptable it has to be accompanied by subsidies and programmes of urban regeneration and revalorisation that make the existing urban area at least as attractive as the periphery as a place in which to invest, develop, produce, live and work, from the perspectives of economic return, social satisfaction and environmental quality.

A more difficult question is: how to control the sort of urban sprawl that occurs through the acquisition and conversion of second homes? Here, land use planning seems less helpful, since the use of buildings may not change. Regulations preventing or controlling second home ownership are difficult to devise and enforce, both for moral philosophical and practical political reasons. In these circumstances policy makers are more likely to look to the tax system to influence consumer behaviour.

The desire to maximise income derived from local taxes appears to be one of the key drivers of competition between core cities and the periphery and between peripheral districts. Changes to systems of local government finance may have an important role to play in reducing the need to compete for development, and therefore take some pressure off urban sprawl. Similarly, changes to the size and competence of local authorities may also have benefits in broadening the local tax base, reducing dependence on a small number of developments, and increasing the capacity of local authorities to make and enforce effective planning policies. However, such major structural changes are complex and whilst strengthening planning policy may have costs, such as the loss of local democracy and control, which are not thought desirable.

The provision of infrastructure ahead of development is another field of policy where the likely impact on development pressures must be predicted and accommodated in policy.

Finally, many would argue that there is much to be gained through the use of soft policy instruments, informing and educating policy makers, developers and households in ways that shift expectations and desires and change the cultural view of town and country.

The control of urban sprawl is important because sprawl leads to the unnecessary loss of open land and natural resources and causes ecological damage. It generates unnecessary traffic, wastes energy and leads to atmospheric pollution that contributes to global warming. It imposes economic costs on local authorities as inner-urban services and amenities lie underused whilst new provision has to be made in the suburbs. Sprawl appears to exacerbate spatial social segregation, reduces the mobility of non-car-owning households and makes access to work and leisure facilities more difficult. Through combinations of the policies outlined above – stronger land use planning; powerful subsidies to urban regeneration; changes to systems of local taxation and administration; and careful planning of infrastructure – urban sprawl can be contained and European cities can move towards an urban renaissance.

Notes

1   The planning ideal of 'decentralised concentration', which has been quite influential in regional planning in Germany in the 1990s, has two distinct notions. Firstly, it may indicate that a particular spatial organisation of growth is striven for – with growth mainly taking place in selected locations on the outer periphery of an urban region. Secondly, it may outline a certain policy of regional development, which, committed to the goal of 'equality of living conditions', aims to steer developmental activities into the urban centres of the hinterland so as to ignite economic development there. It is, of course, the first notion which is relevant in terms of urban sprawl management.

2   In Europe, the concept of urban growth boundaries, which is quite famous in the US, is of minor importance. This is mainly due to the fact that on this more densely populated continent a sharp distinction between urban and rural areas is often hardly possible. Inside–outside-dichotomies, however, are quite common in European planning legislations. We find the distinction between 'inside' and 'outside' of urban areas in almost all national planning laws of the continent. In particular, in southern Europe, this has also caused problems in the past when informal settlements emerged on 'outside urban area' land, especially around the big capital cities such as Athens, Rome or Madrid. The inhabitants of these areas usually had to engage in long political struggles in order to get their respective communities officially acknowledged and, consequently, provided with the necessary infrastructure (examples in Kreibich *et al.*, 1993).

3   For instance, after the great flood in 2002, the German city of Dresden had to give up a recently developed suburban residential area on its territory aside the river Elbe because it was built in a floodplain.

4 The federal states of Berlin and Brandenburg in Germany are probably most advanced in the cross-border management of spatial development (including the management of urban sprawl). Both '*Laender*' together have established a planning authority, vested with the legal competences originally accorded to the federal states and staffed by both states.

5 The category of an Eastern European administrative culture is, however, not very convincing. Whereas it may have been reasonable until recently, due to the common socialist legacy in the countries subsumed to this category, with the ongoing transformation process the trajectories, and consequently also the administrative cultures, of these countries have become quite different (see Chapter 5).

6 Similar processes of uncoordinated rural–urban migration could be observed in some socialist countries in Central and Eastern Europe in the 1970s and 1980s – showing that, though socialist planning systems used to be a kind of stronghold of comprehensive planning, they often also defined a sphere of 'wishful thinking' for the realisation of which there was hardly any hope (cf. Grochowski, 2005, p. 38).

References

Atkinson, G. & Oleson, T. (1996) Urban sprawl as a path dependent process. *Journal of Economic Issues* **30**(2): 609–15.

Bengston, D. N., Fletcher, J. O. & Nelson, K. C. (2004) Public policies for managing urban growth and protecting open space: policy instruments and lessons learned in the United States. *Landscape and Urban Planning* **69**(2–3): 271–86.

Bizer, K. *et al.* (1998) *Mögliche Maßnahmen, Instrumente und Wirkungen einer Steuerung der Verkehrs- und Siedlungsflächennutzung.* Berlin/Heidelberg/New York: Springer.

Brueckner, J. K. (2000) Urban sprawl: diagnosis and remedies. *International Regional Science Review* **23**(2): 160–71.

Brueckner, J. K. & Kim, H. A. (2003) Urban sprawl and the property tax. *International Tax and Public Finance* **10**(1): 5–23.

Carruthers, J. I. (2003) Growth at the fringe: The influence of political fragmentation in United States metropolitan areas. *Regional Science* **82**(4): 475–99.

CEC (1990) *Green Paper on the Urban Environment.* Commission for the European Communities, Brussels.

CEC (1999) *European Spatial Development Perspective.* Commission for the European Communities, Brussels.

Council of Europe (1993) Major cities and their peripheries: Co-operation and co-ordinated management. Local and regional authorities in Europe 51, Council of Europe Press, Strasbourg.

DCLG (2005) *Planning Policy Statement 6: Planning for Town Centres.* The Stationary Office, London.

Dear, Michael (1992) Understanding and overcoming the nimby-syndrome. *Journal of the American Planning Association* **58**(3): 288–300.

DfT (2006) *Invitation for Road Pricing Demonstrations and Supporting Research.* Department for Transport, London. Available at http://www.dft.gov.uk/pgr/roads/ roadpricing/pin/invitationsforroadpricingdem4016

Downs, A. (1999) Some realities about sprawl and urban decline. *Housing Policy Debate* **10**(4): 955–74.

European Environment Agency (ed.) (2006) *Urban sprawl in Europe. The ignored challenge.* EEA report No. 10/2006, European Environment Agency, Copenhagen.

Friedman, J. (1987) *Planning in the Public Domain. From Knowledge to Action.* Princeton University Press, Princeton (NJ).

Gihring, T. A. (1999) Incentive property taxation – a potential tool for urban growth management. *Journal of the American Planning Association* **65**(1): 62–79.

Grochowski, M. (2005) Spatial development in the central planned economy. In: M. Gutry-Korycka (ed.), *Urban Sprawl: Warsaw Agglomeration.* Warsaw University Press, Warsaw.

Gutry-Korycka, M (ed.) (2005) *Urban Sprawl: Warsaw Agglomeration.* Warsaw University Press, Warsaw.

Haase, A., Kabisch, S. & Steinführer, A. (2005) Reurbanisation of inner-city areas in European cities. Scrutinizing a concept of urban development with reference to demographic and household change. In: I. Sagan & D. Smith (eds), *Society, Economy, Environment – Towards The Sustainable City*, pp. 75–91. Bogucki Wydawnictwo Naukowe, Gdansk/Poznan.

Healey, P. (1997) *Collaborative Planning. Shaping Places in Fragmented Societies.* Macmillan, London.

Healey, P. & Williams, R. (1993) European urban planning systems: diversity and convergence. *Urban Studies* **30**(4/5): 701–20.

Kline, J. D. (2000) Comparing states with and without growth management analysis based on indicators with policy implications comment. *Land Use Policy* **17**(4): 349–55.

Knieling, J. (2003) Kooperative Regionalplanung und Regional Governance: Praxisbeispiele, Theoriebezüge und Perspektiven. Informationen zur Raumentwicklung **8**(9): 463–478.

Kolyvas, A. (2003) *URBS PANDENS. Analysis of Present Policy Structures and Concepts.* Draft Version, ICLEI – International Council of Local Environmental Initiatives, European Secretariat, Freiburg.

Kreibich, V., Krella, B., von Petz, U. & Potz, P. (eds) (1993) *Rom – Madrid – Athen. Die Neue Rolle der Städtischen Peripherie.* Universität Dortmund, Institut für Raumplanung (IRPUD), Dortmund.

Leontidou, L. (1996) Athens: inter-subjective facets of urban performance. In: C. Jensen-Butler, A. Shakhar & J. van den Weesep (eds), *European Cities in Competition*, pp. 244–73. Avebury, Aldershot.

Matthiesen, U. & Nuissl, H. (2002) Phasen der Suburbanisierung seit 1989: Stichpunkte zum Berlin-Brandenburgischen Verflechtungsprozess. In: U. Matthiesen (ed.), *An den Rändern der deutschen Hauptstadt: Suburbanisierungsprozesse, Milieubildungen und biographische Muster in der Metropolregion Berlin-Brandenburg*, pp. 79–90. Leske + Budrich, Leverkusen-Opladen.

Municipal Administration of the City of Vienna, Department of Urban Planning (1995) *The Vienna Urban Development Plan*, Vienna.

Nelson, A. C. (1999) Comparing states with and without growth management – Analysis based on indicators with policy implications. *Land Use Policy* **16**(2): 121–27.

Newman, P. & Thornley, A. (1996) *Planning in Europe*. Routledge, London.

Novy, A., Hamedinger, A., Redak, V. & Jäger, J. (2001) The end of red Vienna: recent ruptures and continuities in urban governance. *European Urban and Regional Studies* **8**(2): 131–44.

Nowakowski, M. (2002) *Rozpraszanie Zabudowy Metropolii Warszawskiej (Dispersion of the Built-up Areas of the Metropolitan Area of Warsaw)*, pp. 38–41. Miasto za miastem – Instytut na rzecz Ekorozwoju, Warsaw.

Nuissl, H. (1999) Suburbanisierung und kommunale Entwicklungsstrategien an den Rändern der Hauptstadt. *Archiv für Kommunalwissenschaften* **38**(2): 237–58.

Nuissl, H. & Rink, D. (2005) The 'production' of urban sprawl in eastern Germany as a phenomenon of post-socialist transformation. *Cities* **22**(2): pp. 123–34.

NWRA (2006) *The North West Plan*. Wigan, North West Regional Assembly. Available at: http://www.nwra.gov.uk/downloads/documents/dec_06/nwra_1165321319_Submitted_Draft_Regional_Spati.pdf

Office of the Deputy Prime Minister (2005) *Land Use Change Statistics for England (20)*. National Statistics, London.

Razin, E. (1998) Policies to control urban sprawl: planning regulations or changes in the rules of the game? *Urban Studies* **35**(2): 321–40.

Rivolin, U. J. & Faludi, A. (2005) The hidden face of European spatial planning: innovations in governance. *European Planning Studies* **13**(2): 195–15.

Schmalholz, M. (2004) *Steuerung der Flächeninanspruchnahme: Defizite des Umwelt- und Planungsrechts sowie alternative Ansätze zur Reduzierung des Flächenverbrauchs durch Siedlung und Verkehr*. phD thesis, University of Hamburg, Books on Demand Ltd, Norderstedt.

Siedentop, S. (1999) Informationsinstrumente in der Raumordnung. In: A. Bergmann, K. Einig & G. Hutter (eds), *Siedlungspolitik auf neuen Wegen – Steuerungsinstrumente für eine ressourcenschonende Flächennutzung*, pp. 159–80. Edition Sigma, Berlin.

Town and Country Planning Association (1999) *Memorandum to the House of Commons Select Committee on Environment, Transport and Regional Affairs*. Available at: http://www.publications.parliament.uk/pa/cm199899/cmselect/cmenvtra/477/477mem12.htm

Urban Task Force (1999) *Towards an Urban Renaissance: Final Report of the Urban Task Force*. Spon, London.

Vickerman, R. (2005) Evaluating the wider economic impacts of congestion charging schemes: the limitations of conventional modelling approaches. Paper to the *45th ERSA Congress*, Amsterdam.

Ward, S. V. (1994) *Planning and Urban Change*. Paul Chapman Publishing, London.

Wassmer, R. W. (2002) Fiscalisation of land use, urban growth boundaries and non-central retail sprawl in the western united states. *Urban Studies* **39**(8): 1307–27.

Williams, K., Burton, E. & Jenks, M. (eds) (2000) *Achieving Sustainable Urban Form*. E & FN Spon, London.

Wirral Metropolitan Borough Council (2000) *Wirral Unitary Development Plan*. Available at: http://www.wirral.gov.uk/udp/

9

Urban Sprawl and Hybrid Cityscapes in Europe: Comparisons, Theory Construction and Conclusions

Lila Leontidou and Chris Couch

This chapter summarises our findings about urban sprawl and peri-urban hybrid landscapes around Europe. Beyond urbanism and suburbanism, there is a third concept, a phenomenon happening on the outskirts, the city edges, the metropolitan periphery, expanding the urban frontier, opening questions of city limits. 'Urban sprawl' is a phenomenon and a process affecting different cities in a different manner according to this research project. The rural-urban fringe, or the 'rurban fringe' as Firey (1946) calls it, has aroused interest since the late 1940s, especially in the USA, as we already noted in the Introduction. However, though sprawl used to be an American research topic, a revival of interest in Europe indicates the new dynamics of sprawl here (Phelps *et al.*, 2006; Bruegman, 2005; Hoggart, 2005; Richardson, 2004). Urban sprawl was recently renewed as a field of study with new concepts, such as the 'exurbs', 'edge cities' (Garreau, 1991) and, in recognition of its non-residential uses, 'silicon landscapes' (Kling *et al.*, 1995).

In our comparative project, we found that there is nothing at all universal about urban sprawl. Diverse patterns in Europe have been discovered. In this chapter we will contrast and compare cities from the four corners of Europe – South and North, East and West – also informed from our analysis of the contrast between Europe and the USA in the Introduction (cf. also Bruegman, 2005), as well as from the Third World experiences found in literature (McGregor *et al.*, 2006). Our findings about hybrid landscapes of diverse forms are explained by economic forces as well by cultures of anti-urbanism vs cultures of urbanism in Europe.

'Urban', 'suburban', 'post-suburban', and their in-between spaces

Urbanism and suburbanism as ways of life have been at the forefront of geographical and sociological enquiry at least until the 1970s. They figured as a couplet despite their antithesis. Urbanism nurtured generalisations about the anonymity of the urbanite since Wirth (1938) portrayed urban societies as sharing a loss of community, family and networks, echoing Toennies' *Gemeinschaft/Gesellschaft* (Leontidou, 2005); or since Alonso (1964) whose ambition was to present a universal land use model which did not work, after all, in Mediterranean cities, or continental Europe for that matter. Generalisations have not ceased today, with essentialist claims that 'the city' can be defined, and its recent definitions stressing its role in maintaining 'local-global connectivity' (Amin & Thrift, 2003, p. 27, 135).

As for suburbanism, according to Gans (1968) a specific way of life, it has been caricatured in fiction and film with unforgettable cinematographic suburbanites until very recently, with films like *Edward Scissorhands* or *The Witch*. Jacobs (1961) sharply contrasted the boredom of suburbanisation with the vitality of inner-city neighbourhoods, which she depicted in a manner very different from Wirth's anonymity. She was re-discovered by postmodernists as the first ideologue of the lively mixture of uses and cultures in a postmodern urban mosaic (Harvey, 1989; Leontidou, 1993). Jacobs' view of the suburb was as dismissive as Mumford's (1966 edn, p. 553) who also considered it as a unified cultural landscape with uniform inhabitants, as follows:

> 'a multitude of uniform, unidentifiable houses, lined up inflexibly, at uniform distances, on uniform roads, in a treeless communal waste, inhabited by people of the same class, the same income, the same age group, witnessing the same television performances, eating the same tasteless prefabricated foods, from the same freezers, conforming in every outward and inward respect to a common mould, manufactured in the central metropolis. Thus the ultimate effect of the suburban escape in our time is, ironically, a low-grade uniform environment from which escape is impossible.'

Even if this is only an American caricature, there is indeed something too uniform about the middle-class suburb, inhabited by families with young children; while elite suburbs with their diverse architectural styles designed by celebrities do not escape from the modalities of a certain way of life with car dependency, white appliances, commuting and the like.

Works on post-suburbia followed, referring to the *exopolis* (Soja, 2000, p. 250), the exurbs or the edge city (Garreau, 1991). In this book, too, we have gone beyond suburbia and focused on space in-between urban and rural. In the peri-urban landscapes examined, we discovered the opposite of uniformity. There is a great diversity in European urban sprawl, both among cities, and in intra-urban landscapes beyond suburbia, on the urban periphery and sprawling fringes around cities. In every city researched, we have encountered diverse mosaics of activities on the 'rurban fringe' and we have found 'nature in fragments' among other types of land use (Johnson & Klemens 2005; Phelps *et al.*, 2006). Here, uniformity has not been stressed: on the contrary, hybrid landscapes are the rule, that is, landscapes undergoing mutations, but to a larger or lesser extent keeping the characteristics of previous states of being. Hybridity is usually discussed through the merging of nature and culture (Whatmore, 2002), extended to the rural within the urban, the agricultural within the industrial, so forth. Such mosaics of activities and land use patchworks are frequent in most peri-urban landscapes and make them different from cityscapes, suburbs and satellite towns. They are spaces in-between suburbs and villages beyond the metropolitan regions.

Because of the great diversity in urban material cultures in space and time, we have to build arguments gradually in order to understand and contrast our findings on models of urban sprawl across Europe. We will start with a macroscopic analysis of our findings on causes and consequences of urban sprawl in Europe, continue with a summary of city-by-city findings, and end up with a systematisation and peripheralisation of urban types in Europe. In the conclusion we will show that, besides the important differences between Europe and the USA in urban sprawl already pointed out in Part I of this book, there are intra-European variations too.

Deconstructing the dualism of causes/consequences of urban sprawl

At the beginning of the project we distinguished between causes and consequences of urban sprawl, but as the research process continued this dualism was deconstructed. Urban sprawl is caused by a complex set of inter-related forces. These can be identified at three levels of analysis: macro, meso and micro. At the macro-level are the political-economic paradigms and trends that shape the nature of our urban societies: the nature of capitalism, political ideologies, economic globalisation, so forth. The meso-level is where much of the discourse about the causes of urban sprawl can be found: demographic change and migration waves; local political structures and policies; local geographical, economic and social circumstances. Finally, the micro-level

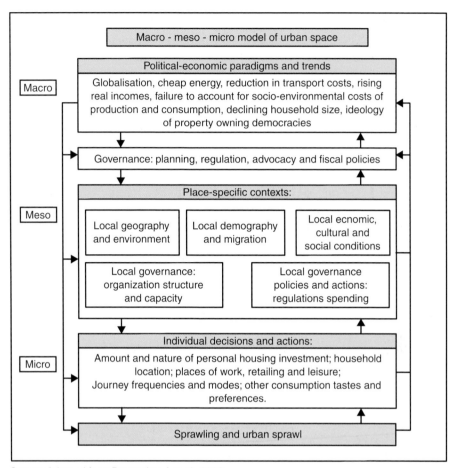

Source: Adapted from Dangschat J *et al.*, 2003.

Figure 9.1   A multi-level theory of urban sprawl.

captures the decisions of individual actors in the urban system: households, firms and other organisations – individual decisions about the location of housing and workplaces; use of services and amenities; choices of transport mode and so forth. Figure 9.1 summarises this approach to the analysis of the causes of urban sprawl.

Macro-level causes

At the highest level it is possible to see how macro-economic and social trends pressurise cities to develop in certain ways. The globalisation of economic activity, accompanied by sharp reductions in long-distance transport costs, has led to increasing competition between cities for economic activity.

On the one hand this has led to urban dereliction in uncompetitive locations, whilst on the other hand it has given birth to the entrepreneurial city, providing the sort of development that capital requires, frequently at or beyond the existing urban periphery – such as office parks or sports infrastructure.

The failure of macro-economic accounting systems to take account of the social and environmental costs of development and transport are another macro-level feature that allows sprawl to take place without consideration of the full costs of such decisions. The promotion of the notion of a 'property-owning democracy' has been favoured by many governments, especially in Western Europe. This notion leads on to demands for the construction of individual private dwellings, frequently in the form of low density peripheral estates. Such housing can be contrasted with the more 'collective' housing built by private landlords or the state in earlier generations under 'laissez-faire' or 'welfare' models of political economy.

It is in the fundamental nature of market economies that all firms are in a permanent state of competition that forces a constant drive to improve productivity (reduce costs). One of the main ways in which costs are driven down is through technological innovation. There is therefore an evolution in the nature of economic activity (whether manufacturing or service provision) that is constantly changing its shape, size, nature and location. For example, the search for reductions in transport costs led industry to adopt the motor lorry in preference to rail or water-borne transport and freed it from its historic central urban locations. The introduction of mass production, assembly-line techniques led to economies of scale that forced industries to seek large extensive production sites on the cheaper land that could be found at the urban periphery. Fothergill and Gudgin (1982) have pointed out that the constrained nature of inner-urban sites, and the problems of land assembly in such areas, have been major inhibitions to indigenous industrial growth and a spur to relocation beyond existing urban boundaries.

On the supply side, certain economic sectors benefit particularly from urban sprawl. Housebuilders can obtain greater productivity from large-scale developments on greenfield sites than can be obtained from smaller and more complex urban redevelopment sites. Then there are the suppliers of household equipment: white appliances, furniture, furnishings and so forth: the more dwellings are built, the more of these secondary goods will be sold. The suppliers of infrastructure – highways, utilities and so forth – also gain from urban sprawl. The more the urban area extends, the greater the demand for their goods and services. Out-of-town hypermarkets, discount stores and shopping centres all offer more efficient ways of retailing, often by passing on to the customer a proportion of the costs involved (such as some transport costs).

Land owners are continually seeking to maximise the returns from their holdings. On the edge of cities this means that most landowners (excluding not-for-profit landowners such as charities) are constantly seeking to convert their agricultural land into urban land. According to Adams & Watkins:

> 'In the South East of England, the average value of 1 hectare in spring 1999 was £1 370 000 if traded as bulk residential building land, but only £8 000 if traded as mixed agricultural land….(Thus) the potential supply of land for greenfield development is driven primarily by the sheer scale of the development value that can be realised from transferring the land from one sector of the market to another'.   (Adams & Watkins, 2002, p. 184)

On the demand side, ever rising real incomes, both terms of total national production and individual incomes, lead to pressures for the development of housing, the enjoyment of goods and services (and therefore their production), and for seemingly ever-increasing mobility. All of which leads on to increasing demand for residential development, building factories, distribution centres, retail and leisure parks and the means of transport to convey people and goods between all of these places.

In addition to economic aspects, there appears to be a social aspiration for suburban living that creates its own demand for urban sprawl. It has been suggested in this and other works, that there is a deep Anglo-American tradition of idealising rural life that drives the demand for suburban and ex-urban living (Schorske, 1998; Newman & Kenworthy, 1999; Leontidou, 1990; 2001; Adams & Watkins, 2002). In more practical terms, in England, for example, the purchase of a new suburban home offers not only the attraction of living near the countryside, but also more generous housing space, lower levels of maintenance and greater investment gains compared with equivalent properties in inner-urban areas. Our own surveys have shown that:

> 'the search for low-crime and quiet neighbourhoods is amongst the most important influences on household location decisions. Especially, amongst younger and middle-aged households….affordability is also very important. For older households and higher income groups and in the outer areas the proximity to the countryside and coast is an important secondary influence. Older and lower income households are also influenced by the proximity of shopping and public transport facilities. The implications for urban sprawl are so long as peripheral developments are perceived as lower in crime, quieter and nearer the countryside than other areas, demand for

sprawl will continue, especially if real incomes continue to rise. If these areas are also perceived as offering affordable housing to younger age groups demand for sprawl will be increased'.   (Couch & Karecha, 2002)

This point has been reinforced by Senior, Webster and Blank who, in an analysis of residential preferences in the Cardiff area concluded that 'the dominant preferences remain, as they have been historically, for semi-detached and detached properties with their own private gardens in suburban areas' (2006, p. 41).

Although this is put forward mainly as an explanation of British and North American urban form, we would argue that similar, but weaker, forces are also at work in much of continental Europe, but not in Southern Europe (Leontidou, 1990, 2001). It is noteworthy that peri-urban criminality in Athens at the turn of the millennium has actively discouraged residential sprawl. The changing structure of households also plays a key role in the process of urban sprawl. Average household size is falling across most of Europe. In 1951 around 286 dwellings were required to house 1000 people in England. Today that figure is nearer to 420. Much of this reduced population density has to be accommodated by urbanising additional rural land. The only household groups known in the UK to have a significant preference for urban living as opposed to suburban living are younger, single or childless households. It is these households who are increasingly occupying dwelling units closer to city centres as families become more concentrated in the suburbs in Britain and to some degree in Western Europe. This change alone, without a single dwelling being built or demolished, will lead to a reduction in the population density gradient.

It has already been mentioned that improvements to the public transport system were fundamental to the emergence of urban sprawl. Throughout the twentieth century the combination of rising car ownership and high-way building continued to reduce transport costs and allow developments to sprawl at greater distances from each other at no financial cost. Technological changes and increases in the efficiency of transport systems have brought down the unit costs of travel, enabling greater distances to be travelled for the same cost. This has allowed cities to sprawl over a larger area without economic loss. Residents can live at greater distance from their places of work, shopping and leisure without additional travel costs. Similarly, firms can deliver goods and services over larger areas without additional travel costs. If the size of the city, in terms of population and economic activity, remains constant, but transport improvements enable it to cover a larger area of land, then the gradient of the bid-rent curve will be flattened. The average rent and density of development would tend to fall in

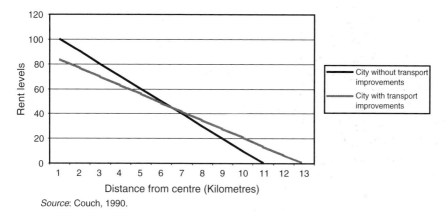

Source: Couch, 1990.

Figure 9.2   The effect of transport improvements on urban sprawl.

the vicinity of the city centre and rise towards the periphery. The total aggregate value of rents within the city would be unchanged (because the total amount of economic activity and profit had not changed) but urban activity would have sprawled over a larger area (See Figure 9.2) (Couch, 1990, p. 20).

Within this overall context individual national governments create their own social, market, fiscal and regulatory environments that encourage or discourage sprawl to differing degrees. In the UK, for example, the government has not discouraged the growth of employment in London and the South-East at the expense of the rest of the country. In consequence, the pressures for urban growth and sprawl are stronger in that region than elsewhere. On the other hand, the UK government has an impressive record of limiting urban sprawl through tough controls on the development of greenfield land and vigorous urban regeneration policies in place for more than a quarter of a century. The Netherlands also have strong policies for the development of 'compact cities', but face high levels of housing demand that have meant continuing urban growth, albeit generally well planned, at relatively high densities and well served by public transport.

Meso-level causes

Within these macro-contexts, the circumstances of individual regions or cities become significant at the meso-level, in determining the extent and nature of urban sprawl. The affluence, social and economic structure of a city will affect the extent to which there is pressure for sprawl and how those pressures can be accommodated.

Many older urban areas have experienced processes of de-industrialisation over recent decades. On the one hand this has resulted in mass unemployment, falling incomes, hardship, regional out-migration and falling demand for housing, particularly in the inner-urban areas. On the other hand it has led to the availability of large tracts of urban land, whose owners are under an economic imperative to seek its early and profitable re-use. At the same time, local governments, keen to attract replacement jobs, are willing to sacrifice greenfield land to industrial use. Thus de-industrialisation has a dual impact upon urban sprawl: the demand for residential sprawl is reduced but inner-urban and rural landowners are pitted against each other in a competition to attract new uses in a declining market for land. The extent to which this has happened and the particular character of the industrial closures leads to distinct local pressures encouraging or reducing urban sprawl. The waterside and warehousing associated with former ports in cities such as Rotterdam, lends itself to redevelopment for residential purposes, as do the mill buildings found in the textile towns of West Yorkshire. In these circumstances, pressures for urban sprawl might be ameliorated. On the other hand, the former coal mines and steel works that scarred the landscape of the Ruhr present more difficult regeneration challenges. Here, with less scope for the intensive re-use of buildings, urban regeneration is more difficult and there is less to discourage urban sprawl.

On the other extreme, there are cities urbanising by migration, which revitalises the centre but often also contributes to sprawl outwards. European cities have been receiving a lot of migrants from rural areas of Southern Europe in the past century, who have led uncontrolled sprawl and popular land colonisation. Later international migrants from Asia and Eastern Europe have followed more dispersed residential patterns.

The strength of the local economy has important implications for sprawl. In Liverpool, for example, relatively weak economic performance over many years has limited demand for housing, industrial or commercial development, and created many vacant sites within the urban areas: in consequence the level of urban sprawl is relatively modest. In contrast, Cambridge, with a booming economy based upon higher education, research and services, has a high demand for development and very few developable sites within the urban fabric: in consequence the demand for urban sprawl is more difficult to resist.

Local government structures and tax systems can also have an impact on urban sprawl. In the UK local government system many urban cores and their peripheries fall within the same strong planning regime but across many parts of continental Europe this is not the case. There are many instances where the pressure to increase local tax revenues has encouraged suburban local authorities to permit urban sprawl: typically commercial developments or middle class housing, frequently to the detriment of the core city. Local plans and planning decisions have important meso-level implications for urban sprawl. Development plans may make generous or restrictive provision for peripheral expansion. They may impose tough or weak density requirements. They may encourage or discourage mixed uses. They may lead to the building of infrastructure that may in turn itself encourage urban sprawl. For example, in the early part of the twentieth century the building of the 'metropolitan' railway into the countryside north west of London was done with the specific intention of encouraging urban sprawl – at a profit to the railway company. Elsewhere in the book we see how similar concerns created Kifissia, to the north of Athens, in the nineteenth century (Leontidou, 1990), which switched to post-suburbia during the new millennium (Phelps *et al.*, 2006). In Attica, the building of the new airport and associated transport infrastructure has created major pressures for urban sprawl outside the city. However, the impact of local plans was very weak in this case.

Micro-level causes

Though micro-level causes are analysed in depth in Chapter 8, it can be stressed here that the location decisions made by a multitude of agents have a profound effect on urban sprawl (cf. also Phelps *et al.*, 2006). Decisions made by employers are influenced by the local interplay of the macro- and meso-level factors described above. Each firm will make decisions and the scale and location of production that will have a direct effect on urban sprawl, and will take into account local plans and policies, infrastructure, utilities, land costs, tax regimes, labour costs and so forth. For each firm these factors may impact in different ways, leading to different location decisions. Similarly, individual household location decisions will be determined by local economic and social conditions, local environmental circumstances, infrastructure provision, the quality of services, such as schools; costs and value for money; and the perceived qualities of individual neighbourhoods. Other agents include developers and building entrepreneurs, who create expensive or affordable housing and shops in different locations.

Consequences of urban sprawl

Identifying and evaluating the consequences of urban sprawl is a challenging and complicated task of great interest to planners and all actors seeking sustainable development. However, though many of them are well researched and seem indisputable, some are still ambiguous or lacking in precision or difficult to attribute to the process of urban sprawl. Difficulties also arise with respect to appropriate indicators to measure the effects of urban sprawl. In part, the problem is attribution, that is, the extent to which a potentially negative phenomenon, for example, air pollution, can actually be attributed to sprawl, as distinct from say, a general rise in car owner-ship. This difficulty arises especially in the post-socialist cities where the rapid change of almost all parameters of urban development made it nearly impossible to retrace in particular the economic or social processes of urban sprawl.

Moreover, normative aspects are quite ambivalent, because consequences can be positive for one person but negative for another: building a house in the green belt might bring enormous satisfaction to the owner but might be per-ceived as a blot on the landscape by others (cf. also Bruegmann, 2005). Indeed, there are many instances where the private costs and benefits of sprawl differ from the social accounts, or where a sprawling decision might have benefits for one social group and costs for other groups. This two-sidedness needs to be kept in mind and dealt with.

The multitude of consequences of urban sprawl has been grouped under three headings:

- transport related;
- density related; and
- related to the conversion of rural to urban land.

The logic behind these categories is as follows. By definition, sprawl leads to greater distances between homes, between homes and workplaces and between urban activities generally, so generating more demand for travel and improvements in transport systems. Secondly, sprawl leads to changes in urban densities, most commonly a reduction in densities towards the urban centre and an increase in densities towards the periphery. Thirdly, urban sprawl usually, but not necessarily, involves the conversion of previ-ously rural land into urban use. As with many classification systems in the urban sciences, this typology does not allow a neat division of the effects of urban sprawl uniquely into any of the three categories. Consider, for exam-ple, the effect of ecosystem fragmentation, which is often mentioned as an important consequence of urban sprawl. It can be seen as an effect, which is due to the conversion of land, but which should, in terms of *fragmentation*, probably be better attributed as a density-related consequence. In contrast, surface sealing is independent of the density issue, but solely related to land conversion.

It seems generally accepted that urban sprawl leads to an increase in the number and length of transport journeys and shift in modal split towards the motor vehicle. These changes then have environmental consequences (increased energy consumption, air pollution by CO_2, NO_x, water pollution by oil, petrol, rubber so forth, noise pollution, land consumption, that is, surface sealing, and ecosystem fragmentation); economic consequences (including infrastructure construction and maintenance, vehicle production and maintenance, the personal costs associated with vehicle ownership and use, the amelioration costs of dealing with the socio-environmental costs of transport); and social consequences (including accidents, stress, loss of time spent travelling).

The density topic is at the very heart of urban sprawl consequences, as almost all its phenomena can be described as a change in density of people, firms, houses, so forth, and a reallocation of land by the establishment of settlements in rural areas and at the same time decrease in average density of the agglomeration. In this book we have considered the consequences of 'low density development', including environmental consequences (increased rural land consumption due to scale effects, increased energy use for heating (CO_2), ecosystem fragmentation); economic consequences (changes in the viability of local amenities, public services and retailing, increased public costs for infrastructure investments and maintenance); and social consequences (greater amount of living space, weakened sense of community, increased distance from the centre to the rural edge). In addition, changes in density affect life quality in various ways (Craglia *et al.*, 2004). In particular, as people spread out their place of living through an entire region, children are going to school in one place, having friends in another, and are joining sports clubs in again another locality, there is the loss of urbanity and 'sense of place'.

The effects and consequences of urban sprawl with regard to the conversion of land into urban use can again be classified along the three dimensions of environmental, economic and social effects. Environmental consequences range from violent conversion of land – even through arson, as it is quite common for forest fires in Spain, Portugal and Greece to make way for land development and this leads to more long-term loss of agricultural and forested land with a destruction of natural habitats – a general deterioration of landscapes; and surface sealing with impacts on runoff and possible floods, pollution (air, water, ground, noise, light). Economic consequences include increase of land value due to conversion and development, increased 'hope' values and speculation on adjacent rural land, changing local tax revenues and requirements for infrastructure investment. Social consequences emanate from the urbanisation of the countryside with increasing economic activity, changing social values and potential social conflicts between the new and the old residents.

Table 9.1 summarises these consequences. Some problems are commonly more severe in one region and less in another. For example, in regions with sprawling second homes, the problems that arise are mainly associated with public infrastructure: insufficient water supply, sewage, social services and public transport at times of peak occupation. These issues are not frequently cited as problems in declining regions. Here, the problematic consequences of sprawl are more likely to be physical degradation and vacant land in the inner-city with little economic pressure for investment or improvement. Some problems, such as environmental consequences and surface sealing, are more common among various sprawling cities.

In many cases, some of the negative consequences of sprawl are felt in inner-cities as departure points for people or enterprises moving outward, or in other regions adjacent to the sprawling areas. It is possible to see increasing degrees of spatial segregation, social exclusion and social retreat (such as the development of gated communities) as negative consequences of sprawl that are felt in other areas. For that reason, a distinction between the problematic consequences in the sprawling area and the region seems necessary. One well-cited phenomenon related to urban sprawl is often referred to as the downward-spiral (Roberts & Sykes, 2000) of urban areas.

In the course of research, we have realised that causes and consequences (effects or impacts) of urban sprawl are culturally diverse and even contrasting, and also in constant interaction with each other and with the phenomenon of urban sprawl, since a cause at one time may become a consequence in another. It appears that some of the consequences of sprawl become causes of future sprawl, for example, if sprawl leads to investment in new facilities such as schools at the periphery and a closure or deterioration in the quality of schools in the inner city, then further demands for sprawl are likely to be stimulated. In general, the relationship of amenities – such as schools, – and infrastructure – such as transport, – to urban sprawl has been both a cause and a consequence in different cities and historical periods, thus deconstructing dualism. There is also the ambivalence of 'causes' – for example, criminality may create urban sprawl in the UK, but it certainly discourages urban sprawl in Greece, where isolated country homes are frequently raided by petty criminals. All these are strong indications of the impossibility of generalisation. We have come to the conclusion

Table 9.1   The consequences of urban sprawl

	Transport related changes	Density related changes	Changes related to the conversion of rural to urban land
Environmental consequences	+ energy consumption for transport use + air pollution (CO_2, NO_x) + water pollution (petrochemical run off) + noise pollution + land consumption and surface sealing + ecosystem fragmentation	+ energy consumption for domestic use + ecosystem fragmentation	 + arson, forest fires + land consumption and surface sealing + ecosystem fragmentation − landscape quality at the urban fringe
Economic consequences	+ costs of infrastructure provision and maintenance + costs of vehicle production and maintenance + costs of vehicle ownership and use + costs of ameliorating adverse socio-environmental effects of transport growth	 − viability of local services	+ costs of infrastructure provision and maintenance + land values due to conversion and speculation + property tax revenues in areas of sprawl
Social consequences	+ accidents + stress + time spent travelling	 + living space per capita − sense of community − sense of place	 + urbanisation of 'rural society' + spatial social segregation − inner urban social conditions

+ = increases − = decreases

that an iterative process of causes-and-consequences of urban sprawl is set in motion by key-variables, such as, for example, an infrastructure-attracting land colonisation, or an infrastructure-driven settlement or a large migration wave, but also the outbreak of an earthquake or fire, which reproduces such phenomena via sprawl.

A systematic comparison of city case studies

In trying to compare models of urban sprawl, to classify land use models and landscapes and to systematise urban restructuring more generally, for the purpose of theory building we have opted to depart from models seeking homogeneity and universality of causes/consequences and to escape the essentialism of urban models. We also avoided the evolutionist perspective relating sprawl with rising prosperity, which stereotypes Southern cities as 'lagging economies' (Bruegmann, 2005, pp. 10, 77). Rather than economic growth, we have researched cultures of urbanism. On a broad spatial scale, we have underlined a contrast between Northern anti-urbanism and Southern urbanism. After the industrial revolution, representations of cities as spaces of vice or risk prevailed in British and other European geographical imaginations, and the escape to the countryside was sought by those who could afford it (Schorske, 1998). By contrast, Mediterranean societies have portrayed cities as spaces of virtue, of culture and creativity, and the affluent classes have chosen to live closer to the historic core (Chapter 2 and Leontidou, 1990, 2001). Further, our comparative analysis revealed a triplet of contrasts discovered in the course of research:

1. Cultures of urbanism in **Southern** Europe have created compact cities in combination with *infrastructure-related* urban sprawl after long periods of popular suburbanisation as a means to survival.
2. Anti-urbanism in **Northern** Europe created *lifestyle-related* urban sprawl, by the elites and middle classes wishing to escape urban squalor by moving to the countryside.
3. *State-induced* sprawl in **Eastern** Europe has *deconstructed* the compact city/pastoral landscape antithesis through the development of post-suburban landscapes which are usually not residential after the transition in the 1990s.

These types of cities in North vs. South vs. East Europe are constructed on the basis of our few urban case studies and research in current bibliography. They involve several urban formations within each type. Most continental European cities fall in-between types, and they will be discussed in this last section, where models are deconstructed and re-interpreted. Let us first examine the city case studies one by one, in the three broad regions in turn, in the light of conclusions about urban sprawl in each city.

Northern and Western Europe

Liverpool. The UK case study was based around the Liverpool conurbation, in Wirral. During the first half of the twentieth century Liverpool was the second most important port in England and the centre of a conurbation of 1.8 million people by 1961. From the late 1960s economic *decline* and urban restructuring brought about a dramatic reversal of fortune and a fall in the population of the conurbation to a low point of about 1.4 million in 2001. Since the millennium there have been some signs of recovery in the local economy, and some stabilisation in population trends. Despite these economic changes, the urban area *continued to sprawl* into the surrounding countryside. However, since the early 1980s a combination of strong restrictions on peripheral development (notably through the 'green belt') and the implementation of vigorous policies for urban regeneration have proved to be a very effective barrier to further urbanisation. Over the last two decades both aspects of policy have been refined and strengthened by successive national and local administrations. Today, virtually all housing developments occur within the existing urban area and in this sense urban sprawl is under *control*. However, there are a number of other aspects of urban sprawl, such as 'leapfrogging' over the green belt, and office parks or recreation and leisure activities, that have been less well controlled and still remain issues of concern for planners.

Stockholm. During recent decades the population of the Stockholm region has expanded at a rate of around 1% per annum, leading to a total population of about 1.8 million in 2001. This growth, however, did not necessarily mean a continuing process of urban sprawl. Stockholm is situated in a landscape with plenty of water, which has affected and restricted the physical enlargement of the city. Also, since the mid-1980s, supported by regional planning measures, much of the expansion has been accommodated through more intensive use of land in the central city or the re-use of derelict land. A significant feature of Swedish urban life is the ownership and use of 'summerhouses' as *second homes*. The rising density of the city is one of the reasons why summerhouses in the area around Stockholm are increasingly being transformed into permanent homes. It could be suggested that Stockholm has a process of demographic sprawl rather than land use sprawl, what we have called *life style-driven urban sprawl*. Nevertheless, this sprawling population, even accommodated within existing buildings, has adverse consequences. Our case study was focused on Värmdö, a municipality situated in the Stockholm archipelago with a very high number of summerhouses and one of the fastest growing places in Sweden. Here sprawl has been life style-driven urban sprawl, but it has led to difficulties with commuting, infrastructure provision and resource use.

Vienna. The capital of Austria has a population of around 1.6 million and is situated on the Danube in the north-east corner of the country, only 40 km from the border with Slovakia. Vienna is not only a capital city but a major historical and cultural centre of European importance. After the fall of the 'iron curtain' in 1989 the region felt an upswing as immigration, commuting and foreign direct investments rose, which increased the pressures for development. Excellent communications and its geographical position at the centre of South-Central Europe suggest that the conurbation will play a growing role in the commerce and governance of the enlarged European Union. Vienna has a lot of the urbanist culture of compact cities encountered in Southern Europe, with affluent classes living closer to the decorous imperial centre. One of the problems with planning the Vienna region is the *division of powers* between municipalities and between regions of Vienna and Lower Austria. Various attempts have been made to coordinate planning between these two regions since the 1960s. In 1995 the 'Settlement Concept East Region' (SKO) was established which aims to control suburban development, protect the environment and encourage a process of decentralised concentration by strengthening existing smaller towns outside the inner suburban ring.

Southern Europe

Athens. Around 4 million people, or 39% of the population of Greece, live within Attica, which is centred on Athens and its suburbs. In the twentieth century and especially after the interwar period, when Athens was flooded by refugees from Asia Minor and became an important metropolitan centre, popular initiative in urban sprawl became one of the major issues (if not the dominant one) in urban restructuring processes and public policy (non-)responses. Until the 1970s, *illegal self-built* housing sprawled onto cheap suburban land. After the 1980s, then, internal migration slowed but several types of sprawl emerged around Athens. After 2000 the picture changed again. Illegal building continued in a new speculative – rather than popular – guise, second homes were turned to main ones, and increasingly population and industry followed new infrastructure created in anticipation of the 2004 Olympics, creating post-suburban landscapes in the Mesogeia plane. This event has created a new set of urban dynamics as the building of the major transport infrastructure – the new airport, motorways, urban metro and an extended suburban railway system – created a new wave of urban sprawl: *infrastructure-led urban sprawl* has replaced the previous model of sprawl without prior infrastructure provision in Athens and Attica more generally. The new pattern, however, kept excluding infrastructure of lesser interest to investors, like water and sewage systems.

Eastern Europe

Leipzig. Together with the city of Halle (population around 270 000), Leipzig (population around 500 000) has historically been at the heart of one of the largest industrialised regions in Central Europe. The population of Leipzig has been in *decline* since the early 1960s, a process which accelerated with the building of new social housing estates on the periphery of the city in the 1970s. Through the last two decades of the German Democratic Republic (GDR), residential areas continued to decay and urban infrastructure became ever-more worn. As everywhere in the former GDR, the economic and societal transformation of the 1990s imposed heavy structural changes on the region. Today, industry is no longer the region's leading economic force, and the growing service sector has by no means made up for the tremendous loss of industrial workplaces. Leipzig has lost almost one fifth of its inhabitants within less than ten years; approximately half due to migration to more prosperous regions and half due to suburbanisation, that is, urban sprawl. These trends have given Leipzig the peculiar character of a massively sprawling, though generally declining, urban region.

Warsaw. The city of Warsaw has a population of 1.6 million people within an agglomeration of over 2.4 million. The characteristic feature of this conurbation is the *dominance* of Warsaw city as well as significant variations in the social, economic and environmental conditions between the central city, its suburbs and the periphery. The 1990s saw an increase of the importance of the suburbs as locations for economic activity and residences. The main driving forces were investment and employment growth, which have then increased the attractiveness of these suburbs as living areas, in another version of infrastructure-led urban sprawl. Expansion of these suburbs has been fuelled, not so much by outward migration from the central city, but by people moving *inwards* from peripheral districts to the suburbs. Since the 1970s, development had 'leapfrogged' over the suburban areas, where strict planning controls were in place, to peripheral areas beyond the city administration. With the change to a market economy after 1989, a strong suburbanisation process might have been expected to start. However, due to a combination of circumstances this has *not* been the case. The reasons include: difficulties with commuting; the continuing availability of building land within the central city; the interests of investors; the traditional low mobility of people; the high costs of new apartments and the relatively good quality of life within the central city.

Ljubljana, with almost 300 000 inhabitants, is the capital city and economic and cultural hub of the Republic of Slovenia. It is also an important cross-road between Central Europe, the Mediterranean and South-East Europe. Slovenia's independence (1991) from the Yugoslav Federation, and democratic and economic reforms with internationalisation and capital city formation in 1990s, have had important effects on the administrative, morphological and functional transformation of Ljubljana. PPP The effects of political, economic and institutional reforms in the 1990s are profoundly visible in the transformation of land use and the built environment around Ljubljana to a post-suburban landscape: selective new housing development, expansion of office and commercial activities, enterprise zones, new cafes and restaurants, upgrading of hotels, development of large shopping centres, so forth. Urban planning was neglected in the 1990s because of the priorities of macro-economic reforms, and the connotation of such planning within the former socialist regime. Market forces prevailed until the end of the 1990s, by which time the need for stronger planning of development in and around Ljubljana had been recognised. A comprehensive development strategy for the City of Ljubljana was adopted in 2002 under the paradigm of sustainable development. The strategy specifies programmes and projects needed to improve the competitiveness, quality of life and international role of Ljubljana. One of the most important policy objectives is how to regulate, control or upgrade areas affected by non-sustainable patterns of urban sprawl.

Cultures of urbanism and sprawl in Europe

The above summary stresses the diversity of urban sprawl in Europe, caused by intertwined socio-economic, political and cultural forces, but also reveals some regularities in hybrid landscapes and multiple interactions of forces, which 'produce' infinite processes that create the city as a sprawling formation. Though not necessarily representative, the seven case studies illustrate heterogeneous trajectories of sprawl as a process of urban change. The origins of this heterogeneity lie in the diversity of European geography, society, culture, politics and history and have to be taken into account when discussing urban sprawl in Europe. Our approach to dealing with this heterogeneity was to identify underlying antitheses or similarities, and group the cities into major archetypal fields of sprawl processes. Due to the limited number of case studies the archetypes identified should not be seen as systematically representative or comprehensively covering the whole of Europe. Through a finite set of case studies, we have identified the following three archetypal processes related to sprawl, which we can systematise into three broad sets of dynamics – with the constant risk of stereotyping – as follows:

- **Life style-driven** urban sprawl in Northern and Western Europe relates with pastoral utopias in cultural representations, especially in Malmo and around Stockholm, and other green villages. Inhabitants of Wirral near Liverpool also seek a better way of life away from congested cities. This mindset belongs to the anti-urban cultures of Northern and Western Europe, in stark contrast with South European urbanism. However, urban competition and the entrepreneurial city type have revived urbanism in the North. There is no evidence that either urban decline, or re-urbanisation as such, slow the process of urban sprawl. Their coincidence is noteworthy, and urban regeneration or 'Mediterraneanisation' – which was first named in Liverpool during urban renewal – constitutes a major change in North European urban material cultures coming to converge with the South.
- **Infrastructure-related** urban sprawl in Southern Europe and across the Mediterranean, relates to urbanism or *'astyfilia'*, that is, 'friendliness to the city' in Greek, as analysed in Chapter 3. Infrastructure-attracting urban sprawl in the popular suburbs of post-war Athens was followed by its opposite, infrastructure-driven urban sprawl, which emerged at the turn of the millennium. These have been the two facets of *infrastructure-related urban sprawl*. In the twentieth century, infrastructure followed settlement which was attracted, in turn, by a demand for a stake in the city, being in a sense a survival-seeking urban sprawl as in the Third World (Leontidou, 1990; McGregor *et al.*, 2006): internal migrants arrived to approach urban infrastructure and the labour market of the city for their livelihood and were hanging as close as possible to the dense urban agglomeration, in places where housing was affordable. They usually *built illegally*, then pressurised the authorities to 'legalise' their settlements. However, infrastructure was *not* automatically provided. The Southern European urban model of the *compact city* was thus reproduced, despite popular suburbanisation. This pattern was terminated during the dictatorship and reversed by the turn of millennium, as Athens was preparing for the Olympic Games of 2004, which contributed in urban sprawl overflowing from the agglomeration to east Attica.

  At present, in many cities of Mediterranean Europe, mega-events have created infrastructure-related urban sprawl. The Athens case shows that the urban fringe has a big population turnover, small households now, maybe nuclear families of suburbanites later. As many regions, the Mesogeia plane grew because of a drive to proximity to the city as well as transport expansion. It has been transformed from a predominantly agricultural area in the past, into a *hybrid urban* landscape, which deconstructs the rural/urban dichotomy, as in the Third World (McGregor *et al.*, 2006). The post-modern collage finds here a perfect expression (Leontidou, 1993).

- **State-regulated** peri-urban areas do *not* experience marked sprawl in post-socialist Eastern Europe. Leipzig, Ljubljana and Warsaw focus on regeneration and protection of heritage in central cities (Gutry-Korycka, 2005). The East European peri-urban landscape is mostly characterised by post-suburban developments, especially commerce. Leipzig is a case of sprawl and *decline*. One interesting feature is the *coexistence of low- and high*-density settlements. High-rises in the outskirts of Leipzig, Warsaw and Ljubljana are to an extent a heritage of socialist estates, but now housing is privatised and expensive on the periphery. The coexistence of estates with sparsely settled land on the urban periphery deconstructs the widespread dualisms of compact (urban) vs. pastoral (sprawl) landscapes and establishes the uniqueness of Eastern post-suburbia. These cities, like the Southern ones, also combine urbanism, re-urbanisation and gentrification with controlled suburbanisation and sprawl, which is not always attractive to their residents, because of high costs.

The contrast between cultures of Southern urbanism and Northern anti-urbanism in the past, and the emergent culture of urbanism spreading from South and Central Europe to the North, constitutes our main background, based on earlier research (Leontidou, 1990; 2001). Aspects of differences such as rental systems and functional heterogeneity (e.g. Hoggart, 2005) have been expected at the outset, unlike issues of cultural diversity around geographical imaginations of urbanism and their material impact on landscapes. New findings about urban sprawl during the recent period of urban competition, and the creation of the entrepreneurial city, reveal new kinds of differences and a broad range of issues which can probably also be found in and around many other urban agglomerations in Europe.

Throughout the post-war period during the past millennium, Mediterranean cultures of urbanism and urbanity have usually led to compact cities and an inverse-Burgess urban model, which is also to be found in Vienna and Paris. The preference of more affluent classes for the centre has reproduced its gentrification, and the very fact of poverty around the city means that suburbia as a desirable way of life should be not taken for granted. In Rome, Barcelona and Athens, semi-squatters predominated in the suburbs from the interwar period until at least the 1970s; in other Mediterranean cities such as Lisbon they are still today very numerous (Leontidou, 1990; Beja Horta, 2004). Though France is barely Mediterranean, a lot of the Parisian *banlieu* were colonised by poor migrants, and the violent riots there in 2005 are adequate evidence of the suburban unemployment and poverty which now hits the second-generation migrants (Leontidou, 2006). By contrast, Anglo-American inner-city poverty has been reproduced by cultures of anti-urbanism, which also affected sprawl by middle and upper classes. Most suburbanites sought pastoral lives in the countryside in homes adjacent to the city in the cases of England and Scandinavia.

These contrasting North/South cultures have been modified since the post-socialist transition and during the present millennium by developments towards urban competition and the creation of the entrepreneurial city. The contrast and dualism of the past now fades, as an emergent *culture of urbanism* spreads from South to North Europe and reproduces re-urbanisation and gentrification (Leontidou, 2001; 2005). Neoliberal entrepreneurialism and the 'commodification' of cities in Western and Eastern Europe were combined with urbanism. Already in 1999, the ESDP expressed urbanist values and promoted the compact city as well as anti-sprawl policies. This is in harmony with processes of gentrification and planning by public–private partnerships in entrepreneurial cities (Jensen-Butler *et al.*, 1996; Bailly *et al.*, 1996); but, as argued in previous chapters, in fact they also emerge easily and smoothly in Southern Europe (Leontidou, 1993; 2001; 2005) and are introduced very fast in Eastern Europe.

The coincidence of re-urbanisation with urban sprawl, which in material terms is also reflected in gentrification and the protection of heritage on the one hand, and innovative design on the other – in a sense, the 'glocalisation' of the cityscape (Beriatos *et al.*, 2004) – constitutes one of the most important changes in European urban material cultures over the past two decades and opens up a new theoretical ground about urban convergence. Reconquering the inner city with the regeneration of local heritage has been described as 'Mediterraneanisation' in the North. Affluent social strata return to urban living inward from sprawling suburbs and re-discover street life, outdoor cafes and compact cities in gentrifying European urban cores (Bailly *et al.*, 1996; Craglia *et al.*, 2004). The urban periphery also benefits from this regeneration process, mostly as a place for innovative design, especially in connection with international mega-events. These experiences have many different causes, especially economic, demographic and cultural ones; but they all exemplify ways in which, in post-modern times, Southern urban-oriented cultures have profoundly influenced and literally penetrated the North, rather than the inverse development posited by evolutionists (Leontidou, 1993, 2001). These new lines of convergence among European cities and urban development stimulate interesting reflections about the future of Europe. Post-modern Europe does not see the South lagging behind or following the development path of the North. Southern cities are *not* developing towards Northern models during postmodernity, as conventional convergence theories claimed and 'urban life-cycle' models posited. On the contrary, the metropoles of Mediterranean Europe slide easily from informality to neoliberal entrepreneurial cities during the past two decades, while at the same time iinfluencing the North and thus reversing evolutionist perspectives of the past (Leontidou, 1993).

Hybrid landscapes and questions of sustainability

Our findings about types of urban sprawl diverge from those of other recent European comparative studies, which are usually policy oriented (Richardson, 2004; Hoggart, 2005; Bruegmann, 2005). In the present project we have not focused much on the ESDP (CEC, 1999). In line with current policy papers, however, this project began with a sort of prejudice against the environmental consequences of urban sprawl and a hope to contribute towards their control. Conforming to the international bibliography and the traditional campaigns against sprawl, we raised a series of questions about 'sustainability' and the compact city and against sprawl, before the Johnson & Klemens (2005) book of critique was published. Among researchers, hybrid landscapes have been considered 'unsustainable' for a long period (Newman & Kenworthy, 1999), and in fact we, too, started with a negative disposition; but we ended up neutral and comparative, recognising the quality of life in European sprawling areas, which is a world apart from that in developing areas (McGregor, 2006) and is often better than in the inner city (Craglia *et al.*, 2004; Bruegmann, 2005). We have exposed the diversity of peri-urban landscapes as well as cities, and different positionalities therein: life patterns of different population groups, urbanites and suburbanites, and among them various types – for example, residents, commuters, visitors, cosmopolitans, migrants (Martinotti, 1999) – create a multitude of adaptations, interactions with and actions on urban space.

Maybe sprawl is not anything sustainable, but again, it is no more unsustainable than other types of urban development. Environmental policy for sustainability in sprawling areas of our city case studies was weak or nonexistent, except perhaps in some instances in the North. The 'Third Sector' of NGOs has rarely taken over the issue of urban environmentalism in many European countries, and this was the worst in the South, despite the fact that Greek NGOs have mushroomed since EU accession. Among them, environmental NGOs were more interested in provincial Greek landscapes, though there were interesting mobilisations during the Olympics.

Spatialities have changed in the new millennium and urban sprawl in Europe is increasingly balanced by inner-city revitalisation, gentrification and renewal in the context of urban competition, and the 'Mediterraneani-sation' of North and West European metropoles. This revitalisation takes advantage of and valorises the main characteristic of European cities: the very diversity of their geographies, built heritage and traditions. Around them, landscapes of hybridity and transience are created by peri-urban uneven development. The diversity of urban material cultures in space and time affects the 'urban fringe', so that it is not considered here possible to speak about 'European urban sprawl' in general, exactly as we cannot essentialise 'the city', 'the urban', and generalise about it. Different cities spring up around the world with diverse landscapes and development dynamics. We can speak of Anglo-American and North European variations of 'urban sprawl', of Euro-Mediterranean and Central European ones, of North African, Middle Eastern, or South-East Asian 'urban sprawl', but even using these terms we have to be cautious, not only because they are inwardly so diverse, but also because of the multiple explanations of sprawl, which differ in each and every city, objectively and intersubjectively, among different social classes and positionalities.

Note

1   The Marathon sports centre for rowing was a contested work since its inception and now it is relegated to a garbage dump, after a valuable biotope was exterminated.

References

Adams, D. & Watkins, C. (2002) *Greenfields, Brownfields and Housing Development*, Blackwell, Oxford.

Alonso, W. (1964) *Location and Land Use: Toward a General Theory of LandRrent*. Harvard University Press, Cambridge M.A.

Bailly, A., Jensen-Butler, C. & Leontidou, L. (1996) Changing cities: restructuring, marginality and policies in urban Europe. *European Urban and Regional Studies* 3(2): 161–76.

Beauregard, R. A. & Body-Gendrot, S. (eds) (1999) *The Urban Moment. Cosmopolitan Essays on the Late-20th-Century City*. Sage, London.

Beja Horta, A. P. (2004) *Contested Citizenship: Immigration Politics and Grassroots Migrants' Organizations in Post-Colonial Portugal*. CMS – Center for Migration Studies, New York.

Beriatos, E. & Gospodini, A. (2004) "Glocalising" urban landscapes: Athens and the 2004 Olympics. *Cities* 21(3): 187–202.

Bruegman, R. (2005) *Sprawl: A Compact History.* University of Chicago Press, Chicago & London.

CEC (Commission of the European Communities) (1999) *ESDP – European Spatial Development Perspective: Towards Balanced and Sustainable Development of the Territory of the European Union.* Office for Official Publications of the European Communities, Luxembourg.

Craglia, M., Leontidou, L., Nuvolati, G. & Schweikart, J. (2004) Towards the development of quality of life indicators in the 'digital' city. *Environment & Planning B: Planning and Design* **31**(1): 51–64.

Couch, C. (1990) *Urban Renewal: Theory and Practice.* Macmillan, London.

Couch, C. & Karecha, J. (2002) *The Causes of Urban Sprawl.* Urbs Pandens Working Paper, PIK, Potsdam.

Dangschat, J., Kratochwil, S. & Mann, A. (2003) *On a theory of urban sprawl and sprawling.* URBS PANDENS Working Paper. Vienna University of Technology, Institute of Sociology for Spatial Planning and Architecture (ISRA).

Firey, W. (1946) Ecological considerations in planning for rurban fringes. *American Sociological Review* **11**(4): 411–23.

Fothergill, S. & Gudgin, G. (1982) *Unequal Growth: Urban and Regional Employment Change in the UK*, Heinemann Educational, London.

Gans, H. J. (1968) Urbanism and suburbanism as ways of life. In: R. Pahl (ed.), *Readings in Urban Sociology*, pp. 95–118. Pergammon, Oxford.

Garreau, J. (1991) *Edge City: Life on the New Frontier.* Doubleday, New York.

Gutry-Korycka, M. (ed.) (2005) *Urban Sprawl: Warsaw Agglomeration.* Warsaw University Press, Warsaw.

Harvey, D. (1989) *The Condition of Postmodernity: An Enquiry into the Origins of Cultural Change.* Blackwell, Oxford.

Hoggart, K. (ed.) (2005) *The City's Hinterland: Dynamism and Divergence in Europe's Peri-urban Territories.* Ashgate, Aldershot.

Jacobs, J. (1961) *The Death and Life of Great American Cities.* Random House, New York.

Jensen-Butler, C., Shakhar, A. & van den Weesp, J. (eds) (1996) *European Cities in Competition.* Avebury, Aldershot.

Johnson, E. A. & Klemens, M. W. (2005) *Nature in Fragments: The Legacy of Sprawl.* University of Columbia Press, New York.

King, R. De Mas, P. & Beck, J. M. (eds) (2001) *Geography, Environment and Development in the Mediterranean.* Sussex Academic Press, Brighton.

Kling, R., Olin, S. & Poster, M. (1995) *Postsuburban California: The Transformation of Orange County since World War II.* University of California Press, California.

Leontidou, L. (1990/2006) *The Mediterranean City in Transition: Social Change and Urban Development.* Cambridge University Press, Cambridge.

Leontidou, L. (1993) Postmodernism and the city: Mediterranean versions. *Urban Studies* **30**(6): 949–65.

Leontidou, L. (2001) Cultural representations of urbanism and experiences of urbanisation in Mediterranean Europe. In: King, R., De Mas, P. & Beck, J. M. (eds), *Geography, Environment and Development in the Mediterranean* (Sussex Academic Press, Brington) pp. 83–98.

Leontidou, L. (2005 in Greek) *Ageographitos Chora [Geographically Illiterate Land]: Hellenic Idols in the Epistemological Pathways of European Geography*. Hellenica Grammata, Athens.

Leontidou, L. (2006) Urban social movements: from the 'right to the city' to transnational spatialities and *flaneur* activists. *City: Analysis of Urban Trends, Culture, Theory, Policy, Action* **10**(3): 259–68.

Martinotti, G. (1999) A city for whom? Transients and public life in the second-generation metropolis. In Beauregard, R. A. & Body-Gendrot, S. (eds), *The Urban Moment. Cosmopolitan Essays on the Late-20th-Century City* (London: Sage), pp. 155–84.

McGregor, D., Simon, D. & Thompson, D. (eds) (2006) *The Peri-Urban Interface: Approaches to Sustainable Natural and Human Resource Use*. Earthscan, London.

Mumford, L. (ed.) (1966) *The City in History: Its Origins, Its Transformations and Its Prospects*. Penguin/Pelican, Harmondsworth.

Newman, P. & Kenworthy, J. (1999) *Sustainability and Cities: Overcoming Automobile Dependence*. Island Press, Washington DC.

Pahl, R. (ed.) (1968) *Readings in Urban Sociology*. Pergamon Press, Oxford.

Phelps, N. A., Parsons, N., Ballas, D. & Dowling, A. (2006) *Planning and Politics at the Margins of Europe's Capital Cities*. Palgrave, London.

Richardson, H. W. (ed.) (2004) *Urban Sprawl in Western Europe and the United States*. Ashgate, Aldershot.

Roberts, P. & Sykes, H. (eds) (2000) *Urban Regeneration: A Handbook*, Sage, London.

Schorske, C. E. (1998) *Thinking with History: Explorations in the Passage to Modernism*. Princeton University Press, New Jersey.

Senior, M., Webster, C. & Blank, N. (2006) Residential relocation and sustainable urban form: statistical analyses of owner-occupiers preferences. *International Planning Studies* **11**(1): 41–57.

Soja, E. W. (2000) *Postmetropolis: Critical Studies of Cities and Regions*. Blackwell, Oxford.

Whatmore, S. (2002) *Hybrid Geographies: Natures, Cultures, Spaces*. Routledge, London.

Wirth, L. (1938) Urbanism as a way of life. *American Journal of Sociology* **44**(1): 1–24.

Index